Evangelical Theology *in* Transition

Theologians

in Dialogue

with Donald

Bloesch

Edited by
Elmer M.
Colyer

InterVarsity Press
Downers Grove, Illinois

InterVarsity Press
P.O. Box 1400, Downers Grove, IL 60515
World Wide Web: www.ivpress.com
E-mail: mail@ivpress.com

InterVarsity Press® is the book-publishing division of InterVarsity Christian Fellowship/USA®, a student movement active on campus at hundreds of universities, colleges and schools of nursing in the United States of America, and a member movement of the International Fellowship of Evangelical Students. For information about local and regional activities, write Public Relations Dept., InterVarsity Christian Fellowship/USA, 6400 Schroeder Rd., P.O. Box 7895, Madison, WI 53707-7895.

ISBN 0-8308-1594-5

Printed in the United States of America ∞

Library of Congress Cataloging-in-Publication Data

Colyer, Elmer M., 1956-
  Evangelical theology in transition : theologians in dialogue with
Donald Bloesch / Elmer M. Colyer.
    p.   cm.
  Includes bibliographical references and indexes.
  ISBN 0-8308-1594-5 (pbk. : alk. paper)
  1. Bloesch, Donald G., 1928-   . 2. Theology, Doctrinal.
3. Evangelicalism.   I. Title.
BT75.2.C655 1999
230'.04624—dc21

                                                              99-21811
                                                                CIP

20	19	18	17	16	15	14	13	12	11	10	9	8	7	6	5	4	3	2	1
15	14	13	12	11	10	09	08	07	06	05	04	03	02	01	00	99			

CONTENTS

Preface

Donald G. Bloesch, in his various roles as a scholar, theologian, teacher and mentor of a whole generation of students, has made an unparalleled contribution to a renaissance of evangelical theology in the final decades of the twentieth century. The genesis of this volume developed out of a desire to honor Don and his work on his seventieth birthday (May 1998). A festschrift was already on the way to publication,[1] so rather than undertake another, the contributors and I decided on a different way to honor my former professor and present colleague.

The following chapters examine Donald G. Bloesch and his theology. The essays are written by some of the best-known and most respected theologians in the evangelical world and beyond. This in itself symbolizes something of the respect for Bloesch and his work in evangelicalism and the wider scholarly community. It is particularly fitting to have chapters by noted Roman Catholic and Reformed theologians Avery Dulles and Thomas Torrance since Bloesch's goal has been to develop a theology that is not only evangelical, but catholic and reformed.[2]

The first chapter of this volume summarizes Bloesch's life and career; the second locates him within evangelicalism and assesses his influence on evangelicalism and evangelical theology. The remaining chapters analyze key themes in Bloesch's theology and enter into critical dialogue with him. All of the main loci developed in his seven-volume systematic theology, Christian Foundations, are covered here, except for subject matter of the final two volumes on ecclesiology and eschatology which will not appear for several years.

There is convergence between the three chapters on method, revelation and Scripture, as one would expect on three closely related themes. This is beneficial in light of the diversity in perspective of the authors who represent Roman Catholicism and two very different strands of evangelicalism, and also because this is the area of Bloesch's theology that has proved to be particularly controversial.

The essays on Bloesch's Christology and doctrine of God are written by theologians currently engaged in constructive work in these areas. Thomas

Torrance's volume, *The Christian Doctrine of God, One Being Three Persons*,[3] and Bloesch's book, *God the Almighty: Power, Wisdom, Holiness, Love*,[4] were published within a few months of each other. Gabriel Fackre wrote his essay on Bloesch's Christology while he was working on his own volume on that theme.

Clark Pinnock's essay on pneumatology is unusual in that he was given the unenviable task of writing on the subject without seeing Bloesch's final synthesis of it in volume five of Christian Foundations. That volume was not available when Clark wrote the essay.

Chapter nine outlines Bloesch's doctrine of the Christian life, which is so integral to his overall theological horizon. And chapter ten examines the way in which Bloesch's theology and view of the Christian life intersect American culture in the second half of the twentieth century.

In the final chapter Bloesch reenters the dialogue directly and responds to the essays by his colleagues and friends.

This way of honoring Donald Bloesch in the form of a dialogue about his work seems especially appropriate in light of the fact that one of the main goals of his career has been to enrich evangelical theology by his own encyclopedic dialogue with the catholic history of Christian faith and thought, past and present. Yet, since these essays are about one of the premier evangelical theologians writing today, the book is much more than a tribute to Don Bloesch and his work.

This collection has multiple ends. It is an introduction to Bloesch's theology and provides a useful guide for those researching his work. The biographical chapter and bibliographic material in the endnotes and the selected bibliography orient readers and researchers to Bloesch, his career, his publications and secondary materials. These essays provide the most significant and comprehensive analysis and evaluation of Bloesch's theology to date. Finally, the book is theology in its own right and at its best, for here are some of the outstanding contemporary theologians in creative and constructive dialogue with one of the most important evangelical theologians writing in North America at the turn of the century.

The timing for this collection of essays seems particularly auspicious for several reasons. The dawning of the new millennium is our immediate horizon. Evangelical theology is in transition. Bloesch is one of the authors of that transition and he is at the pinnacle of his career. The central volume (on Christology) of his systematic theology has been published, and volume five on pneumatology is forthcoming. It is an ideal time for a dialogue with

Donald Bloesch about the future of evangelical theology.

I want to thank the contributors for their fine essays on various themes in Bloesch's theology, and Rodney Clapp and InterVarsity Press for their support in publishing the book. Everyone's enthusiasm for the project and cooperation made my editorial tasks a pleasure. I also express my appreciation for the editorial suggestions of my colleague Dr. Bradley Longfield on several of the chapters, and for the work of my student research assistant James Dauer, whose careful handling of all manner of mundane tasks has made my part of this endeavor much easier. Most of all I want to thank Donald and Brenda Bloesch. The book is dedicated to them in gratitude for their contributions, which have enriched the lives of so many.

One

Donald G. Bloesch & His Career

ELMER M. COLYER

DONALD G. BLOESCH IS ONE OF NORTH AMERICA'S PREMIER EVANGELICAL theologians. His literary productivity has been amazing: he has over thirty books and nearly three hundred published articles and book reviews to his credit.[1] He is in the midst of writing a seven-volume systematic theology, Christian Foundations, which will be the most significant evangelical theology at the turn of the millennium.

Bloesch's first systematic presentation, *Essentials of Evangelical Theology*,[2] generated his substantial recognition in the evangelical world and the wider theological community. The publication of this creative two-volume work was a landmark event within evangelicalism because it provided younger scholars and pastors with a new way to be theologically evangelical.[3]

Two points are significant. Bloesch's deep piety pervades the work as it does his life and has had an alluring influence on seminarians and other readers.[4] In addition, the panoramic scholarship evident in *Essentials of Evangelical Theology* is nearly without peer in North American evangelicalism, though there are now many younger evangelicals following his lead.[5]

This has earned Bloesch a reputation as an outstanding and creative thinker, one of the most quoted evangelical theologians in the United States.[6] Yet his real agenda has been to lead North American evangelical theology into dialogue with the wider church and evangelical impulses throughout the history of Christian thought. Bloesch's goal is a broader and more dynamic evangelical theology with deeper historical roots and a bold confessional stance that will call the church back to the gospel and to a life of piety and service befitting the God encountered in Christ. Bloesch believes that such a refurbished evangelical theology can provide a credible witness in the postmodern era and a viable alternative to fundamentalism and sectarian evangelicalism on the right, and the latitudinarian and accommo-dationist tendencies of liberal and neoliberal theologies on the left.[7]

Early Years

Donald G. Bloesch was born in Bremen, Indiana, on May 3, 1928, to Herbert and Adele (Silberman) Bloesch.[8] His father was a pastor in the local German Evangelical Church, part of the Evangelical Synod of North America which had its roots in Lutheran and Reformed Pietism. This was also the church of Reinhold Niebuhr, a personal friend of Bloesch's father.[9] Both of Bloesch's grandfathers were also pastors in the Evangelical Synod.[10] They studied at evangelical mission schools in Switzerland (St. Chrischona and the Basel Mission) before coming to the United States as missionaries to German-speak-ing immigrants.[11]

The Evangelical Synod merged with the Reformed Church in the United States in 1934 to form the Evangelical and Reformed Church, which later joined the Congregational Christian Churches creating the United Church of Christ (UCC) in 1957. Bloesch remains a member and ordained minister in the UCC, though at times a somewhat disgruntled member, disturbed by what he considers latitudinarian tendencies within the denomination. The most evident legacy of the Bloesch family in Donald Bloesch's theology is the influence of Pietism which still permeates significant areas of his thought.[12]

The Bloesches moved to Monee, Illinois, when Don was six years old. Monee at the time was a country town of about five hundred people, but has since been swallowed by the urban sprawl of the Chicago area. There Bloesch came to personal faith, and during his high-school years sensed a call to ministry.[13]

Also during high school Bloesch learned the meaning and value of hard work. He grew up during the Depression. His family was relatively poor, so he felt the need to work. While in high school he delivered papers and worked on the farm or in factories in the summer. During his college years Bloesch worked on the assembly line in factories and in the college kitchen.[14]

Theological Education

After high school, in 1946, Bloesch entered Elmhurst College in Elmhurst, Illinois. This was the preparatory school for pre-theological students in the

Evangelical and Reformed Church; here he majored in philosophy and minored in sociology.[15] Bloesch particularly remembers an important course in Kant's philosophy taught by Dr. William Halfter, an excellent teacher.[16]

Most students at Elmhurst College intent on entering the ministry in the Evangelical and Reformed Church continued on to Eden Theological Seminary. Instead, Bloesch chose Chicago Theological Seminary (CTS), partly because of his growing interest in sociology of religion, but also due to his desire to pursue Ph.D. studies.[17] At CTS he could proceed directly on to the doctoral program once he had completed his Bachelor of Divinity degree.

Despite his broad exposure to theology and philosophy in his undergraduate studies, Bloesch was not prepared for what he describes as "the extreme liberal theology" he encountered at CTS. Most of the theologians there "identified themselves as neo-naturalists and appealed to the writings of Alfred North Whitehead."[18] There Bloesch discovered neo-orthodoxy, which has played a pivotal role in his theological development. He read major works by Kierkegaard, Brunner, Barth, Tillich and Bultmann, with favorable reaction.[19] For a budding young theologian from a Pietist background, who had passed through the fires of modern thought epitomized in Kant's philosophy, these authors must have seemed effective alternatives to the process philosophy and theology Bloesch encountered at CTS.[20]

Bloesch, however, gradually shifted his allegiance to Brunner and especially Karl Barth. None of the leading evangelical theologies in America at the time provided viable options, according to Bloesch, because their rationalist approaches were inadequate in the face of the kinds of problems created for traditional theology that Bloesch encountered in his study of modern philosophy and theology.

After graduation from CTS in 1953, Bloesch was ordained in the UCC and served as minister of St. Paul's United Church of Christ in Richton Park, Illinois, from 1953 to 1956 while pursuing Ph.D. studies at the University of Chicago Divinity School.[21]

At the university Bloesch studied under Charles Hartshorne, Daniel Jenkins, Wilhelm Pauck, Jaroslav Pelikan and Daniel Day Williams.[22] Bloesch also participated in InterVarsity Christian Fellowship, where he sensed a spiritual bond that he had not experienced with the neo-orthodox students in his program.[23] In 1956 he completed his dissertation on "Reinhold Niebuhr's Re-Evaluation of the Apologetic Task" under Bernard Meland.[24]

After completing his Ph.D., Bloesch left for Oxford University to pursue postdoctoral studies through a scholarship from the World Council of

Churches.[25] There he studied Anglo-Catholic monasticism. Bloesch had been fascinated with religious community life for some time and even considered embracing it himself. The motive behind this interest lay in his growing concern for renewal in the church. Religious communities seemed to provide a concrete way to embody these interests. Thus Bloesch's first book called for centers of Christian renewal, spiritually and theologically vital monasteries and family-oriented religious communities that would pour new life back into the churches.[26] Most of Bloesch's early books are oriented around this concern for renewal in mainline churches.

Teaching Career

In the fall of 1957 Bloesch began his thirty-five-year teaching career at the University of Dubuque Theological Seminary (UDTS) in Dubuque, Iowa.[27] The administration hired Bloesch partly to counteract the influence of the noted Barthian theologian Art Cochrane, assuming that Bloesch would reflect the more liberal theology of his alma mater, the University of Chicago. Bloesch, however, developed a friendship with Cochrane and regards him as one of his mentors.[28]

UDTS is affiliated with the Presbyterian Church (U.S.A.). The seminary has an ecumenical faculty and student body (predominantly Presbyterian and United Methodist) and a long history of preparing pastors for mainline churches in the Upper Midwest. There has been a consortium of several theological schools in Dubuque for many years, including Wartburg Seminary (Lutheran) and the Aquinas Institute (disbanded in 1982). UDTS was housed at the Aquinas Institute from 1968 to 1982, though ecumenical relations between the schools go back to 1959.[29] This placed Bloesch in continual dialogue across several theological traditions and helps account for the ecumenical and catholic flavor of Bloesch's theology and for his reputation as a bridge-builder.[30]

There have been some colorful moments in Bloesch's life at UDTS. For example, in 1960 he and six other colleagues signed "A Statement Concerning the Use of Weapons of Mass Extermination as a Means of Waging War."[31] At the height of the Vietnam era, Bloesch produced and distributed a tract entitled "This Unholy War." In 1974, during a period of tension between the faculty and administration, Bloesch and other faculty affiliated with a labor union and even demonstrated, protesting what they considered arbitrary firings and inappropriate contractual negotiations.[32]

In November 1962, after five years at UDTS, Bloesch married Brenda Mary

Jackson, a charming British woman he had met while studying in Geneva, Switzerland. She holds a Ph.D. in French literature from the University of London. Brenda is Bloesch's copyeditor and research associate. She is staunchly evangelical and theologically insightful. Brenda has created an environment conducive to the single-minded vocation of research, reflection and writing they embody in their life together. Few people realize what a strategic role she has played in Bloesch's career as an author. They have a remarkable partnership in ministry.

Again in 1963 and 1964, through the financial support of a faculty fellowship of the American Association of Theological Schools, Bloesch returned to Switzerland and Germany for postdoctoral research at the Universities of Basel and Tübingen. There he studied under Karl Barth and Hans Küng. Bloesch served as the president of the Midwest division of the American Theological Society from 1974 to 1975. In 1983 he received an honorary doctorate from Doane College.

Publications

The majority of Bloesch's early books focus on various aspects of Christian renewal. *Centers of Christian Renewal* (1964) and *Wellsprings of Renewal: Promise in Christian Communal Life* (1974) deal with renewal through religious communities. *The Reform of the Church* (1970), *Servants of Christ: Deaconesses in Renewal* (1971), *The Invaded Church* (1974) and *Light a Fire: Gospel Songs for Today* (1975)—a collection of hymns with music and words composed by Bloesch,[33] outline a program for reviving the church's life, ministry and outreach in light of the secularization infiltrating the church. Bloesch's vision for spiritual renewal in the Christian life is found in *The Christian Life and Salvation* (1967), *The Crisis of Piety* (1968) and *Christian Spirituality East and West* (1968). All of these books are deeply theological, as is true of everything Bloesch has published.

Many of Bloesch's other works deal with themes related to this emphasis on renewal.[34] Richard Lovelace has astutely observed that "Bloesch has made spiritual and theological renewal more central in his writings than any other systematic theologian in our century."[35] Part of the reason for this is that Bloesch has been a catholic evangelical ordained in a mainline denomination and a professor in a mainline seminary. Because of this, a significant segment of Bloesch's audience has been evangelicals, charismatics and moderates in mainline denominations. He has also served as an advisor to renewal groups in the United Church of Christ (Biblical Witness Fellowship), Presbyterian

Church (U.S.A.) (Presbyterians United for Biblical Concerns) and United Methodist Church (Good News).

Since the mid-seventies formal theology has been at the forefront of Bloesch's publication: *Jesus Is Victor! Karl Barth's Doctrine of Salvation* (1976), the two-volume *Essentials of Evangelical Theology* (1978-1979), *The Struggle of Prayer* (1980), the two-volume *Theological Notebook* (1989-1991)[36] and his current seven-volume systematic theology, Christian Foundations (1992-). Bloesch has also written in the areas of social prophecy (*Crumbling Foundations,* 1984), theological ethics (*Freedom for Obedience,* 1987) and current issues (*Is the Bible Sexist?,* 1982; *The Future of Evangelical Christianity,* 1983; and *The Battle for the Trinity,* 1985). Close scrutiny of Bloesch's complete bibliography reveals an impressive topical breadth of research and publication.[37]

Bloesch has lectured at colleges, seminaries and conferences throughout North America, and has had an extensive ministry of correspondence.[38] His theological and spiritual orientation developed out of his family heritage in Pietism, and gradually moved through existentialism in college and seminary (including a brief flirtation with liberal existentialism). Neo-orthodoxy was significant for Bloesch during his Ph.D. studies at the University of Chicago and early years of teaching. From that time on, he has become progressively more evangelical in the deeper and broader "catholic" sense he has injected into that term. This means that the trajectory of Bloesch's theological pilgrimage from CTS onward has been conservative in direction—conservative in the sense of striving "always to maintain the truth of Scripture and tradition."[39]

In May 1993 Bloesch retired from teaching at the University of Dubuque Theological Seminary in order to devote all of his energies to completing his new seven-volume systematic theology, Christian Foundations. Volumes one, *A Theology of Word & Spirit: Authority & Method in Theology;* two, *Holy Scripture: Revelation, Inspiration & Interpretation;*[40] three, *God the Almighty: Power, Wisdom, Holiness, Love,*[41] and four, *Jesus Christ: Savior & Lord,*[42] are published. The Bloesches continue to reside in Dubuque, where they are currently working on volume five, which focuses on pneumatology. The remaining two volumes deal with ecclesiology and eschatology.

The completion of Christian Foundations, however, is not likely to be the conclusion of Bloesch's career. Beyond Christian Foundations, Bloesch has plans for several books on subjects in the area of spirituality: *Spirituality Old and New, The Doctrine of the Saints, The Christian Meaning of Love in*

Light of the Cross, The Paradox of Holiness, and a lay theology, *The Faith We Uphold.* In a sense, this will bring Bloesch's career full circle to where it began, to Pietism's concern for spiritual renewal; however, the fruits of Bloesch's rich career will have transformed his family heritage in Pietism as that career has transformed segments of North American evangelicalism.

The Man Behind the Persona

I would be remiss if I did not say something about Donald Bloesch, the man behind the public persona and scholarly career. Bloesch is not only a person of deep faith, he is also a person of humility and great generosity.[43] More than a few students at UDTS have been the recipients of that generosity without ever knowing it. Bloesch has secretly channeled contributions through financial aid and other avenues to students in need.

Bloesch is also a gracious person even to those who resist his theology. I have never seen him manifest a mean spirit or discourteousness in the classroom or at public lectures. A number of years ago, after a lecture at another seminary, a professor launched a rather vitriolic attack on Bloesch and his theology. It was evident that Bloesch could have run scholarly circles around the professor. Yet Bloesch graciously answered his questions. Finally, after the other man had badgered Bloesch to the point that everyone in the room was mildly embarrassed, Bloesch replied that perhaps the professor was right and that he had learned a great deal from the professor's questions and would reflect on them further.

In light of his generosity and liberality of spirit, it is no surprise that Bloesch has a wide circle of friends and admirers. He continues his extensive correspondence with scholars, pastors and laypersons from all over the globe.

Two

Locating Donald G. Bloesch in the Evangelical Landscape

ROGER E. OLSON

L OCATING A PARTICULAR THEOLOGIAN'S PLACE IN THE LANDSCAPE OF EVAN-
gelical Christianity is a daunting task, especially in light of the debat-
ableness of the concept "evangelical." Complicating the effort further
in this case is the fact that the theologian in question, Donald G. Bloesch, is
at this time in the midst of writing his theological magnum opus: a
seven-volume systematic theology with the overarching title Christian Foundations. Pinpointing Bloesch's location within evangelicalism, then, must be
seen as a tentative task open to possible revision.

The Evangelical Landscape

Before we attempt to place Bloesch on the map of evangelical theology, we
must describe that map itself (or better, the territory it charts). What is this
theological landscape we are describing as "evangelical Christianity"? Bloesch
has himself expended great creative energy describing it, as well as urging
revision of some traditional maps of its territory. In *The Evangelical Renaissance* (1973) he celebrated the new vigor and vitality of evangelical Christianity in America and attempted to pinpoint its authentic heritage within the
historical Pietist movements of Protestant Christianity. Ten years later in *The
Future of Evangelical Christianity* (1983) Bloesch identified the tensions
within evangelicalism and warned of dangers in the road ahead of it.

Bloesch's vision of evangelical Christianity is broad. I concur with that
vision and have been greatly influenced by it. Some may say that "evangelical" is an essentially contested concept and for all practical purposes useless.

Like Bloesch, I would prefer to think of it as an ideal sought after by a large and diverse group of Christians who, in spite of many differences, all seek to proclaim and live out the great gospel of Jesus Christ in today's world. Bloesch tends to give the benefit of the doubt to all who sincerely and proudly claim the label "evangelical" for themselves. So do I. It does not describe a "party" or an "ideology" and it has no headquarters or pope. At the same time, however, it is not a meaningless concept consistent with anything and everything. It has contours and flexible boundaries, and sometimes the effort must be made to map its authentic territory while keeping in view the broader horizons all around it.

In *The Future of Evangelical Christianity* Bloesch wrote

> "Evangelical" can . . . be said to indicate a particular thrust or emphasis within the church, namely, that which upholds the gospel of free grace as we see this in Jesus Christ. An evangelical will consequently be Christocentric and not merely theocentric (as are the deists and a great many mystics). Yet it is not the teachings of Jesus Christ that are considered of paramount importance but his sacrificial life and death on the cross of Calvary. The evangel is none other than the meaning of the cross.[1]

Few contemporary theologians have done more to define evangelicalism and map its landscape than Bloesch. The above statement provides just a hint of his approach to that task to which he devotes many pages. While my own map of the evangelical landscape is profoundly influenced by Bloesch's, our maps may not be identical at every point. My task here is to locate his theological contribution in that landscape as I see it. It will be helpful to readers, then, to know how I map its contours and landmarks before discovering where I place Bloesch in it.

Evangelicalism is, historically speaking, a form of Protestant theology with antecedents in the early church and pre-Reformation thought and parallels in Eastern Orthodoxy and Roman Catholic theology. Some would like simply to identify "evangelical" with "authentic Reformation theology," but, in fact, what we now know as evangelicalism grew out of a second Reformation after the great Protestant split from Rome in the sixteenth century. This second Reformation that gave rise to what we now call evangelicalism began with German and Swiss Pietism in the seventeenth century and gained further impetus and shape from the various great awakenings of Europe and North America in the eighteenth century.

Early evangelicalism's giants stood on the shoulders of men like Luther and Calvin, Zwingli and Bucer, Menno Simons and other radical reformers. They were the preachers, writers and spiritual directors of renewal who emphasized "experimental" (experiential) Christianity and exalted the importance of personal conversion (even within the framework of infant baptism and a high view of the sacraments) as the sine qua non of authentic Christian life. Without denigrating orthodox belief or the church and its liturgy, the founders of evangelicalism wished to add into the Protestant recipe for renewal the dimension of heartfelt experience with Christ, daily devotional life, love for Bible reading, solicitation of faith (witnessing), and holy living (sanctification). To their enemies (even within the magisterial Protestant traditions) they were "enthusiasts"—fanatics, dreamers, extremists.

During the nineteenth and early twentieth centuries, earthquakes of liberal theology and higher criticism of the Bible shook many Protestant denominations to their foundations. Also during this period these Pietists and scholastic defenders of orthodox Protestant belief discovered each other and forged an alliance against encroaching spiritual deadness and intellectual apostasy within Protestant Christianity. For all their disagreements over propriety and the authentic marks of true Christianity, they could agree on one thing: Unitarianism in the guise of "new theology" was a greater threat to the gospel within the churches than was either dead orthodoxy or "enthusiasm."

And so throughout the great liberal-fundamentalist conflicts of the early decades of the twentieth century, the conservative antiliberal wing of Protestant Christianity in Europe and America held within its ranks both pietist-revivalist Protestants who emphasized "personal experience of Jesus Christ" and orthodox-scholastic Protestants who emphasized "adherence to the faith once for all delivered to the saints" (Luther, Calvin) as the sine qua non of true Christianity. Both groups called themselves evangelicals in distinction from explicit or implicit Unitarianism, liberalism and modernism. Both groups valued the unique emphasis of the other group and, faced with a common enemy, stuck together for the sake of Christ and the gospel.

After the Second World War, however, latent tensions within this coalition of conservative Christians began to widen during formal attempts to institutionalize it in parachurch groups, evangelistic ministries, educational efforts and publications. Evangelicalism became a subculture within North American Christianity in part, at least, because of the success of the various ministries of Billy Graham and his associates. Those who rejected his "broad tent" approach to evangelism became known as "fundamentalists" rather than "evangelicals," although they thought of themselves as the truer evangelicals and called the others "neo-evangelicals" as a pejorative label.[2]

With the founding of the National Association of Evangelicals—a rival umbrella organization to the National Council of Churches (formerly Federal Council of Churches)—in the 1940s and *Christianity Today* in the 1950s, and with the 1970s designated by major secular media as the "decade of the evangelicals," the evangelical subculture ripened and came of age. The question of its theological identity gradually came more and more to the fore. Because of his close association with Billy Graham and his prolific prowess as author, editor and speaker, conservative theologian Carl F. H. Henry was identified by many as the spokesman for evangelical theology. *Time* magazine seemed to baptize him as such in a full-page article with his photograph.

However, tensions remained between those evangelical spokespersons who emphasized the pietist-revivalist (experientialist) roots of the movement and those who emphasized its orthodox, confessional (doctrinal) roots. Some on each side of the evangelical tent would go so far as to reject the authenticity of the other side's evangelical credentials. That would be especially true whenever the experientialists paid less than enthusiastic homage to conservative hallmarks such as the inerrancy of the Bible and whenever the confessionalists were less than enthusiastic in their support of evangelistic or spiritual renewal movements.

In the face of the perceived overwhelming threat of liberal and radical theologies, however, the evangelical tent held both groups together in spite of occasional squabbles, excommunications and aspersions cast from one side to the other.

Everyone within the tent of this evangelical movement in the second half of the twentieth century agreed on certain hallmarks of experience and belief: a supernaturalist worldview, Scripture as supernaturally inspired and the ultimate authority for Christian faith and life, Jesus Christ as divine Savior and Lord for all people, the cross as the event of divine-human reconciliation, salvation by grace alone through faith alone and the importance of evangelism. All evangelicals agreed also that authentic Christianity necessarily involves a personal decision of repentance and faith, even though they disagreed about the exact meaning of the sacraments or ordinances such as baptism and communion.

Bloesch's Location in the Evangelical Landscape

Donald Bloesch's place within this evangelical milieu depends very much on one's perspective. For those evangelicals who see evangelicalism as a large, diverse movement that is basically synonymous with twentieth century Protestantism that emphasizes the gospel and resistance to subversion by forces of secularity and political ideologies, Donald Bloesch stands at its center. For those evangelicals who view evangelicalism as a very specific subculture within twentieth-century Protestantism that has emerged from fundamentalism, Bloesch is on its fringe somewhere. He is not an insider to that subculture; he lives and works within a more mainstream Protestant environment. His own theological and spiritual journey has been almost untouched by fundamentalism.

When Donald Bloesch writes about evangelicalism and evangelical theology, he means Christ-centered, gospel- and cross-centered, thoroughly biblical Christianity with an emphasis on encounter with Christ in a life-transforming experience. He is not obsessed with boundaries of the subculture, however. He is an ecumenical evangelical and is more interested in building bridges between diverse strands of the evangelical spectrum than in identifying who is in and who is out of the movement.[3] He recognizes the need for evangelicals to find one another and learn to appreciate each other in spite of genuine differences of interpretation. The danger to the gospel lies not in nuances of difference over interpretation of inspiration or eschatology but in the rising tides of liberalism, paganism and politicized Christianity that threaten to swamp the gospel in cultural accommodation. Without backing away from tough-minded and vigorous critique of fellow evangelicals' theological proposals and contributions, Bloesch has consistently called for a renewal of the evangelical consensus to ward off those increasingly dangerous trends in the churches.

For those evangelicals who have one foot still firmly planted in the strictest versions of Protestant orthodoxy, such as fundamentalism, Bloesch is too ecumenical to be at the center of authentic evangelicalism. For those evangelicals who are pushing the envelope of orthodoxy or reveling in sheer experiential Christianity, Bloesch is too cautious, confessional and conservative. For those evangelicals who value a clarion call for theological balance and moderation without mediocrity or blandness, Bloesch is a giant who has contributed as much as anyone to evangelicalism's maturity and self-confidence as a twentieth-century theological phenomenon.

In fact, to many observers and interpreters of evangelicalism, Donald Bloesch is the model evangelical theologian, a scholar who combines within himself and his work the two sides of this century's evangelical movement in intimate union: historic Protestant orthodoxy and Pietism. Bloesch has allowed both to have their full weight in his work without allowing either one to go to an extreme. Bloesch's theology is passionately yet irenically confessional and at the same time intellectually pietistic.

Bloesch's Theological Mentors

Every theologian, no matter how creative, passes along through his or her contributions the influences of earlier theologians and schools of theology. Bloesch is no exception. In order to understand his place in evangelicalism, it is imperative to examine his own theological heritage—both in terms of that which he absorbed through his early training in home and church and that which he adopted during his formative theological education.

Bloesch's own testimony credits his warm, pietistic European Protestant heritage with shaping much of his spirituality and theology. His autobiographical reflections and mature writings reveal further influences by the great Protestant reformers Luther and Calvin, Protestant Pietism (Spener, Zinzendorf) and mediating theologians such as turn-of-the-century British thinker Peter Taylor Forsyth. Also evident in Bloesch's writings is critical appropriation of the theologies of Karl Barth and Emil Brunner, two leading Swiss shapers of dialectical theology (neo-orthodoxy). Lurking far in the background of Bloesch's thinking are the philosophers Immanuel Kant and Søren Kierkegaard. Notably missing from the theologians he credits with shaping his thought are those so often mentioned in lists of movers and shapers of evangelical theology: the Princeton theologians Charles Hodge and B. B. Warfield, the Scottish commonsense realist Thomas Reid and his heirs, and twentieth-century evangelical rationalist thinker Gordon Clark.

Throughout his theological career Bloesch has also turned more and more to the early church fathers, especially Athanasius and the Cappadocian Fathers Basil and the two Gregorys. His relationship with the great Augustine is more ambiguous. Almost entirely missing, however, is any appreciation for or influence by the medieval scholastics. While Thomas Aquinas merits an occasional reference or quotation, his overall influence on Bloesch's thought is minimal. Finally, Arminian theologians rank very low on the list of influences that shape Bloesch's thought. He rarely quotes Arminius or Grotius or any other Arminians appreciatively, and Wesley shapes his thought only in the area of spirituality. Bloesch is thoroughly Reformed in his overall approach to theology. His Reformed thought is not mediated to him via the Dutch Calvinists, Scottish commonsense realists or American Puritans, however. Its main channels to him seem to be his own Evangelical and Reformed heritage of Swiss and Southern German Protestant Confessionalism and the Swiss dialectical theologians Barth and Brunner.

This lineage of theological influence helps explain some of the labels that he has himself given to his theological approach. He eschews labels such as "liberal" and "fundamentalist" as well as their euphemistic counterparts "revisionist" and "conservative evangelical," preferring for himself and his own theology the terms "ecumenical evangelical," "progressive evangelical," and, showing his leanings toward Barth and Brunner, "biblical personalism," and even "neo-orthodoxy." By the latter label he means the search for a "new articulation of faith that speaks to the contemporary situation."[4]

A Mediating Theologian

Bloesch clearly sees his own theology as an alternative to the two-party system in modern American Protestant thought. His is self-consciously a mediating theology similar to that espoused by Philip Schaff and P. T. Forsyth a century before. One large and diverse theological alternative Bloesch clearly wishes to avoid is Protestant accommodationism: the liberal and revisionist theologies that give maximal acknowledgment and authority to the claims of modernity or postmodernity in Christian theology. He tasted and rejected this approach during his doctoral studies at the University of Chicago at a time when that venerable institution was dominated by process theology and so-called empirical theology.

Just as unacceptable to Bloesch as liberal-revisionist accommodationism in theology is the reactionary maximal conservatism of fundamentalism. In that he sees a kind of biblical-propositional rationalism and literalism, individualistic piety and backward-looking flight from cultural engagement that amounts to obscurantism. It also divides orthodox Christians from one another over hair-splitting debates that have nothing to do with the gospel itself, thus undermining the unity of authentic Christianity.

Many other people who proudly wear the label "evangelical" will agree with Bloesch in rejecting these two extremes within twentieth-century Protestant thought. Discomfort mounts, however, when Bloesch levels milder but distinct criticisms against evangelicals whom he perceives as veering too close to liberal-revisionist accommodationism or fundamentalism. Evangelical revisionists who believe that theology's constructive task is unfinished and seek to revise traditional formulations of doctrine in light of newer cultural-philosophical developments such as postmodernity come in for sharp correction, if not rebuke, from Bloesch. At the same time he criticizes evangelical traditionalists who see theology's constructive task as closed and engage only in rear-guard defenses of past theological systems.

Donald Bloesch is without any doubt or dispute one of the most irenic theologians on the scene in twentieth-century Protestantism. He is far from a theological pugilist and eschews polemics while reserving the right to ask critical questions of all theological proposals and systems. Even with regard to those with whom he most firmly disagrees, he remains more than merely civil. He is extremely friendly, gentle and kind. Nevertheless, after reading his critiques of almost every alternative in modern and postmodern theology, one cannot help envisioning a man sitting on a mountain peak of clear perception of truth warning fellow climbers below of loose handholds and pitfalls. To be completely fair to Bloesch, one would have to add to such a caricature the ghostly figures of Schaff, Forsyth, Barth and Brunner on slopes above Bloesch smiling in satisfaction that another has come along to replace them in helping living theological pilgrims and climbers out of the valleys of distortion, extremism, cultural accommodation and reactionary traditionalism and onto the bright plateau of balanced, biblical truth for this day and age.

In sum, then, Donald Bloesch is a theologian of reconciliation without compromise of the gospel. Throughout his theological career he has stood firmly within the classical, historic evangelical-Protestant tradition (committed by ordination to the Augsburg Confession, Luther's Small Catechism and the Heidelberg Catechism) while seeking to find common ground and points of possible reconciliation between modern theologies of various kinds. In *The Evangelical Renaissance* (1973) Bloesch announced his vision for theological reconciliation:

> Evangelicals and liberals can only be reconciled through a common rededication to the message and imperatives of Holy Scripture, and remote though the possibility may seem we should certainly strive toward this goal. Cannot we even learn from liberal scholarship concerning the historical and cultural background of Scripture? The denial of the principle of historical criticism can be just as mindless as the acceptance of the rationalistic philosophy of some of the higher critics.[5]

Although Bloesch's dream of a reinvigorated classical, evangelical-ecumenical Protestant theology may have dimmed a bit in his more recent writings, it remains alive as an ideal for the twenty-first century in his work in progress, the seven-volume magnum opus *Christian Foundations*. In its first volume (1992) Bloesch decries the present theological malaise and blames it on "heresies on the right as well as on the left."[6] But even though this later work breathes a more pessimistic spirit than *The Evangelical Renaissance,* Bloesch nevertheless holds out hope that he can contribute to "the recovery of a centrist position standing thoroughly in the tradition of orthodoxy but not averse to articulating the faith in new ways that relate creatively to the contemporary situation."[7]

Discerning Alternatives

Donald Bloesch's specific location within evangelicalism can best be charted by reference to several major theological issues. Throughout his career he has been keenly interested in theological methodology. Like many other critical and constructive theologians, he believes that starting points are all-important. If someone begins thinking about God with the wrong sources and norms, for instance, it should be no surprise if that person gets lost in the wilderness of heresy or the desert of irrelevance to culture.

While disagreeing with the early church father Tertullian on many details, Bloesch clearly believes that his rhetorical question "What has Athens to do with Jerusalem?" is still relevant to Christian theology today. Bloesch believes that Christian thinkers on *both* ends of the modern theological spectrum are guilty of accommodating to culture by overrationalizing the biblical message. He has always been extremely wary of rationalistic apologetics and of linking proclamation with any particular extrabiblical, philosophical or cultural process of reasoning or worldview.

Bloesch has consistently called in various ways for evangelical theology (centrist orthodoxy) to rediscover its true kerygmatic rather than modern apologetic foundations. With Tertullian he rejects too close of an alliance between theology and philosophy. With Luther he warns against imprisoning God's freedom with chains of logic. With Calvin he emphasizes the priority and primacy of the Holy Spirit as the "ground of Christian certainty." With Kierkegaard he rejects Hegelian logical synthesis and embraces paradoxes required by divine revelation. And with Barth he rejects natural theology and affirms theology's sole starting point and norming norm in God's Word understood as special divine revelation centering on Jesus Christ and Holy Scripture.

Bloesch never tires of warning both liberal and conservative Protestant theologies against seeking intelligibility or certainty outside of God's Word and Spirit in union. To American evangelicals obsessed with grounding the truth of Christian claims in rational apologetics (whether presuppositional-propositional or empirical-evidentialist) he writes, "The ground of certainty is not what reason can show or prove but what faith grasps and knows as the human subject is acted upon by the Holy Spirit in conjunction with the reading or hearing of the biblical Word."[8] In a rare statement of bald displeasure, Bloesch once wrote with regard to that evangelical theology rooted in the scholastic Protestant orthodoxy of the old Princeton school (Hodge, Warfield and their twentieth-century heirs), "The bane of much of modern evangelicalism is rationalism."[9]

To liberal-revisionists among Protestant theologians, Bloesch warns against truncating the biblical message and enervating Christianity itself by attempting to make them intelligible and acceptable by accommodating them to modernity or postmodernity's standards of thought and experience. He accuses them of confusing Christian theology with philosophy of religion (the heresy of philosophism) and with phenomenology of universal human religious experience (the heresy of experientialism) and warns, "Theology is not the verbalization of religious experience (Schleiermacher), even less of common human experience (David Tracy). Instead, it is the articulation of a divine revelation that breaks into our experience from beyond and transforms it."[10]

Without specifying their exact proper roles in theology, Bloesch puts both philosophy and reason in their places as "servants" of divine revelation. Both may serve as tools, but neither may become masters. Against both liberal and conservative rationalists Bloesch affirms the proper evangelical theological method as "fideistic revelationism."[11] However, from this he seeks to exclude every hint of sheer subjectivism: "What I espouse is not fideism but a faith that is deeper than fideism, for it is anchored in the supreme rationality that constitutes the content and object of faith."[12]

Is Bloesch's mature theological method sheer Barthianism? Some critics will surely see it as that. Bloesch is aware of the charge and, while seeking to give Barth his due, argues that his own theological method is not borrowed from Barth, nor identical with Barth's, but one that derives from the Reformers themselves (and ultimately from Paul the apostle!) and has always been the evangelical bulwark against cultural-philosophical accommodation. It is, he says, the method of "faith seeking understanding" espoused in various ways by a long line of Christian thinkers going back to the earliest church. With regard to its relationship with Barth's own theology, Bloesch is content to say,

I am not urging a repristination of Barthian theology (some of Barth's conclusions are problematic), but I believe we need to take his way of doing theology over that of Tillich, Küng, and Pannenberg (and I might add Edward John Carnell, Francis Schaeffer and Carl Henry).[13]

In spite of his protests to the contrary, Bloesch's theological method does seem to be heavily indebted to Barth and Brunner. While not identical with their "dialectical" theologies, Bloesch's is certainly a via media between them and that method so commonly espoused by twentieth-century evangelical rational-propositionalists. Unlike the latter, he is not particularly concerned with the laws of logic or grounding the certainty of faith even partly in rational coherence. Unlike Barth and Brunner, he is very interested in maintaining a link between divine revelation and the propositional content of Scripture itself—but without identifying them, an error he fears too many evangelicals fall into.

Another clue to the proper identification of Bloesch's place in contemporary evangelical theology lies in his doctrine of Holy Scripture. As with theological method, it stands somewhere between the neo-orthodoxy of Barth and Brunner and the rationalist-propositional (and often presuppositional) biblicism of much contemporary evangelical thought about the Bible.

Bloesch was becoming a rising star in evangelical theology at the same time that the so-called battle for the Bible was ripping evangelicalism apart in the mid-1970s. In his typically irenic manner he refused to join in the fighting, but at the same time in his typically centrist-prophetic manner he looked down on the internecine war as almost wholly unnecessary and counterproductive. Against those who were attempting to force a particular vision of Scripture's authority on all evangelicals in a sectarian spirit, Bloesch warned of the greater dangers outside evangelicalism that ought to unite evangelicals around their common confession of the truth of the gospel: "The battle today is not so much for the Bible as for the Gospel, since the innermost content of the church's proclamation and mission is being altered."[14]

The neo-orthodox influence on Bloesch is apparent in his assertion that the Bible itself is not identical with God's Word apart from the internal testimony of the Holy Spirit. In fact, Bloesch avers, the Bible *becomes* God's Word through the Spirit and the encounter with God brought about by the Spirit through the written word: "[Scripture] becomes the revealed Word of God when God himself speaks through the prophetic and apostolic witness, sealing the truth of this witness in our hearts."[15] He seeks to balance the

Barthian emphasis on Scripture's becoming the Word of God, however, by emphasizing equally that the Bible is *always* translucent to the act of Christ through the Spirit. Because of the divine inspiration of the Bible, Bloesch avers, there is an ontic difference between it and other books. But *inspiration* ought not to be understood as dictation of the very words of Scripture to the human authors, or even as verbal if by that is meant a supernatural guidance by God to the very words the human authors chose.

Instead Bloesch affirms a sacramental understanding of God's Word and the Bible: "Inspiration means that the Bible is penetrated and filled with the Holy Spirit; revelation occurs when the Bible transmits the Word of God by the action of the Spirit."[16] He uses the analogy of a light bulb and light to illustrate the connection between God's Word and the Bible. The Bible is the light bulb; God's Word is the light that shines through it. The Spirit is what makes the light bulb glow with God's Word. On the one hand, the light would have no focus and be of little help without the bulb. On the other hand, the bulb would only be glass and filament without the light. Nothing happens without the action of the Spirit of God.

Most conservative evangelicals are not likely to agree with Bloesch's view of the relationship between Scripture and God's Word. One question it raises is of Scripture's trustworthiness: the issue of inerrancy or infallibility. Bloesch tackles that thorniest of all evangelical theological thickets and affirms a "qualified inerrancy" of the Bible: "We must never say that the Bible teaches theological or historical error, but we need to recognize that not everything reported in the Bible may be in exact correspondence with historical and scientific fact as we know it today."[17]

With regard to the doctrine of Scripture, Bloesch's location is very close to that held by his British theological mentor P. T. Forsyth. That some see it instead as sheer Barthianism never ceases to amaze and dismay Bloesch. While there are similarities, Barth's view of Scripture weakens the connection between the Bible and God's Word: the relationship is only accidental, by virtue of the fact that time and again God speaks through it. Bloesch believes that his own sacramental understanding of Scripture avoids both fundamentalist and neo-orthodox errors. Fundamentalism and much conservative evangelical thought emphasize the supernatural aspect of the Bible so much that it is in danger of becoming a talisman. Bloesch criticizes even sophisticated evangelical biblicism for overemphasizing the propositional facticity of the Bible to the point that revelation is reduced to conceptuality or logic.[18]

To many conservative evangelicals Bloesch's views on Scripture place him outside the mainstream of evangelical thought, closer to neo-orthodoxy, and at best in the camp of the mediating theologians such as Herman Bavinck and G. C. Berkouwer. While Bloesch would not reject their company, he does consider himself and his own view of Scripture to be clearly within the evangelical Protestant tradition. He does not see any major differences between his own doctrine of the Bible and that of John Calvin. The truth of the matter may be that Bloesch's view lies somewhere between Calvin's and Barth's, taking something from each. With Calvin he affirms the Bible as the Spirit's unique book, inspired by the Holy Spirit and used by the Spirit to illuminate the darkened hearts and minds of people. With Barth he distinguishes between the Word of God and the words of the Bible. Against Barth he argues that the Bible cannot err theologically or even historically. Against many defenders of inerrancy today, Bloesch argues that God's self-disclosure cannot be focused exclusively on the cognitive-propositional content of the Bible's teachings and that biblical records and reports may err if measured by modern standards of scientific and historical accuracy.

Progressive Evangelical?

If evangelicalism is reduced to a tiny tent of strict propositionalists and literalistic inerrantists, then Bloesch is no evangelical. But if evangelicalism is a tent that includes all who stand firmly and faithfully in the historic, classical Protestant-Pietist heritage, then Bloesch may be the paradigm of evangelical theologians for the late twentieth century.

In fact, though Bloesch labels his own theology "progressive evangelical," many postconservative evangelical revisionists (those who believe the constructive task of theology is open and ongoing) see him as a conservative and a traditionalist. Defenders of Christian feminism, for example, criticize him for his allegedly reactionary rejection of its contributions.[19] Proponents of an evangelical narrative theology are dismayed by Bloesch's criticism of that hermeneutical approach as relativistic and as virtually identical with "story theology."[20] Finally, evangelical adherents of the "open view of God" question how truly progressive Bloesch is in light of his admittedly irenic rejection of their proposals. Their concern is not *that* Bloesch disagrees with their reconstruction of the doctrine of God, but *how* he rejects it. To many of them it seems that he falls back on a confessionalist foundation at this and many other points when confronted with a new theological proposal.[21]

Undoubtedly Bloesch's exact place on the landscape of contemporary evangelical theology is difficult to pinpoint. He wishes to be and is *progressive* compared to fundamentalists and neo-fundamentalists who cherish and defend a particular, narrow vision of tradition that is more indebted to Scottish commonsense realism and Princeton theology than it is to the genuine Reformation and Revivalist heritage of evangelicalism; yet he is *conservative* compared to evangelicalism's postconservative revisionist party that calls for genuine dialogue with moderates among the mainstream of liberal Protestant thought.

Overall it would be fair to say that Bloesch began his writing career among evangelicals with great optimism for new life and vitality for evangelicalism *if* it could overcome parochialism and narrow-minded, backward-looking defensiveness; however, he is ending his writing career on a note of moderate pessimism due to what he sees as a gradual slide away from sound doctrine into cultural accommodation, ideological or therapeutic piety and theology, and flirtation with heresy. What might account for this change of mood?

As one who has tracked Bloesch's theological career for two decades, I will venture a risky hypothesis. The emerging battle for the Bible of the 1970s brought out Bloesch's progressive side. He feared that a narrow, sectarian biblicism was about to capture evangelicalism and reduce it to a dressed-up version of fundamentalism. In response he called for and sought to construct a broader version of authentic evangelical theology that emphasized its Reformation and Pietist roots and highlighted the positive contributions Barth and Brunner and other neo-orthodox thinkers could make to a broad but vital evangelicalism. This spirit shines through his works of the late seventies and early eighties, such as *The Future of Evangelical Christianity* (1983) and his two-volume *Essentials of Evangelical Theology* (1978-1979). But then something happened.

Throughout the 1980s and into the early 1990s Bloesch experienced and observed the dangers of ideological and therapeutic influences in mainstream Protestant theology and became concerned about the future of evangelicalism if it should succumb to the same subversions and distortions. He responded prophetically with two book-length treatises: *The Struggle of Prayer* (1988)[22] and *The Battle for the Trinity* (1985).[23] While no significant theological shift is discernible in these pivotal works, they breathe a new and more conservative spirit. Bloesch's evangelical mood was changing in response to what he perceived to be sea-changes in mainstream Protestant thought that had the potential of corrupting evangelical theology.

In *The Struggle of Prayer* Bloesch warned against new forms of spirituality that tend to reduce prayer, devotion and worship to self-actualizing therapies.

Without in any way rejecting the authentic Christian tradition of contempla-
tive spirituality, he identified true Christian prayer as primarily crisis and
confrontation between the sinner and the holy God that leaves the one
praying spiritually prostrate. This "prophetic prayer," Bloesch argued, is the
true heart of Christian spirituality and is in danger of being swamped in a
morass of self-centered journeys of near-pantheistic meditation and charismatic experience. One thinks of the *New Yorker* cartoon in which a young
woman says to her counselor, "What good is an epiphany if it doesn't make
me feel better?" Bloesch warned prophetically against the dangers of
experientialism that he saw in new forms of evangelical spirituality.

In *The Battle for the Trinity* Bloesch warned against flirtation with
ideological "resymbolization" of Christian truths and used the growing
feminist movement and inclusive language of God as his case study of its
dangers. He compared mainstream Christian feminism such as that espoused
by Rosemary Ruether with the theology of the German Christians of the 1930s.
He more than hinted that a *Kirchenkampf* (church conflict) similar to that
between the German Christians and the Confessing Church in Germany
under the Nazi regime may be needed in America to rescue authentic
Christianity from subversion to radical social and political ideologies.

Bloesch's earlier optimistic, irenic, pietistic spirit was largely eclipsed by
these concerns and his responses to them during the late 1980s and early
1990s. The danger to authentic evangelicalism was different from what it had
been fifteen years earlier. Now the danger was that evangelical distinctiveness
would be swamped completely in charismatic and therapeutic feel-good
spiritualities and their subjective theological counterparts, or that it would be
snuffed out by the left-wing ideologies of the age that seek to force
Christianity into their mold.

One has to wonder if Bloesch's ecclesiastical location shaped his new
mood and the specific concerns on which he focused his attention. Ordained
in the United Church of Christ and teaching in a mainline Presbyterian
seminary (University of Dubuque Theological Seminary) brought these
particular issues to his attention more forcefully than resurgent fundamentalism within the Southern Baptist Convention or alliances between evangelicals
and right-wing ideologies during the Reagan administration. These he said
little about, while other evangelicals saw them as the greater threats to the
broad and inclusive nonsectarian evangelicalism Bloesch had helped identify
and establish during the 1970s and early 1980s.

If the first few volumes of Christian Foundations are true indicators of

Bloesch's mature theology, one may safely say that at the pinnacle of his theological career he is attempting to combine both his progressive, optimistic mood of the 1970s with his more reserved, cautious and even critical mood of the 1980s. The mature Bloesch (now in retirement from teaching, and writing as an elder statesmen of evangelical theology) is still warning both mainstream, left-of-center Protestants and more conservative evangelicals of the pitfalls of cultural accommodation, experientialism, philosophisms of all kinds, rationalism, ideological subversion and subjectivism. At the same time, he is bringing to the fore more than ever before his Barthian, neo-orthodox leanings. While avoiding the uncritical trumpeting of Barth's theology that unfortunately characterized the very end of fellow evangelical Bernard Ramm's theological career,[24] Bloesch is pointing back *through* Barth (as a twentieth-century focusing lens) *to* the Protestant reformers themselves.

A great strength of Bloesch's evangelical neo-orthodoxy is its nonsectarian traditionalism. That is, Bloesch is laying a foundation for future evangelical theology that is firmly planted on the soil of the Great Tradition of the early church fathers, evangelical medieval thinkers and Protestant reformers and pietists. It is a centrist vision that is scriptural without being biblicist, classical and traditional without being reactionary, and ecumenical without being insipid. Harder to recognize so far is how it is truly progressive.

Bloesch's Influence

Bloesch's influence on contemporary evangelical theology is difficult to gauge, as few evangelical scholars have yet responded to his theological contribution. He has not been aggressive in promoting himself or his agenda for theology throughout the land or even throughout the evangelical subculture. His influence has been primarily through his published works: articles, book reviews, monographs and multivolume systematic theologies. These have not given rise to a "Bloesch school" of evangelical thought, but they have provided many an evangelical student and scholar with an alternative to rigid, conservative orthodoxy and many an ecumenical, mainline Protestant with an alternative to liberal theology.

Despite the lack of any Bloesch school of evangelical theology, the Iowa theologian has been hailed by both conservative and ecumenical Protestant colleagues as the most "brilliant, creative evangelical working in systematic theology." That assessment by twenty seminary professors from around the United States was published in the conservative *Moody Monthly* in March 1988.[25] Furthermore, Bloesch's network of influence has extended deeply and widely into the various renewal movements within mainline Protestant denominations such as his own United Church of Christ and the Presbyterian Church (U.S.A.). Many pastors and professors who would not wear the label "evangelical" openly nevertheless look to Bloesch as their theological model and mentor.

Essentials of Evangelical Theology has been in publication continuously for almost two decades, and volume one has gone through sixteen printings (volume two, twelve printings). The book is used in many seminaries, universities and colleges and has deeply influenced students studying to be pastors and church staff persons. This and other of Bloesch's books have been widely and favorably reviewed in a variety of religious publications including *Christianity Today* and *Christian Century*. There can be no doubt or debate about the significant impact of Bloesch's theological contribution within a variety of Christian communities and contexts.

Without doubt, one of Bloesch's main influences within evangelicalism has been a greater openness to Barth and his theology than was the case under the influences of Cornelius Van Til's *The New Modernism*[26] and those conservative evangelicals influenced by its polemic against neo-orthodoxy. Throughout much of the 1950s and 1960s Barth's theology (as well as all neo-orthodoxy and dialectical theology) was condemned by conservative evangelicals as "below the line of despair" (Francis Schaeffer), only a hair's breadth from Bultmann's existentialist demythologizing with regard to the resurrection of Jesus Christ (Carl F. H. Henry) and an ally of liberal theology due to an allegedly low view of Scripture (Van Til).

Bloesch wrote one of the fairest and most incisive evangelical examinations of Barth's theology, *Jesus Is Victor! Karl Barth's Doctrine of Salvation*, in 1976.[27] While criticizing Barth's tendency to overobjectivize salvation by neglecting the role of the human person's decision of faith, Bloesch generally applauded Barth's soteriology as biblically and historically sound: "Barth has for the most part remained true to the Augustinian and Reformed principle of the sovereignty of grace."[28] Bloesch's very positive assessment of Barth's theology in 1976 and in later writings such as *Essentials of Evangelical Theology* and his Christian Foundations series has influenced many evangelicals to reconsider the traditional conservative assessment of Barth as a wolf in sheep's clothing and to embrace him as an ally. This is certainly one way in which Bloesch's theology might be considered progressive.

Three

"Fideistic Revelationalism"

Donald Bloesch's Antirationalist Theological Method

STANLEY J. GRENZ

T HE TWILIGHT YEARS OF THE TWENTIETH CENTURY HAVE WITNESSED A WIDE-spread rekindling of interest in systematic theology that in turn has ignited a flurry of literary activity. In the wake of this theological renaissance, evangelical thinkers have produced a spate of new systematic theologies. Many of these works follow the rationalist theological method that in many conservative circles has come to be viewed as the only proper way of expounding Christian doctrine. Other evangelical thinkers are exploring alternative ways of engaging in theological reflection. They are hopeful that such approaches can link contemporary evangelicalism to a broader and historically longer trajectory of Christian thought while facilitating evangelicals in speaking more clearly within the contemporary situation.

Donald Bloesch belongs to the latter group. In his self-descriptions he readily invokes the labels "evangelical" (by which he means "committed to the gospel and to the New Testament interpretation of the gospel"), "catholic" (that is, faithful "to the historic tradition of the church") and "Reformed" (that is, expressing "allegiance to the basic message of the Protestant Reformation").[1] And he claims as his theological mentors luminaries of the broader Christian tradition such as Augustine, Calvin, Luther, Kierkegaard, P. T. Forsyth and Barth.[2]

In a writing career spanning over three decades, Bloesch has sought to speak as a Reformed, catholic, evangelical theologian. At the midpoint of his career, he offered a preliminary sketch of such a theology in his two-volume

Essentials of Evangelical Theology (1978-1979). In retirement he has expanded this sketch into a multivolume series, Christian Foundations (1992-).

Throughout his distinguished career Bloesch has stood as an example of an irenic yet uncompromising evangelical who purposefully draws from the Great Tradition and fearlessly engages with the contemporary world. As a result, he belongs to a select group of pioneers whose example has given younger conservative thinkers permission to explore new vistas while self-consciously maintaining their moorings within the evangelical movement.

The goal of this essay is to summarize and evaluate the theological method that Bloesch readily admits has set him apart from certain of his evangelical colleagues, yet has pointed many others in fruitful directions. The difficulty of this task is augmented by Bloesch's program itself. His stated preference for paradox and dialectical reasoning is matched by a writing style that eschews the straightforward, linear flow indicative of rationalistic outlooks, demonstrating instead a much more erratic development of thought.

The "Standard" Evangelical Paradigm

Donald Bloesch views himself as somewhat of a "mediating" theologian. Like other evangelicals he forthrightly rejects the various liberal or modernist proposals in vogue today. However, in seeking to carve out a more orthodox alternative, he refuses to fall in line with the rationalist approach that Protestant scholasticism bequeathed to evangelicalism. To understand Bloesch's program, therefore, we must view it in contrast to the method followed by many conservative theologians.

At the heart of the rationalist paradigm is an understanding of theology that proponents claim arises naturally out of the root meaning of the word itself, namely, the organized study (*logos*) of God (*theos*).[3] When viewed from this perspective, the ultimate goal of the theologian's efforts is to articulate in a systematic manner all that can be known about God, that is, to write (as Thomas Aquinas set out to do) a *Summa Theologica*.

Whereas Aquinas drew from various sources, evangelical rationalists tend to look exclusively to the Bible for the truth about God. In charting this narrower focus, they reveal an indebtedness to Francis Turretin (1623-1687), who declared that the purpose of theology is to teach savingly of God.[4] Believing that general revelation, while perhaps valid in its own sphere, can make no appreciable contribution to this task, Turretin argued that the proper object of theology is God as he has revealed himself in his Word.[5] Consequently, theology is the systematization of the teachings of Scripture into a system of "right-doctrine."[6]

In the nineteenth century the Princeton theologians (including Charles Hodge and B. B. Warfield) combined Turretin's vision with the reigning scientific paradigm of the day. Looking to the natural scientist as their model, these thinkers argued that the theologian is likewise a scientist, albeit one who discovers and organizes the "facts" of Scripture so as to crystallize biblical truth into a set of universally true and applicable propositions.[7]

In keeping with this agenda, Wayne Grudem, to cite one contemporary example, announces at the beginning of his *Systematic Theology* this working definition: "Systematic theology is any study that answers the question, 'What does the whole Bible teach us today?' about any given topic." He then explains: "This definition indicates that systematic theology involves collecting and understanding all the relevant passages in the Bible on various topics and then summarizing their teachings clearly so that we know what to believe about each topic."[8] Somewhat more sophisticated than Grudem's "concordance" model, Lewis and Demarest declare that systematic theology "organizes the material of divine revelation topically and logically, developing a coherent and comprehensive world view and way of life."[9]

The rationalist method leads quite naturally to a primarily propositionalist understanding of theology. The central goal of such inquiry is knowledge understood as correct assertions or true statements about God and the world. This focus on cognitive statements arises out of a rationalist understanding of revelation that views it as the communication of information. Hence, Carl F. H. Henry defines revelation as

> that activity of the supernatural God whereby he communicates information essential for man's present and future destiny. In revelation God, whose thoughts are not our thoughts, shares his thoughts with man; in this self-disclosure God unveils his very mind; he communicates not only the truth about himself and his intentions, but also that concerning man's present plight and future prospects.[10]

Consequently, "God's revelation is rational communication conveyed in intelligible ideas and meaningful words, that is, in conceptual-verbal form."[11]

Further, because the theologian's findings take the form of propositions, the veracity of such assertions can be determined. One prominent proposal suggests that the verification process involves comparing alternative theological hypotheses with the biblical data. In this task, evangelical rationalists appeal to the canons of logic, including the principles of identity, the excluded middle and noncontradiction.

Rationalist theologians regularly delineate their approach in elaborate prolegomena to the systematic theologies they compose. These prolegomena generally begin with an introductory chapter delineating the rationalist theological method, followed by a discussion of their stated starting point for theology: revelation understood as God's self-disclosure. The standard approach then gives passing reference to God's revelation to all humankind in creation and in the human person (general revelation), before focusing on God's more complete self-disclosure to special people, such as the prophets and apostles (special revelation), which revelation is inscripturated in the Bible. At this point, evangelical thinkers generally develop a doctrine of Scripture in which they seek to establish biblical authority by appeal to the divine inspiration of the Bible (as well as ongoing illumination of its contents) followed by an attempt to set forth the extent of biblical authority through explications of terms such as *infallibility* and *inerrancy*.

Only at this point do rationalist theologians sense that they have laid a sufficient foundation to launch the systematic theological task itself. Indeed, the explication of Christian doctrine that occupies the bulk of standard evangelical systematic theology texts is the theologians' summary of propositions they believe are embedded within God's self-disclosure in Scripture.

The rationalist method in theology is the outworking of certain theological and anthropological presuppositions (as well as the more obvious beliefs about the nature of the Bible). Above all, Christian rationalists build from the assumption that the human mind (or reason) is capable of gaining access to actual truth about God. Consequently, theological statements can be univocal. Bloesch observes, "Rationalism tends toward a univocal predication of God over equivocity and analogy. It assumes that our language about God directly communicates who God really is and what he demands of us."[12]

Lewis and Demarest provide a clear example of this. Their theological method assumes "that God can reveal information to people who are created in his image to think his thoughts after him."[13] In a similar manner, Carl Henry claims that lying behind the rational character of the Christian faith is "the rational living God"[14] who "addresses man in his Word."[15] The divine address is possible, he adds, because reason is foundational to the human person[16] as created in the image of God.[17] The canons of logic are helpful in theology, therefore, because these "are rooted ultimately in the mind and nature of the

Creator," to cite the words of Lewis and Demarest.[18]

Although sympathetic to his colleagues' desire to maintain a certain objectivity to theology, Bloesch rejects categorically this rationalist theological method.

The Nature of Revelation

Instead of following uncritically the lead of Turretin, Hodge and Warfield, Bloesch seeks to go behind Protestant scholasticism so as to draw from an earlier theological trajectory. His goal is "to discover a new way of doing theology that will establish its continuity with the catholic tradition, especially as this tradition has come alive in the Protestant Reformation."[19] Lying at the foundation of his alternative is what Bloesch considers to be a more Reformed understanding of revelation.

Like his rationalist colleagues, Bloesch believes that the starting point for theology lies in revelation understood as the divine self-disclosure. And he readily acknowledges a type of cognitive component to it:

> Revelation is God's self-communication through his selected instrumentality, especially the inspired witness of his prophets and apostles. This act of self-communication entails not only the unveiling of his gracious and at the same time awesome presence but also the imparting of the knowledge of his will and purpose for humankind.[20]

Yet Bloesch quickly distances himself from the implications that rationalists draw from this. The heirs of Protestant scholasticism conclude that revelation is largely static. Consequently, they focus almost exclusively on the communication of cognitive information. For Bloesch, in contrast, revelation takes on a dynamic character. It is an event. Revelation is what transpires between God and the recipient. Echoing his mentor Karl Barth, Bloesch declares, "Revelation is God speaking and the human being responding through the power of God's Spirit. . . . Revelation is the conjunction of divine revealing action and human response."[21] Above all, revelation is the redeeming, transforming encounter of the individual with the Living God. In Bloesch's words, "It is an act of communication by which God confronts the whole person with his redeeming mercy and glorious presence."[22]

The foundation for Bloesch's alternative. Why does he argue so strongly against the rationalist understanding and in favor of what he sees as the Reformation view? As he himself suggests, Bloesch's program is generated by a thoroughgoing Reformed understanding of the human situation, albeit one filtered through a strong Barthian reading of that tradition. Rather than the optimistic anthropology that drives the scholastic approach with its inordinate trust in our human rational capabilities, Bloesch works out of a profound sense of human fallenness and a thoroughgoing application of the idea of depravity.

The extent of our fallenness, he argues, leaves us devoid of any innate point of contact for the gospel.[23] Even our reason is affected. Rather than a vehicle for knowing God, reason is tainted and therefore untrustworthy. This means that reason cannot bring us into contact with the eternal truth of God. If we are to know God, he himself must take the initiative.

Into this situation Bloesch declares happily, God does graciously speak. But the divine Word is not merely, or even primarily, a cognitive or propositional message. Indeed, given the fallenness of our reason, how could it be? Instead, the Word of God comes to us as transforming power. This, Bloesch adds, is "revelation." And the event of God's powerful self-communication to "a world in darkness," he adds, invariably brings about "a disruption of our thoughts, values and goals."[24]

Not only does human fallenness preclude a purely cognitive understanding of revelation, the nature of God does so as well. In Bloesch's estimation the rationalists draw from a too narrow understanding of God, one that views him as primarily "mind" (that is, "rationality"). Following the volitional dimension present in Reformation theology, Bloesch speaks of God as "will": God "is not simply an all-comprehending mind but dynamic will and energy."[25]

Because God is will, Bloesch concludes, revelation is not chiefly concerned with transferring cognitive information from one rational mind (God's) to another (ours). More importantly it is an encounter of a sinful person with God through Jesus Christ that transforms the human will and thereby issues forth in obedience. Further, because the being of the God who is will is never fully disclosed in revelation, "God remains hidden (*deus absconditus*) even in his revelation." This divine hiddenness, Bloesch avers, precludes the rationalists' claim that our statements about God are identical with God's own being.[26]

The locus of revelation. Bloesch's shift in understanding of revelation has far-reaching consequences for his approach to theology. It leads him, like Barth, to question the typical evangelical use of the concept of general revelation and the openness to natural theology that arises from their acceptance of that concept. Bloesch argues that general revelation contradicts the idea of revelation as essentially a personal encounter. More specifically, "If revelation is defined as God's effectual communication of his will and purpose to humanity, then we have no revelation in nature that can be positively conjoined with the biblical meanings of 'unveiling' . . . and 'manifestation.' "[27]

Bloesch is too good a reader of Calvin to toss out the idea of general revelation completely. He acknowledges the appropriateness of speaking about a general presence of God in nature and history. But he quickly adds that "this general presence does not become a revelation of his grace and mercy until it is perceived in the light of Jesus Christ."[28]

Despite this concession Bloesch simply cannot condone the move from general revelation to natural theology. In fact, like Barth he considers any claim to a natural knowledge of God to be sheer falsehood, even idolatry:[29]

> The knowledge of God through nature and conscience apart from the revelation in Christ is not a true knowledge but a deceptive knowledge. It is not an understanding but a misunderstanding. It is not a saving knowledge but a condemning knowledge. It gives us not a capacity for revelation but an incapacity.[30]

If natural theology is a cul-de-sac, the quest to know God (and hence our theological method) casts us solely and squarely upon special revelation. But what is this "Word of God" that confronts the recipient directly? And where is such revelation found?

The Bible and the Word of God. Here Bloesch tackles the heirs of Protestant scholasticism head-on. The rationalists with their static concept of revelation too readily equate the Word of God with the words of Scripture. Bloesch's dynamic view simply cannot countenance such a mistaken understanding. Pulling no punches, he asserts,

> The bane of much of modern evangelicalism is rationalism which presupposes that the Word of God is directly available to human reason. It is fashionable to refer to the biblical revelation as propositional, and in one sense this is true in that the divine revelation is communicated through verbal concepts and models. . . . At the same time we must not infer that the propositional statements in the Bible are themselves revealed, since this makes the Bible the same kind of book as the Koran which purports to be exclusively divine.

In fact, he adds, "Those who reduce the content of revelation to declarative statements in the Bible overlook the elements of mystery, transcendence, and dynamism in revelation."[31]

Lying behind Bloesch's polemic is his understanding of revelation and its implications for the nature of Scripture. He points out that revelation, which is "the Word of life and redemption that comes directly from God," precedes Scripture, for it "existed before the writing of the Bible and brought this writing into existence."[32]

His concern that the dynamic Word of God not be equated with the propositional statements of the Bible leads Bloesch to posit a distinction between Scripture and the transcendent Word. He declares in no uncertain terms, "The Bible is not in and of itself the revelation of God but the divinely appointed means and channel of this revelation."[33] Bloesch willingly grants a close connection (a *conjunction,* to use his term) between the Bible and the divine Word.[34] Yet lest his view be mistaken for the rationalist position he rejects, he states clearly that the connection between the Word and the Bible does not inhere in the text itself, but in the Spirit who speaks to the reader through the text: "The Bible in and of itself is not the Word of God—divine revelation—but it is translucent to this revelation by virtue of the Spirit of God working within it and within the mind of the reader and hearer."[35]

The Role of Theology

His understanding of revelation requires that Bloesch distinguish between the divine Word of God and the human words that point toward it or bear witness to it. But this distinction raises a crucial question: If theology does not consist in systematizing the revelation inscripturated in the statements of the Bible, what exactly is its task?

The various definitions Bloesch sprinkles throughout his writings carry a strongly practical, even missiological tone. Theology, he writes, is

> the systematic endeavor to render a compelling and faithful witness to the truth of divine revelation. It is addressed primarily to the believing community with the intention of enabling that community to bring all of its thought and action into conformity with the will of God as revealed in Jesus Christ. It nevertheless takes into consideration the thought and plight of the world outside the church, for its ultimate aim is to bring the whole world into submission to Jesus Christ.[36]

In a similar definition (albeit one in which he confusingly seems to use "the Word of God" in two different manners) Bloesch declares,

Theology is the diligent and systematic explication of the Word of God for every age, involving not only painstaking study of the Word of God but also an earnest attempt to relate this Word to a particular age or cultural milieu. Theology in the evangelical sense is the faithful interpretation of the biblical message to the time in which we live.[37]

In keeping with this practical thrust, Bloesch describes his approach to theology by appeal to a widely known dictum that dates at least to Anselm: "The theological method I affirm is 'faith seeking understanding.' " He then explains how this method works:

We begin with faith's apprehension of divine revelation and then endeavor to explore the ramifications and implications of this for daily life. . . . Our starting point is God's self-revelation in Jesus Christ, which creates faith within us.[38]

Statements such as these reflect Bloesch's strong conviction that true theology always points beyond itself to the dynamic of revelation that transcends every human attempt to speak about it. This conviction sets Bloesch apart from rationalists. "The task of theology," he writes, "is to acquire not observational knowledge about God (as in naturalistic empiricism) or conceptual mastery of him (as in idealistic rationalism) but an understanding of his will and purpose disclosed in Jesus Christ, an understanding that eventuates in obedience."[39]

At the same time Bloesch readily acknowledges that divine revelation has a conceptual side.[40] The divine-human encounter is not a subjective experience that arises from within the human person. Instead, in that it is grounded on a message that comes to the recipient from beyond revelation, it is objective. This objective dimension opens the door to theology as intellectual reflection.

In this context Bloesch's somewhat opaque but important distinction between dogma and doctrine becomes important. In the opening pages of *A Theology of Word & Spirit* (1992), he defines dogma as "a propositional truth that is grounded in and inseparable from God's self-revelation in Christ and communicated to the interiority of our being by the Spirit of God. It signifies the divinely given interpretation of revelation." A doctrine, in contrast, "is a propositional affirmation that represents the church's continuing reflection on the dogmatic norm of faith."[41]

Later in the same work Bloesch once again contrasts dogma and doctrine:

Dogma is the divinely inspired apostolic interpretation of the events of redemption. Doctrine is the systematic affirmation of this divinely inspired interpretation by the theologians of the church. Dogma is what God declares; doctrine is what the person of faith articulates. Doctrine is dogma condensed in a propositional statement accessible to human understanding and *eo ipso* distortion. Dogma is irreversible and irreformable. Doctrine is open to reformation and correction, but its dogmatic content is irrevocable and unalterable. Dogma in the plural is equivalent to doctrines, but in the singular it ordinarily indicates the content of revelation.[42]

These statements suggest that in Bloesch's understanding, *dogma* refers to the objective, yet seemingly ineffable, cognitive content of the gospel that the Holy Spirit causes the recipient to "know" in the interiority of the heart. *Doctrine* is a human attempt to state that dogma in the form of an assertion. Doctrine emerges as we try to put into human words the divine truth that in fact cannot be subsumed by cognitive communication.

Viewed in this context, one task of theology becomes that of testing and refining these statements of doctrine. Bloesch himself hints at this role: "Dogmatics is the articulation of the dogma of revelation in the light of the biblical and apostolic witness and in the light of the interpretation of this revelation by the fathers and doctors of the church through the ages."[43] Yet in contrast to the optimism of the rationalists, Bloesch is convinced that we can never hope to "get it right." Only at the eschaton will we be able to state perfectly the objective dimension of our faith.[44]

Bloesch believes that this awareness ought to lead to a certain humility on the part of the theologian. He models this characteristic when he acknowledges, "I believe in one faith—the holy catholic faith, but this faith can never be exhaustively or definitively formulated by mortal human beings, though it can be truly confessed and proclaimed. Every interpretation is open to fresh articulation."[45]

The humility Bloesch advocates extends to the theological enterprise as a whole. He adamantly and consistently asserts that in the end the task of theological reflection is not to construct an all-encompassing worldview. Its purpose is not to set forth the one, all-encompassing metaphysical truth of reality and thereby establish some supposedly Christian philosophy. Instead, theology can only point to the divine revelation that transcends all human assertions: the mystery of God's self-disclosure in Jesus Christ. And its message is simply that of the gracious God who in Christ encounters sinful humans:

> Theology can never perfect a comprehensive, rational system of truth because the Bible presents us not with universal principles related only tangentially to history but with varied and sometimes divergent reports of significant happening in history. We can glean from these reports reliable intimations of God's will and purpose for his people but not final answers to problems that have vexed metaphysicians through the ages. The Bible gives us not an overarching synoptic perspective of historical and spiritual reality but an unfailing impression of God's faithfulness and mercy, which extends even to a recalcitrant and stubborn people.[46]

Bloesch, following the Reformers, declares that this gospel message—the good news about the God who meets us in Jesus—runs contrary to fallen human reason. Because theology speaks about this glorious truth, it may not consistently follow the canons of logic, as the rationalists erroneously claim. On the contrary, theological reflection will by necessity come to expression in paradoxical statements arising through dialectical reasoning. Bloesch explains:

> I agree with Barth and Brunner that dialectical reasoning is necessary in the theological enterprise because the paradox of the eternal God dramatically entering the stream of human history in Jesus Christ can be grasped only through holding together aspects of the truth about God and his plan of salvation that seem contradictory to human reason.[47]

The Sources for Theology

Protestant scholasticism was born out of the Reformation elevation of Scripture as the sole norm of the theology. As a result, evangelical rationalists claim that they look to the Bible as the source for their theological formulations (some even going so far as to suggest that they draw from the Bible alone). Here again Bloesch parts company with his conservative colleagues while claiming to present a richer understanding of the Reformation heritage. And once again his nuanced understanding of revelation forms the foundation of his methodological proposal. If revelation is not simply the Bible but the dynamic of the divine encounter, then Scripture cannot be the ultimate norm for theology. Instead, this norm can only be revelation itself.

At the same time Bloesch admits that the divine revelation never comes to us immediately. It is always mediated through human words. For this reason, he offers an intriguing differentiation between the absolute norm (that is, divine revelation, or the "gospel of God") and what he calls relative (dependent) norms.[48]

In Bloesch's understanding we can never draw directly from the absolute norm. Instead, this norm "descends" into the relative norms to which we have access. In his appraisal of the Wesleyan quadrilateral, he explains this idea:

> I propose a *unilateral* authority—divine revelation—but one communicated through various means. I see divine revelation received through Scripture and tradition and elucidated by reason and experience. Revelation does not so much proceed out of Scripture and tradition as descend into these earthen vessels. It is not based on reason or experience, but it employs reason and experience in making itself credible and effectual.[49]

Above all, however, Bloesch looks to Scripture and tradition (or the church's proclamation) to function as the relative sources for theology. "Scripture," he writes, "is the primary, tradition the secondary, witness to divine revelation."[50]

Biblical authority. In keeping with the heritage of the Reformation, Bloesch adamantly elevates Scripture as the normative (relative) source in theology. Yet he offers a carefully nuanced understanding of what the authority of the Bible entails.

Bloesch sets his proposal apart from what he sees as the two major contemporary options. On the one hand, he rejects the scholastic approach, which he describes as "that kind of theology that emphasizes the accessibility of the infinite to the finite and the possibility and indeed the desirability of systematizing the body of revealed knowledge given in Scripture." On the other hand, he refuses to go along with the liberal or modernist alternative, which, in his words, "stresses the inseparability of the infinite and the finite and sees the infinite as residing in the finite as its ground and depth."[51]

In seeking to carve out a position between these two, Bloesch sets forth what he calls the sacramental model. Like the sacraments and even the church itself, the Bible is "a divinely appointed medium or channel of revelation. The Bible is the earthen vessel in which we have a hidden treasure."[52]

Bloesch readily acknowledges that his view shares a certain affinity with rationalism: "One can see that the sacramental model has much more in common with the scholastic model than with the liberal one, for the first two are united in affirming the reality of an objective, absolute revelation of God in history." But he quickly points out that unlike the rationalist approach, his model "recognizes that this absolute Word of God is mediated through the relativity of human witness."[53]

Bloesch's sacramental model is closely connected to his somewhat enigmatic and clearly Barthian understanding of the normative status of Scripture. On the one hand, he clearly denies that the Bible in itself is our authority:

> The ultimate, final authority is not Scripture but the living God himself as we find him in Jesus Christ. Jesus Christ and the message about him constitute the material norm for our faith just as the Bible is the formal norm. The Bible is authoritative because it points beyond itself to the absolute authority, the living and transcendent Word of God.[54]

On the other hand, Bloesch resolutely refuses to disengage the voice of Christ from Scripture:

> We must go on to affirm, however, that the absolute authority of faith, the living Christ himself, has so bound himself to the historical attestation concerning his self-revelation, namely, the sacred Scripture, that the latter necessarily participates in the authority of its Lord. The Bible must be distinguished from its ground and goal, but it cannot be separated from them.[55]

In his attempt to avoid both fundamentalism and liberalism, Bloesch places himself squarely in the Reformation tradition as he understands it. He forthrightly affirms that the Word of God comes to us through the biblical message. But how exactly does this Word emerge? For Bloesch, there can be only one answer: by the Spirit. Hence, in commenting on the widely held distinction between the sign (which he defines as "the letter of Scripture") and the thing signified (that is, "God's self-revelation in Christ"), he declares, "We do not have Christ apart from the sign, which, by the power of the Spirit, is effectual in communicating the mystery of Christ to us."[56]

In this manner Bloesch seeks to follow the Reformation in holding Scripture and the Spirit together. For him, "The Holy Spirit is not a second criterion alongside the Word [which I take him to mean in this context the Bible as the written word] but one aspect of the sole criterion—the Word enlightened by the Spirit or the Spirit illuminating the Word."[57] By bringing the Holy Spirit and Scripture together, he does indeed attempt to set forth "a theology of Word and Spirit," as the title of his inaugural volume in the Christian Foundations indicates.

Church tradition. For Bloesch the primary (relative) norm for theology is the Bible. He believes that the divine Word comes to us as the Spirit speaks through Scripture. In so doing he raises high his Reformation flag. Indeed, Bloesch clearly sides with the Reformers in their disagreement with the prevailing view of the late medieval church that placed church tradition on a par with Scripture. According to Bloesch,

> The Reformers resolutely maintained that there is only one source of revelation, Holy Scripture. Scripture, moreover, contains not only the revealed, divine truth but the *whole* revealed truth. For the Reformers the church is under the Word and simply attests and proclaims it but does not authorize it.[58]

And for Bloesch, following the Reformers, the Scripture under which the church stands is self-interpreting and self-authenticating.[59]

Although adamant in his affirmation of *sola Scriptura,* Bloesch finds a crucial role for church tradition. He looks to creeds and confessions of faith as "road signs" that direct us to Jesus Christ and the truth of the gospel, thereby "keeping the church in harmony with the faith once delivered to the saints."[60] Yet Bloesch is careful always to place tradition secondary to Scripture. Creeds and confessions of faith carry only "a ministerial authority" in contrast to the "magisterial authority" of Scripture.[61]

This ordering of Scripture and tradition suggests the function the secondary source ought to fulfill: "The role of the church is to clarify and interpret what has already been decisively revealed in the person and work of Jesus Christ recorded in Holy Scripture."[62] And creeds ought to assist in understanding Scripture.[63] For this reason, he believes that such statements are always open to reformulation "as the Spirit brings new light to bear from the Scriptures."[64]

Bloesch is likewise careful to maintain the dependency of tradition (like Scripture) on the controlling authority, the mystery of the divine Word. Just as the gospel ought not to be confused with the words of Scripture, so also it cannot be equated with the church's teaching:

> The ultimate authority for faith is the living Word of God, the gospel of reconciliation and redemption, which is made known to the church

but not delivered into the hands of the church. What the church passes on from one generation to another is teachings about the gospel, not the very gospel itself.[65]

In an intriguing paragraph in the heart of his discussion of Scripture and tradition, Bloesch notes how the dependency of both exegesis and the church's teaching office on the ultimate authority of the transcendent gospel provides the appropriate response whenever the two relative authorities appear to conflict:

> When these authorities seem to disagree, this means that we have not really made contact with the real Word of Scripture or the true head of the church, which are one and the same. We must subject the discordant voices that we hear to Christ's self-witness within the Scriptures thereby bringing a transcendent norm to bear upon the point of contention.[66]

Like Scripture, church proclamation functions sacramentally. For Bloesch, it can become the vehicle through which the divine Word speaks to the hearer. This glorious miracle occurs only by the Spirit:

> Another way to express the dynamics of theological authority is to state that the final norm is Jesus Christ, the living Word of God, who is attested in Holy Scripture and proclaimed by the church through the ages. Both the Bible and church proclamation become transparent to this living Word when they are illumined by the Spirit for the community of the faithful. When confronted by the illuminated text, we are at the same time meeting the risen Christ. Through the agency of the Spirit the understanding of the text becomes a redemptive happening, a breakthrough into meaning.[67]

Bloesch's theological hermeneutic. Bloesch's idea of the "conjunction" of the divine Word with the words of Scripture leads him to a final point of methodological disagreement with the rationalist tradition. Rationalist theologians, assuming that the words of the Bible are identical with divine revelation, go to the Bible to discover the theological truths found in its pages. Bloesch agrees with the rationalists that the text has "objective meaning." Yet he is convinced that the true meaning is not contained in the text itself, but resides in the Spirit "who breathes on the text."[68]

To explain this Bloesch draws a distinction between two levels of meaning.

On the one hand, there is what he calls the "historical meaning" of the text, which includes both "authorial intention and the way in which the text was received in the community of faith." But a text also has a "revelational," "pneumatic" or "spiritual meaning." This is "meaning that the text assumes when the Spirit acts on it in bringing home its significance to people of faith in every age."[69]

Whereas the biblical scholar may devote attention to the former, the theologian Bloesch finds the second meaning far more interesting. In fact, it is this meaning that brings the Word of God to light in our lives leading to our transformation. On this basis Bloesch states quite forthrightly his disagreement with his rationalist colleagues:

> I do not share the vision of much traditional orthodoxy that the Bible is impregnated with universal, unchanging truths that are waiting to be discovered and formulated. Instead I hold that the Bible is filled with the Spirit of God, who brings new light to bear on ancient wisdom—light that leads us not only to renewed understanding but also to obedience.[70]

Were revelation lodged simply in authorial intent, the exegete could be satisfied with the critical, historical methods of interpretation scholars have developed over the years. In fact, however, such critical scholarship is limited, Bloesch avers. By itself it can "do little more than cast light on the Bible as a historical document."[71] But the divine truth of Scripture is not directly accessible to the reader, and consequently a more nuanced hermeneutic is necessary,[72] one which can draw the readers into "the work of the Spirit on the text" so that they "become covenant partners with the Spirit in his work of interpretation." In this encounter with divine grace the interpreter's horizon is overturned (rather than "fused" as Gadamer proposed) and a "wholly new horizon" dawns within the interpreter.[73]

But how does one gain access to this "revelatory meaning" and come to be drawn into the process of encounter with the divine Word? Bloesch believes that this requires that we go beyond the typically evangelical method of exegesis with its quest for authorial intent. The "theological exegesis" he proposes entails four moments. First, it requires that the reader comes to the text with "an open heart and a searching mind." This is crucial, because the spiritual meaning of the text is only accessible to those who "are in experiential contact with the realities to which the text witnesses."[74] Second, it involves the attempt to ascertain authorial intent through historical-grammatical exegesis. But third, the interpreter must then seek to see the text "in the light of its theological context, relating the text to the central message of Holy Scripture," and listening "to the voice of the living Christ within Scripture." Finally, the hermeneutical task entails interfacing the text with the cultural situation of one's own time.[75]

Only when we engage our efforts toward this kind of expectant listening, can we anticipate that the "miracle of divine grace"[76] will occur. Only then can we expect the Spirit to break into our lives from beyond and speak the divine truth of the Bible to us. For Bloesch, only this kind of genuine "hearing" of the Word of God can give rise to true theology.

Theology and Culture

Bloesch's "theology of divine-human encounter" or "theology of crisis," as he on one occasion characterizes his program,[77] leads him to an inevitable clash with the advocates of a theology of culture in its various forms. If humans are fallen, if all humanly devised statements about God are idolatry, if humans lack an innate point of contact for the gospel, if revelation is a transcendent power that transforms the human recipient, then what possible contribution could culture make to this process?

This foundational stance leads Bloesch to display a thoroughgoing distrust for culture that at times approaches a fundamentalist diatribe. In his estimation many of the harmful tendencies at work today are the outgrowth of certain misguided theological methods that draw too much from culture. Chief among these is a naive theology of accommodation that attempts to find some "underlying unity between secular and religious wisdom and thereby forge a vision of God and of the world that can elicit support from all quarters."[78] Equally onerous is a misdirected theology of correlation that seeks to bring together "the creative questions of the culture and the answer of Christian revelation."[79]

In contrast to the accommodationists and correlationists, Bloesch advocates "a theology of confrontation," that is, a theological approach that militantly confronts culture with the divine Word. In a lucid description of the response to modern society he advocates, Bloesch sets his program apart from the accommodationist theological agenda:

> The goal in this kind of militant theology is not synthesis or correlation but the conversion of culture and philosophy to the new values and transcendent perspective of the kingdom of God. The gospel is not

added to what is already known; instead, it overturns human knowledge and calls us to break with our past orientation.

A theology of confrontation is primarily kerygmatic, not apologetic: its first concern is to make known the claims of the gospel without any desire to bring them into accordance with the preconceived wisdom of the culture. It is a theology of crisis rather than process. It sees humanity as the question and the gospel as the answer. But humanity can see itself as the question only in the light of the answer, which is given in revelation.[80]

Bloesch's confrontational stance precludes him from viewing culture as making any normative contribution to theology:

Against the harmonizers and syncretizers I maintain that culture is not a bona fide source of theology but the catalyzing material that theology uses in the application of the Word of God. Our task is to make the faith intelligible but not credible or palatable, for only the Spirit does that. Our aim is to clarify the gospel, to set forth its scandal without ambiguity, not to remove or mitigate this scandal.[81]

Bloesch extends his quarrel with the theologians of culture by characterizing his program as a confessional theology. In a manner that would make many fundamentalists proud, he speaks about a conflict looming on the horizon between those who want to bring theology into harmony with the world and those (like him) who would speak the Word of God to the world:

The real battle lines in the future will be between those who espouse a revisionist theology bent on updating theology and bringing it into greater harmony with contemporary experience, and those who uphold a confessional theology that witnesses to the claims of the gospel as presented in Scripture and church tradition.[82]

Titles of works like *Faith and Its Counterfeits* (1981) and *The Battle for the Trinity* (1985) suggest that Bloesch has already entered the fray.

Yet despite his rhetoric of militant confrontation Bloesch has not joined cause with those on his right. Even here, he sets himself apart from what he sees as the errors of the rationalists.

While bemoaning the unfortunate ramifications of accommodationism, Bloesch chides evangelicals for not offering a viable alternative. Evangelicals all too readily respond to the modern situation with a "theology of restoration," he asserts, that advocates a simple return to "older methodologies and theological formulations in the sincere belief that these past positions can still be a viable alternative to seekers after meaning and truth."[83] This restorationist impulse, Bloesch adds, has led evangelicals to gravitate to "a rationalistic orthodoxy that views the Bible as a compendium of propositions or a storehouse of facts inviting systematic analysis."[84]

Bloesch remains at all times a "Reformed, catholic evangelical." Rather than the narrow, backward-looking confessionalism he finds widespread among evangelicals, the theology of confrontation he advocates is a "catholic confessional theology" that seeks to interface the gospel with the contemporary situation. Bloesch explains the difference:

> Confessional theology in the catholic sense will not be reactionary. It advocates not a return to the past but a critical reappropriation of the wisdom of the past. It espouses continuity with tradition but is willing to subject even church tradition to the judgment of the Word of God. It is evangelical and catholic but not sectarian or restorationist.
>
> The confessional theology I uphold will be both conservative and radical (in the sense of going to the roots, *ad fontes*). Its theologians will respect and try to learn from the creeds and confessions in their own traditions, but instead of remaining with them, will aspire to go through them to a fresh articulation of the faith for our day.[85]

Bloesch's unabated quest for "a fresh articulation of the faith for our day" births in him a burning desire to engage constructively with culture. Despite all the rhetoric chastising the accommodationists, Bloesch's agenda demands that he create a culturally sensitive theology, a theology that speaks to the contemporary situation. And this goal requires a theological method that takes culture seriously. Bloesch acknowledges the cultural dimension when he defines theology as

> the systematic reflection within a particular culture on the self-revelation of God in Jesus Christ as attested in Holy Scripture and witnessed to in the tradition of the catholic church. Theology in this sense is both biblical and contextual. Its norm is Scripture, but its field or arena of action is the cultural context in which we find ourselves.[86]

Yet he remains adamant in refusing to give culture a place alongside Scripture and tradition as a source for theology in his description of the proper theological method.

In the end, Bloesch's opponent in the discussion of culture is not merely the accommodationists and correlationists on his left, but also the rationalists on his right. He is convinced that at a deeper level evangelical rationalists are as captive to modern culture as are their liberal opponents. They too have jettisoned the biblical understanding of truth in favor of the modern, scientific conception. And it is ultimately at this level that he sees the battle being waged. Bloesch explains:

> The debate today revolves around conflicting understandings of truth. In modern parlance the true is the historically and scientifically demonstrable. In biblical perspective the true is the spiritually and redemptively transformative. For moderns the true is that which can be empirically verified. For the prophets of biblical history the true is that which authenticates itself through the power of the Spirit.[87]

What is the solution? Bloesch is clear as to which theological programs cannot carry the day. In a single hard-hitting discussion early in *A Theology of Word & Spirit* he distances himself from a gamut of approaches to theology—revelational positivism, presuppositionalism, foundationalism, evidentialism, coherentism—to which he attaches the names of some of the most revered thinkers within evangelicalism. From Bloesch's perspective, all these proposals are suspect because they all fall under the overarching rubric of rationalism. They are simply varieties of the same flawed rationalist theological method with its erroneous modern conception of truth and its inordinate trust in reason to provide the foundation for faith.

As the antidote, Bloesch offers what he calls "fideistic revelationalism":

> The decision of faith is as important as the fact of revelation in giving us certainty of the truth of faith. The revelation is not simply assented to but is existentially embraced as the truth or power of salvation. Certainty of its truth becomes ours only in the act of decision and obedience by which the external truth becomes internalized in faith and life.[88]

Only by recapturing this biblical outlook, Bloesch believes, can we once again hear the divine Word spoken by the divine Spirit.

Bloesch's Program in Contemporary Perspective
His thoroughgoing dissatisfaction with options on the right and the left marks Donald Bloesch as one of the key mediating evangelical theologians of our

day. He calls for a method that balances the insights from both sides of this somewhat erroneous theological divide, while placing himself squarely within the broader evangelical trajectory.

Bloesch speaks with prophetic clarity in calling the church to a renewal of catholic and Reformed concerns within the contemporary context. His elevation of the gospel as God's gracious provision for human sin and his emphasis on the necessity for a personal reception of the gospel are needed reminders in a day in which self-help programs abound not only in society but within the church as well. His chastened view of what human reason can accomplish and consequently of the extent to which theology can articulate ultimate truth is a welcomed antidote to the triumphalism displayed by many evangelicals today.

Bloesch is likewise to be lauded for his attempt to bring doctrine and experience together and thereby to combine "head" and "heart." In so doing he stands as a contemporary heir to his own Puritan-pietist heritage. This strand becomes visible as well in Bloesch's helpful emphasis on the practical dimension of theology.

But perhaps the central feature of Bloesch's theological method is the foundational role played by his rediscovery of the dynamic character of revelation. His delineation of a method that takes seriously the mystery of the divine Word as the paradoxical unity of the written Word and the Spirit in the event of God's transforming self-disclosure comes as a fresh breeze at a time when a propositionalism born out of a rationalist approach to theology has become the quasi-orthodox approach in many circles.

On this basis Bloesch rightly calls evangelicals to think through the nature of biblical authority in a manner more in keeping with the heritage of the Reformers who did not focus on the Bible alone but, like Bloesch, conjoined Scripture and Spirit. And Bloesch puts his finger on one of the crucial methodological issues of our day: the tendency among evangelicals to collapse the Spirit speaking through Scripture into human attempts to gain access to authorial intent through critical exegetical tools.

Despite my great appreciation for Bloesch's contribution, I nevertheless come away from this central dimension of his methodological proposal with several gnawing questions.

Reformed pessimism. One question focuses on what I see as the thorough-going pessimism driving Bloesch's theological method. I agree wholeheartedly with his fundamentally Reformed take on the human predicament. I too affirm that humans are depraved, even totally depraved (so long as that phrase is understood in the manner the Reformers meant). And he is surely correct in upholding the central Christian conviction that God's gracious response to human sin comes to us in and through Jesus Christ. Yet I wonder if Bloesch (like Barth before him) does not take a too dim view of the human situation, a view that at times appears to lead to a truncated theological method.

For example, in his concern to uphold the Christocentric focus of divine revelation, does Bloesch pay adequate attention to the universal activity of divine grace? Special revelation is, of course, crucial for human salvation as Bloesch so faithfully upholds. At the same time, the Bible seems to indicate the presence of a divine activity directed toward all humankind. While not operative apart from Christ, this "true light that gives light to everyone" (Jn 1:9) does appear to be active apart from the specifically salvific message of the gospel of Jesus Christ. In this sense we might speak of a general revelation at work prior to or even beyond the pale of the church's proclamation of Jesus as the Christ, even if this work is not adequate for human salvation. An acknowledgment of this kind of prevenient grace would lead us to look for a point of contact for the gospel not so much as an innate possession or a structure of the human person, but as the gracious operation of God in our lives even before we knew God's name.

Bloesch's pessimism moves in another direction as well. In his concern to uphold the transformational effect of the gospel, he posits a radically disjunctive view of the new life and original creation. In so doing, he stands in a venerable tradition of theologians who see salvation as a total contradiction to human existence (or at least existence after the Fall). Yet the Christian tradition contains a stream of thought boasting an equally long pedigree that views salvation as the completion of human existence. While agreeing that such a completion requires that we be redeemed from the Fall, proponents of this view are more willing to speak of salvation as a continuation, albeit in a heightened manner, of what God inaugurated in the Garden of Eden. But if there is indeed both discontinuity and continuity between creation and new creation, then as theologians we must be open to finding traces of divine grace within our present situation, even in its depravity and fallenness.

Bloesch's anthropological pessimism is one crucial factor that generates both his critique of rationalism and his uneasiness with anything that smacks of cultural accommodationism. In both areas, I wonder if Bloesch's laudable critique is not potentially as one-sided as the theological programs he opposes. In fairness I must quickly add that Bloesch the theologian seems to back-pedal from the bold condemnatory utterances of Bloesch the prophet. While arguing for "fideistic revelationalism," the theologian does readily acknowledge a cognitive and rational dimension of faith. And in the midst of his campaigning for a militaristic "theology of confrontation," he highlights the importance of taking seriously our contemporary cultural context. But I would want to push Bloesch further here.

I must admit that when the dust settles I find myself—contra Bloesch—sympathizing with Brunner in his famous dispute with Barth. Similarly, I find a host of traces of divine grace present in the midst of human brokenness. Consequently, I am willing to speak of culture as a source for theology (to the horror of some evangelicals), albeit not in the sense of being the normative standard determining the nature of the gospel message itself but as a conversation partner that as theologians we must take seriously in our constructive articulations of the "faith once delivered." Observing how Bloesch in fact does theology leads me to suspect that he might go at least part way with me on this matter. But I fear that his commitment to a Barthian reading of the Reformed tradition prevents him from spelling this out more explicitly in the theoretical formulation of his theological method.

The gospel of individualism. Second, I come away from Bloesch's theological method wondering if the focus of his methodological proposal is simply too individualistic. He is surely correct in highlighting a dynamic view of revelation in the context of a staid rationalism that narrows it to a deposit of propositions. In response, Bloesch offers an intriguing retrieval of Barth's idea of revelation as the transformative encounter of the recipient with the gracious God in Christ through the Spirit, which Bloesch traces back to the Reformers. Yet I wonder if in his reformulation he has in fact introduced an equally problematic narrowing of the dynamic of faith in another direction.

Bloesch is surely correct in upholding the individual dimension of the gospel. God's Word does cut to the human heart, as Bloesch so eloquently asserts. But I am convinced that there is more to the story than his method suggests, at least as I read him.

One of the major developments in recent years has been the rediscovery of the social or communal dimension of the human phenomenon. Under the rubric of "the sociology of knowledge," contemporary communalists have rejected the modern individualist epistemologies. Crucial to the knowing process, they argue, is a cognitive framework (a web of belief) that is mediated to the individual by the social group (one's community of reference).[89] Similarly, communalists theorize that the community is crucial to personal identity formation. None of us creates our own identity, they declare. Instead, our sense of self is socially produced.[90] More specifically, identity develops through the telling of a personal narrative in connection to which our lives make sense.[91] And this narrative is always embedded in a transcendent story—the stories of the communities in which the person participates.[92]

These contemporary ideas have sparked some Christian theologians to rediscover a more profound sense of the social or community nature of the faith. Indeed, while God may save us one by one, God's goal is in fact not an aggregate of saved individuals. Consequently, the purpose of the in-breaking divine Word, a pervading theme of Bloesch's writings, is the bringing together of a reconciled people. I believe this understanding of God's eschatological goal provides a fruitful foundation for bringing creation, redemption and new creation together. If God is at work establishing community, then the divine salvific work mediated through Christ that brings the church into being as its sign and foretaste constitutes the completion of what God began in creation.

Related to the role of community in identity formation is the connection between theology (in the sense of doctrine) and experience. In the preface to his earlier volume *Essentials of Evangelical Theology* (1978), Bloesch sounds a helpful note in suggesting that the two must be brought together.[93] What I find missing in the fuller formulations of his theological method is a detailed explication of the connection between these two.

Here again, contemporary insights into the sociology of knowledge could help fill in the gaps. Contrary to what many theologians often suggest, experience never occurs in a vacuum. There is no such thing as "brute" experience. Rather, experience is always facilitated by and mediated through an overarching view of reality, a web of belief about the world as a whole, that is, a theology. This suggests that a person's belief system, which is mediated to a large degree by one's community of reference, provides a crucial foundation for the experience of faith that Bloesch finds so crucial as a defining moment of the revelational dynamic.

I know that Bloesch has a far more profound understanding of the Christian community and a far more nuanced view of the role of Christian doctrine in the experience of faith than my remarks suggest. Yet I wish he would have given us a more complete presentation of these dimensions in his discussion of theological method. I would like to see him take contemporary findings as to the social dimension of faith, as well as the interaction of worldview with experience, into the heart of how he proposes we engage in theological reflection on the event of faith.

The Bible and the Word. We have noted Bloesch's intriguing and paradoxical understanding of the relationship between Scripture and the Word of God that stands at the heart of his theological proposal. Like his theological mentor Karl Barth, Bloesch's understanding of revelation as a divine dynamic transforming the recipient demands that he posit a distinction between the transcendent Word and the Bible as the written Word. At the same time his commitment to the Reformation principle of *sola Scriptura* requires that he elevate the Bible as the norming norm for the church. How can this apparent tension be maintained?

As we have seen, Bloesch attempts to solve this problem by advocating a sacramental model of the role of Scripture. The Word of God comes to the recipient through the words of the Bible. In developing this model Bloesch draws from the distinction between the sign (the Bible) and the thing signified (divine revelation or the transcendent Word). I applaud Bloesch for this ingenious way of handling a vexing theological problem. But I come away wondering if he has in fact pulled off what he hopes to accomplish.

My uneasiness is ignited by what seems to me to be an apparent inconsistency in the use of terms at certain places in his writings. Perhaps the problem lies with me; perhaps I have not read Bloesch correctly, or perhaps I am oblivious to the workings of dialectical reasoning in these passages. Nevertheless, at times I perceive him using "the Word" (or "the Word of God")—which I would anticipate as referring exclusively to the dynamic of the divine revelation—as a synonym for the Bible.

More telling, however, is the question as to whether or not Bloesch has overcome the Nestorian approach to the Bible that he himself criticizes the Barthian turn in theological method for fostering. On several occasions in his writings, the divine Word and the human words of the Bible seem to drift apart. This leads the reader to wonder what cords bind them together beyond the gracious, sovereign will of the Spirit. And if the divine choice is the bond, what prevents the Spirit from choosing other great literature as well?[94]

Once again, I think contemporary communitarian concepts could assist Bloesch in this matter. They offer a helpful point of departure in the quest to understand the dynamic of the Spirit speaking through Scripture, which Bloesch so faithfully upholds.

Recent insights into the role of narrative in identity formation suggest that the Spirit brings sinful humans to change direction by leading them to reinterpret their own personal narratives according to the categories set forth in the biblical story, especially as it is focused in the story of Jesus. In this process the recipients of the gospel link their own stories with the story of the people of God. Thus as we proclaim the "old, old story," the Holy Spirit calls its hearers to participation in the family of God.

Again in fairness I must quickly add that in his recent writings Bloesch has interacted quite consciously with the narrative approach. I am not pushing him to become a thoroughgoing narrative theologian. However, I am convinced that a more explicit use of insights such as these could assist Bloesch in clarifying a dimension of his understanding that will remain the focus of criticism. But more important, I think the recent discovery of the dynamics of narrative could provide Bloesch with the concepts out of which to develop an even stronger methodological foundation for his theology of the Word.

Conclusion

Donald Bloesch calls us to reevaluate the rationalist propositionalism so pervasive within evangelicalism. He is convinced that a "fideistic revelationalism" leading to a "theology of Word and Spirit" is more in keeping with the wider evangelical and Reformation trajectory. As a fellow heir of the Puritan-Pietist heritage, I resonate well with much of what Bloesch is attempting to do.

At the same time, I must admit that in the end I stop short of Bloesch at one point and move farther at another. As one schooled in rationalist theology I am reticent to shed this side of me to the extent to which Bloesch demands, even though I, like he, am highly critical of the excesses of the rationalist approach. My hesitancy to move completely in Bloesch's direction at this point is paralleled by my greater openness to take culture seriously, as is evident in my willingness to draw from current insights into the social nature of the human phenomenon. I of course affirm Bloesch's elevation of Scripture as the primary source for theology and placement of tradition as secondary. But I think we as theologians would do well to admit that we do in fact look to culture as a tertiary source in our theological reflections and that throughout the church's history its theologians have indeed viewed theology as a "trialogue" involving the biblical message, the theological heritage and the contemporary culture. Such a trialogue, I am convinced, provides the foundation for what I would see as the more complete method to which I see Bloesch pointing.

Despite these reservations, I come away from reading Bloesch challenged to think more clearly and admonished to listen to and for the Word of God more carefully. And encouraging us to do this, I believe, is the ultimate goal of Bloesch's theological method.

Four

Donald Bloesch on Revelation

AVERY DULLES, S.J.

DONALD BLOESCH IS A MAN OF PEACE AND CONCILIATION, A MODERATE WHO has read widely and appreciated the wisdom embedded in a great variety of traditions. He intends to be firmly evangelical but at the same time broadly catholic. His very desire to be inclusive leads him, by an irony of fate, into disputes with many leading theologians and theological schools. He rejects, above all, the narrowness that has often inclined others, whether Protestant or Catholic, to take one-sided and unbalanced positions. Attempting to pick his way through the maze of theological opinions, Bloesch can easily appear to be rather contentious. By agreeing with one author he finds himself thrown into a position of disagreement with others. And by trying to save the elements of truth in a number of schools of thought, he finds himself driven to disagree in part with all.

As befits the subject matter Bloesch's doctrine of revelation is complex and comprehensive. He recognizes that revelation is not a simple matter. When God speaks it is rarely God alone who speaks. God addresses his people through creaturely structures including historical events, persons of faith, inspired writings, sacraments and traditions that interpret the legacy of the past.

Bloesch's doctrine of Word and Spirit does remarkable justice to both the objective and the subjective aspects of revelation. The Word represents that which comes from outside; the Spirit, that which emerges from within, enabling recipients to recognize and interpret the external Word. In revelation the Word never comes apart from the Spirit, nor is the Spirit given without the presence of the Word.

The Word, the objective element in Christianity, is found most saliently in Jesus Christ, and we apprehend it in a privileged way in Holy Scripture. Scripture, however, never comes to us in isolation from the tradition of the church, which thus becomes, under Scripture, a secondary authority. The inner testimony of the Spirit authenticates Scripture as divine, and guides the church to grasp the divinely intended meaning. Without Scripture, tradition and the receptive attitude of faith, revelation itself could never come to term.

Five Models

Some years ago I staked out five models of revelation theology that are operative in twentieth-century theology, both Protestant and Catholic. According to the first model, which I characterize as doctrinal, revelation is divinely authoritative teaching inerrantly proposed as God's Word by the Bible or by authoritative church teaching. According to the second model, which I describe as historical, revelation is the manifestation of God's saving power by his great deeds in history. The third model, which I designate as experiential, depicts revelation as the self-manifestation of God through his intimate presence in the depths of the human spirit. The fourth model, which I call dialectical, views revelation as God's address to those whom he encounters with his Word in Scripture and in Christian proclamation. The final model, which I characterize as a consciousness model, understands revelation as a breakthrough to a higher level of awareness that occurs as individuals and humanity at large are drawn into a fuller participation in the divine creativity. Revelation, therefore, is variously identified with divinely authoritative propositions, with historical persons and events, with an inner experience of the divine, with a mysterious paradoxical encounter and with a transformed state of consciousness.[1]

In *Models of Revelation* I sought to recognize and appropriate the positive values in each of these five models and to bring them into harmony by adding, as a dialectical tool, an epistemology of symbol. My final position can perhaps best be described as "symbolic realism."

Using my five types as a grid, I would say that Bloesch recognizes elements of truth in all five, or at least the first four, and is most inclined toward the fourth. As evidence of his appreciation of the first three models, one may cite his statement: "Revelation has three facets: historical, propositional, and experiential."[2] Quite properly, he is unwilling to see revelation reduced to any one of these facets alone.

Revelation and History

Recognizing that Scripture deals in great part with what God has done, Bloesch begins with the historical ingredient. God speaks, he says, in the pivotal events of history.[3] In speaking of the loci of authority Bloesch writes, "From my perspective, the ultimate norm is the gospel of God based on the mighty acts of God."[4] Basic to faith is that which God has accomplished for us in sacred history and in Jesus Christ, in whom the will and purpose of God are fully and truly revealed.[5] The climax of revelation is Jesus Christ, but Christ does not first emerge in the New Testament; he was already present in a hidden way in the sacred history of the Old Testament.[6] After Christ there is no new revelation that completes or supersedes that which has been given in Holy Scripture.[7]

Notwithstanding the importance he attaches to history, Bloesch maintains that history, even sacred history, falls short of actually being revelation. History, he writes, is "the occasion, not the source, of revelation."[8] The events of sacred history are both the medium through which revelation is given and the material of revelation.[9] But for history to qualify as revelation its divine significance must be disclosed from above.

Because of the gap that he finds between revelation and history, Bloesch reacts unfavorably to authors such as William Temple, George Ernest Wright, Gordon Kaufman and Wolfhart Pannenberg, who identify revelation with history. He prefers the position of Barth, whom he quotes as saying, "Whoever says history is not yet saying revelation, nor Word of God as the Reformers called the Bible, nor the subject to which man must submit himself with no possibility of becoming its master."[10]

Revelation and Doctrine

The Reformed tradition has commonly emphasized the verbal component in revelation. Standing as he does in this tradition, Bloesch finds himself obliged to deal extensively with the Word of God, which is central to my first model: revelation as doctrine. He accepts as helpful Karl Barth's distinction between the three forms of the Word of God: the revealed or living Word (Christ), the written Word (Scripture) and the proclaimed Word (the church).[11] These three forms interpenetrate, since the revealed Word never comes to us apart from the Word written and proclaimed. But in the three forms there is an order of priority, dependence and importance—descending from the first to the second and from the second to the third.

In the course of his dialogue with William Temple, to which I have already alluded, Bloesch insists that revelation is the speech of God as well as the action of God. The Word of God is transmitted through Holy Scripture, which bears witness to the great deeds of God. God speaks in the Bible because it both contains the inspired words of prophets and apostles and gives an account of the events of saving history. A merely narrative approach to Scripture is insufficient, because revelation is not simply a story about what God has done; it is the Word of God. God's commandments and promises come to us in the form of written commandments and written testimonies, which are intelligible.[12] The Bible contains propositional truths about persons, about events and about God and his will for human beings.

While giving due emphasis to the propositional, Bloesch, with his customary balance, addresses some criticism toward propositionalist colleagues in the Reformed tradition. He takes Gordon Clark, Carl Henry and James Warwick Montgomery to task for their excessively propositional emphasis. For them, he says, "the Bible becomes a book of revealed propositions which are directly accessible to reason and which contain no errors in any respect."[13] For Bloesch, on the contrary, Scripture contains a great variety of literary forms besides the descriptive and the didactic. Much of its language is symbolic and mythopoetic.[14] Biblical revelation, therefore, cannot be reduced to a series of declarative sentences.[15]

Is the Bible revelation? As we have seen him doing in response to the question about revelation and history, Bloesch walks a very fine line between saying yes or no to this second question. The Bible, he says, "is not in and of itself the revelation of God but the divinely appointed means and channel of this revelation."[16] He compares the presence of divine truth in the Bible to the presence of the divine Son in the humanity of Jesus Christ. He wants to acknowledge the full humanity of the Bible while avoiding any separation of the divine and human elements. With some indebtedness to Barth, and in opposition to strict inerrantists like Gordon Clark and James Packer, he holds that there is no absolute identity between the written and revealed Word. But he does not settle for Barth's actualism. He insists that the written word of Scripture is itself revelation, though it still needs to be actualized in the consciousness of the reader or hearer. Revelation is both objectively given truth and actual event.[17]

Although he does not equate inspiration with revelation, Bloesch sees the two as closely interconnected. "Inspiration concerns the reliability of the scriptural witness; revelation refers to the self-disclosure of Jesus Christ in the biblical witness."[18] "By the gift of inspiration the biblical writings are made the repository of divine truth as well as the unique channel of divine revelation."[19] While allowing for the historical and cultural conditioning of the human writers, Bloesch adheres to the view that God is the primary author of the Bible in such a way that everything written by the human authors has the sanction of God himself.[20] From this he infers that the church is forever bound to the concepts and images of Scripture. He accordingly resists the call for reconceptualization that has been issued by some Catholics such as Karl Rahner.[21] From Thomas Torrance he takes over the thesis that the language of Scripture, given as it is by God, cannot be changed. Although we may clarify and illuminate the contents of Scripture with additional concepts and metaphors derived from contemporary thought, we must return again and again to the original. God has set his seal upon the inspired text as providing the language we are to use in praying to him and speaking of him.[22]

In terms of my symbolic realism I myself have spoken of the irreplaceable foundational images and metaphors of biblical revelation. In my words, "The biblical symbols of marriage and family, deserts and animals, kings and warriors, even when they do not exactly correspond to the conditions of our own life, remain powerfully evocative."[23] Bloesch's position on this point appeals to me, but I am not convinced that his views on inspiration are sufficiently strong to give canonical status to the concepts and images of Scripture. It is unclear to me how much he wishes to ascribe to the divine author and how much he is prepared to concede to the culturally conditioned and fallible human elements in Scripture.

Catholics will tend to applaud Bloesch's insistence that the biblical revelation contains truths of a conceptual type. Bloesch, however, distances himself in a very subtle way from the practice of many Catholics, who are accustomed to speak of "revealed truths."[24] He prefers to speak of "truths of revelation," truths that arise out of revelation and therefore presuppose a conceptual content in revelation. He goes so far as to say that dogma articulates the truth of revelation in the form of a guiding standard or normative witness. With this commentary he can approve of my formulation when I state that "right doctrine, insofar as it accurately mirrors the meaning of the original message is, in its content, revealed."[25]

Bloesch makes a distinction between dogma, as divinely given and unalterable truth, and doctrine, which in his view consists in the historically and culturally conditioned expression of dogma. Dogma demands our submission in the obedience of faith; doctrines are to be respected to the

extent that they serve to communicate infallible truth.[26] Although Bloesch's
terminology is somewhat unusual, his position on this point appears to be
sound. To the Catholic it recalls the familiar distinction between the unalterable deposit of faith and the time-conditioned formulations in which the
deposit is presented.

Revelation and Experience

We may now turn to my third model, that of revelation as experience. The
mystical tradition, according to Bloesch, regards God as basically unknow-
able and incommunicable. It speaks of an ineffable encounter with a divinity
that is beyond the grasp of human understanding. As a representative of this
tradition, Bloesch mentions Gregory of Nyssa, who maintained that the cloud
of unknowing could not be pierced except by those who ascend the ladder
of love.[27] While he does not ignore modern authors, Bloesch does not have
much to say in this connection about Evelyn Underhill, Dean William R. Inge
and William Ernest Hocking, all of whom may be seen as identifying
revelation with a direct experience of the divine.

Bloesch asserts at one point that the mystical tradition has a Neo-Platonic
tinge that stresses the immanence of God and frequently ends up in a form
of pantheism or panentheism.[28] But elsewhere he informs the reader that
according to the mystics God is immeasurably remote and can be approached
only by negating statements.[29] In partial agreement with the second position,
Bloesch as an evangelical holds that God is infinitely distant from all that the
human mind can comprehend, but he dissents from the view that any process
of inward preparation is necessary before we can encounter the divine.
Bloesch apparently suspects that this position implies a Pelagian attitude. For
him the process of revelation takes place only from God's side, through his
free and sovereign initative.[30] Like many Protestants he seems reluctant to
acknowledge that God normally works through gradual steps, first preparing
the soul to receive and then conferring on it his choicest gifts. Bloesch is
correct, however, in holding that the power of God can effect sudden and
surprising conversions.

When he speaks of experiential views of revelation, Bloesch seems to
have in mind not so much the mysticism of Gregory of Nyssa and Pseudo-
Dionysius as the liberalism of Schleiermacher, Ritschl, Herrmann and Har-
nack. These authors dwelt on religious experience to such a degree that they
practically made it a substitute for revelation. Bloesch finds some of the same
liberal experientialist tendencies at work in Paul Tillich, Langdon Gilkey,

Elton Trueblood, Eugene Fontinell and Gregory Baum.[31]

Bloesch gladly concedes that experience plays an essential role in faith. In opposition to the objectivism of biblicist Protestants who neglect the working of the Holy Spirit in the reception of revelation, Bloesch insists that an experience of the inward working of the Holy Spirit confirms and illumines what is taught by the revealed Word. Although he wants to "reintroduce into theology the critical role of the experience of faith," he firmly maintains that authentic faith-experience is qualitatively different from ordinary human experience and even from religious experience. The experience of faith is correlative with, and is specified by, God's self-revelation in Jesus Christ.[32]

As an evangelical Bloesch feels a particular responsibility to assert the primacy of Scripture over religious experience.[33] "It goes without saying," he writes, "that evangelicalism is diametrically opposed to liberal-modernist Protestantism, which substitutes the authority of religious experience for that of a divine revelation given in sacred Scripture."[34] Revelation, he insists, is always more than religious experience; it is the divine criticism and transformation of that experience.[35]

I personally appreciate Bloesch's insight into the ambiguities of human experience. I can only agree that experience is not normative unless it is itself normed by revelation. The current tendency to revise the Christian heritage according to the promptings of common secular experience represents a threat that should be resisted.

One of Bloesch's objections to modern experientialism is that it depicts revelation as affective rather than cognitive.[36] He quotes Schleiermacher, Herrmann, Schillebeeckx and others to the effect that revelation does not consist in information but in an immediate awareness and an affective response.[37] Bloesch admits that revelation does not take place without experience, but he views experience as secondary. In a formula I find captivating he declares, "Truth descends into experience, but it does not arise from experience."[38]

Revelation and New Awareness

Bloesch does not distinguish sharply between the experiential model and my fifth model, which I characterize in terms of altered consciousness or "new awareness." But the two models do not fully coincide. In the latter, God is not regarded as the direct object of an experience. Rather, God works subjectively from within to give the believer new eyes with which to contemplate the world and discern God's latent presence in past and current events.

Bloesch is keenly aware of what he calls the "new mysticism," which finds the locus of the sacred in nature and depreciates the rational. He speaks of Teilhard de Chardin, Joseph Campbell, Theodore Roszak and Fritjof Capra as the heralds of a synthesis in which mysticism becomes a technique for gaining access to the creative power immanent in the universe, harnessing that power for the sake of human expansion and domination.[39] In opposition to evolutionary monism Bloesch denies that the divinity of Jesus Christ is to be seen as a mutation in the evolutionary process and as "a breakthrough of cosmic consciousness."[40] He is apprehensive that the new Catholicism (represented by theologians such as Schillebeeckx, Küng, Tracy and Baum) seems to understand revelation not as the impartation of cognitive truth but as the breakthrough into a higher consciousness.[41]

In the theology of the religions, Bloesch notes, revelation is increasingly coming to be seen as "the breakthrough into a higher form of consciousness."[42] He disapproves of the audacity with which Raimundo Panikkar, Paul Knitter and others contend that a distinctly Christian consciousness needs to give way to a global consciousness that makes room for truth to unfold itself in myriad ways and experiences.[43] In opposition to John Hick he denies that the great world faiths constitute bona fide ways of salvation that should command our respect.[44] Bloesch is commendably resistant to soteriological relativism of this type.

I have had my own reservations about the consciousness model of revelation, which can easily take the form of secular humanism or New Age syncretism, but I am not as absolute as Bloesch seems to be in rejecting it. Vatican II, as I read it, did not endorse the idea of revelation as emergent consciousness, but in its Pastoral Constitution on the Church in the Modern World it did reckon with the shift of consciousness brought about by modernization. The council there urged Christians to be alert to the presence and activity of God in the happenings of our age, to discern the "signs of the times" and to judge them in the light of the gospel.[45] Bloesch's work could be enriched, I think, by greater attention to the ways in which Christians might enter into livelier dialogue with the world by drawing on their experience as participants in contemporary history.

Revelation and Personal Encounter
Among the five models of revelation, the fourth (dialectical) is the one that, by and large, most closely approximates the position of Bloesch. He castigates fundamentalists for depicting revelation as a static deposit of truth and insists

that God is sovereign even in his revelation, remaining hidden until he gives himself to be known.[46] God, according to Bloesch, is supremely personal and transcendent. The paradox of God's entering history, he believes, can only be grasped by a kind of Barthian dialectic, in which our formulations are necessarily tentative, broken and refracted.[47] In somewhat Barthian style, he asserts, "The Word of God exists for us only when God is actually speaking and we are actually receiving his Word."[48]

While he does not wish to deny that Holy Scripture is objectively God's Word, Bloesch asserts that "it becomes revelation for us only in the moment of decision, in the awakening to faith."[49] Bloesch considers himself the faithful disciple of Luther and Calvin in affirming that the authority of Scripture is self-authenticating by virtue of its divine content, and that the object of faith is from first to last Christ himself. Protestant biblicism erred in directing faith first of all to the Bible as a sacred object rather than to Christ, the Lord and content of Scripture.[50]

During the years when existential and dialectical theology were dominant, it became almost axiomatic to hold that there is no such thing as revealed information. Bloesch is properly skeptical of this position. While respecting the element of personal encounter in revelation, he holds that God discloses not only himself but objective information about his plan for the world. This information, however, is not at our free disposal; it must be given ever anew by the operation of the Holy Spirit.[51]

With Barth, Bloesch seeks to affirm the paradox of the divine infallibility of the Bible and its human fallibility.[52] He admits, however, that Barth can be criticized for not clarifying his position on biblical inerrancy.[53] Under his leadership neo-orthodoxy fostered a Nestorian approach to the Bible.[54] Barth himself in his later work could no longer speak of the Bible as the Word of God.[55]

In the face of these difficulties Bloesch strives mightily to add the necessary clarification, but it may be questioned whether he completely succeeds. He speaks of "the impenetrable mystery of the dual nature of the Bible,"[56] which is both a divine Word to sinful humanity and a human witness to an incomparable divine action. It is fallible insofar as it reflects the cultural and historical condition of the writers, but it is not mistaken in what it purports to teach: God's will and purpose in the world.[57] For Bloesch, as for Barth, there can be only an indirect identity between revelation and the Bible.[58]

My principal difficulty with this explanation is that it makes no mention of the authorized interpreter of the Bible: the church to which the Bible was entrusted. I would like to add that the true and revelatory meaning of the Word of God is discerned and authoritatively proposed by the church. I do not see how the Bible can be considered either self-authenticating or self-interpreting unless the statement means that it authenticates and interprets itself to the church, which is animated by the same Spirit who inspired the Bible itself. I shall presently have more to say about this topic.

Summary Evaluation

To summarize Bloesch's position on the nature of revelation, one may say that for him revelation is an act of communication by which God confronts human beings with his redeeming mercy and glorious presence. The reception of revelation involves the mind, the will and the affections. Revelation has a cognitive and conceptual component that may be articulated in propositions, but it is also existential, and for that reason defies adequate formulation in propositions.[59]

The event of revelation, for Bloesch, has two poles. He describes these sometimes as Word and Spirit, and sometimes as the historical and the experiential. Revelation is God speaking and the human being responding through the power of the Holy Spirit. Revelation consists in the conjunction between the divine act of self-disclosure and the human act of acceptance.

Everything in the last two paragraphs seems to me to be true and harmonious with Catholic teaching, as found, for example, in Vatican II's Constitution on Divine Revelation. Although Bloesch's doctrine of revelation is broad and comprehensive, it could, I think, be profitably broadened still further in several areas where he is unduly influenced by a somewhat restrictive earlier tradition. My criticism will cover four principal themes.

The Bible, Church and Tradition

The first of these themes has already been indicated: the relationship between the Bible and the church. Bloesch is not a narrow biblicist. Revelation, he acknowledges, has an ecclesial dimension. The ecclesial tradition constitutes "the matrix in which revelation comes to us and is interpreted by us."[60] But all church tradition, he believes, is subordinate to the primary revelation contained in Scripture. "Scripture," he writes, "is the primary, tradition the secondary, witness to divine revelation."[61] The church's doctrinal definitions may on occasion be guided by the Holy Spirit, but all creeds and church pronouncements are reformable as the Spirit brings new light to bear from the Scriptures.[62] As expressions of tradition, doctrines can never be the final word.[63]

Although he does not hold that revelation is found in the Bible alone, Bloesch continues to adhere to the formula, *sola Scriptura*. In a curious turn of phrase he asserts that *sola Scriptura* is not *nuda Scriptura*. For him *sola Scriptura* apparently signifies the primacy, not the aloneness, of Scripture.[64]

In an effort to build ecumenical solidarity Bloesch points out that a number of distinguished Catholic theologians have recently come to recognize that Scripture is the "one source of revelation."[65] But notwithstanding the assertions of theologians, which can sometimes be ambiguous, it is best to acknowledge that according to Catholic doctrine the gospel is the one source and that the Word of God comes through Scripture and tradition in unison. Vatican II is clear in teaching that the Word of God never exists as Scripture alone.[66] In taking up the theme of tradition before Scripture in its Constitution on Divine Revelation, Vatican II made it clear that apostolic tradition comes directly from Christ and the Holy Spirit. Although tradition can never contradict the inspired Scripture, it is not simply derivative from Scripture.

The magisterium, to be sure, must serve the Word of God. In teaching this[67] Vatican II did not imply that the magisterium depends on Scripture alone, for the Word of God comes equally in the forms of Scripture and tradition. The definitive teaching of popes and councils is always perfectible, but perfectible does not mean erroneous.

Bloesch refers to theologians such as Rahner and me as holding the "neo-Catholic" position that the living magisterium has authority from Christ to interpret the Word of God for the community.[68] But this position is not a novel one, and is not peculiar to a particular school. It is the settled doctrine of the Roman Catholic Church, authoritatively taught by the councils of Trent, Vatican I and Vatican II.

On this point it is best to acknowledge that a difference remains between the Catholic Church and the churches of the Reformation. As Vatican II declared in its Decree on Ecumenism, "When Christians separated from us affirm the divine authority of the sacred Books, they think differently from us—different ones in different ways—about the relationship between the Scriptures and the Church. In the Church, according to Catholic belief, the authentic teaching office plays a special role in the explanation and proclamation of the word of God."[69]

Faith and Reason

A second theme on which I find Bloesch's position somewhat unsatisfactory has to do with the relationship between faith and reason. Here again, he is no extremist. He disavows the *credo quia absurdum* of Tertullian and Søren Kierkegaard. Against extreme Barthians such as Jacques Ellul he insists that faith is neither absurd nor is it a blind leap into the dark.[70] Once faith has been given, he maintains, reason can explicate its claims.[71] But the truth of revelation is not empirically accessible.[72] Reason, Bloesch maintains, cannot prepare the way to faith or establish its truth.[73] Nor can reason constitute a criterion whereby an alleged revelation could be judged as credible or incredible.[74] In his critique of foundationalism Bloesch denies that there are any indubitable and incorrigible premises in which human thought can be anchored.[75] Revelation, he says, overthrows and disrupts human reason, placing it on a new foundation.[76] Reason needs to be shattered and transformed in order to accept revelation.[77] Faith contravenes the direction of our reasoning prior to the act of faith.[78]

I agree in part, since it is true that reason cannot antecedently demonstrate the claims of faith. Revelation contains certain mysteries that are contrary to what the exercise of unaided reason on the part of fallen human nature would lead us to expect. But if revelation is not absurd, there must be some rational norms by which its nonabsurdity can be vindicated. It cannot, for example, violate the principle of contradiction and still be true. Bloesch perhaps intimates as much when he asserts that the Word of God "does not contradict the structure of reason."[79] If he holds this, he might wish to qualify statements about reason being overthrown, disrupted and shattered by revelation.

Bloesch vigorously denies the possibility of any natural or general revelation that would lead to truth about God.[80] Since human beings are in a condition of total depravity, he asserts, they cannot know God except through supernatural revelation. Natural theology in Bloesch's estimation falls under the same condemnation as natural religion and general revelation. "Natural theology can only result in the manufacture of idols, since the true God cannot be identified with the constructs of man's vain imagination."[81] Bloesch is convinced that unaided human reason can know nothing about the existence and attributes of God from the order of the cosmos or the intimations of conscience. Proofs of God's existence may have a certain value in helping believers to gain a clearer understanding of the relationship between God and the world, but apart from faith, such proofs cannot disclose the truth about God.[82]

At this juncture Bloesch manifestly separates himself from medieval scholasticism and from modern Catholic teaching. He likewise reproves several contemporary Protestants, such as Wolfhart Pannenberg and Gordon Clark, for holding that the truth of revelation can be demonstrated.[83] Bloesch is evidently afraid that natural theology might become a substitute or competitor for revealed theology, and that the God of the philosophers might be worshiped in place of the God of Jesus Christ. In denying that the credibility of the faith can be perceived by reason, Bloesch falls into what Catholics would regard as undue fideism.

In connection with Bloesch's antirationalism one must consider his views on philosophy. I would have expected him to emphasize the limitations of philosophy and its need to undergo correction in the light of revelation, but I was genuinely surprised to find him sweepingly rejecting the very idea of philosophic thought. With uncharacteristic bluntness he declares,

> I contend that every philosophy represents a rationalization for a false theology or religion and that true theology necessarily excludes philosophy—not its concerns, not even its language, but its world view, its metaphysical claims. In contradistinction to Tillich, I hold that theology and philosophy are not simply two ways of approaching reality, but they speak fundamentally of two different realities. I agree with Pascal that the God of the philosophers is something other than the God of Abraham, Isaac and Jacob. It is the difference between an idol created by the imagination and the experience of the true God. The relation between theology and philosophy is not one of synthesis or correlation but one of conflict and contradiction.[84]

Personally, I owe a great debt of gratitude to Plato and Aristotle for having brought me to the point where I could take the New Testament seriously. Great Christian converts such as Justin, Clement and Augustine had similar experiences in their search for truth. Nearly all great systematic theologians have accepted the principles of some philosophical system to give coherence and credibility to their conclusions. Many important questions that are relevant to theology are not directly answered by revelation. Bloesch's failure to grapple with the perennial philosophical questions might be regarded as one of the principal weaknesses in his systematic theology.

Implicit Faith

A third theme has to do with the spiritual condition of the unevangelized. Bloesch is extremely pessimistic. He is convinced that the redemptive grace of God "is given only in the Word and the sacraments."[85] Salvation is not possible, he maintains, without explicit faith in Jesus Christ.[86] "To speak of implicit or latent faith as itself being sufficient for salvation or as meriting eternal life has absolutely no scriptural warrant and is indeed a grave error."[87] Bloesch denies that nonbiblical religions can have any redemptive value and repudiates the proposal that Christians should enter into dialogue with them.[88]

On this question the Catholic Church for the past century has been more optimistic. The idea of "seeds of the Word," which occupied a prominent place in the speculations of early patristic writers such as Justin, Clement of Alexandria and Origen, was picked up by Vatican II[89] and occurs frequently in the writings of John Paul II.[90] According to this view the philosophies and religions that have arisen prior to, or independently of, biblical revelation may be salvifically oriented to Christ in a hidden way that is manifest to the eyes of God. By adhering to this seminal divine revelation, persons ignorant of God's full revelation in Christ may be associated with Christ and the church in a measure sufficient for them to attain eternal life. However that may be, we may be sure that God will somehow make salvation possible for persons inculpably ignorant of the gospel. Bloesch himself concedes that "no person is bereft of the opportunity to come to Jesus Christ . . . even if this be not in this life."[91]

Revelation and Symbol

As a final theme I should like to raise the question of symbol and its role in revelation. In his discussion of biblical language Bloesch concedes that symbol and metaphor play a prominent role.[92] He approvingly quotes me as saying that Christian doctrines live off the power of the original revelatory symbols.[93] But he takes Tillich and me to task for allegedly holding that symbols lead to God rather than that God uses symbols to come to us.[94] This must, I think, be a misinterpretation of the authors cited. Certainly in my doctrine of symbolic realism I have insisted on the priority of God's revelatory action in bringing us into communion with himself. But still, if God can use symbols such as flowing water, bread and wine, and wooden crosses, these realities must have naturally knowable characteristics that render them suitable for use as redemptive symbols. By familiarizing ourselves with these characteristics, we can come to a greater appreciation of the revelatory symbolism. The supernatural presupposes the natural and builds upon it.

Again, a little later, Bloesch objects against me that the content of theology is not what the symbols evoke but what revelation proclaims.[95] He opts for a language of faith that is explanatory rather than doxological. Is he at this point falling back into a narrow propositionalism? Is he denying the revelatory value of the symbols and metaphors of Scripture? I certainly do not question the truth expressed in doctrines, but I would refuse any reduction of revelation to the propositional mode. God uses symbols, both physical and verbal, precisely to evoke meanings so rich that they cannot be encapsulated in explicit doctrinal statements. At certain points Bloesch seems reluctant to admit that a meaning that is evoked can yield any real knowledge.[96]

Although he is ill at ease with symbol, Bloesch is more positive toward sacrament. When discussing biblical authority, he favors what he calls the "sacramental" model.[97] I can heartily agree, but in so doing I would like to add that a sacrament is a kind of symbol: a sign instituted by God to signify and existentially communicate a spiritual reality that cannot be conveyed by merely conceptual language. Because of their transformative power, symbols and sacraments are vitally important in mediating a salvific personal encounter. If this be conceded, I can applaud Bloesch's statement: "Evangelical theology will regain its vitality and relevance when it rediscovers the sacramental understanding of truth, authority, and revelation."[98]

As an evangelical, however, Bloesch insists that Christianity is a religion of the word rather than of images.[99] Faith, he holds, comes by hearing, not by seeing. Christianity, as Bloesch understands it, is a prophetic religion, not a ritualistic or mystical religion. Catholic and Orthodox communions, in his estimation, err by accepting the priority of sight over hearing and of images over language.[100]

Bloesch may have a point here. At certain points in history the Catholic Church has magnified the importance of visible signs, rituals and sacraments at the expense of Scripture and proclamation. But this is only a question of emphasis, and the evidence points in different directions. Bloesch, for instance, is able to quote a Catholic theologian, Thomas Aquinas, to the effect that even in the Eucharist, the sacrament of faith par excellence, the senses are deceptive, and hearing alone gives assurance.[101]

Conclusion
It has been a particular pleasure for me to review Donald Bloesch's writings on revelation in preparation for this essay. As I have discovered in personal conversation with him in 1986, and in my study of his books before and since that date, we share many of the same interests and concerns. For both of us the theology of revelation has been central. He, as a catholic evangelical,

seeks to serve the evangelical cause by adhering to its rich legacy and enriching it with contributions from the broader and more ancient catholic tradition. I, as a somewhat evangelical Catholic, strive to maintain the Catholic heritage while reenergizing it with the ferment of evangelical conviction.

In our theological methods the two of us exhibit notable similarities. We seem to agree that the paramount need today is not for radically new and venturesome hypotheses but for assessing the divergent theories that have already been proposed by others. We seek to listen carefully to what others are saying and to learn from every serious theologian, while sounding the alarm against proposals that we regard as antithetical to the gospel. Without relishing controversy, we recognize that we cannot responsibly give an appearance of agreeing with everyone. Both of us are apprehensive that authentic Christianity could be corrupted by the influence of triumphant secularism, even when that influence masks itself as a new and more relevant form of faith. Like Bloesch, I am convinced that the fullness of revelation has been given in Jesus Christ and in the Spirit-guided foundation of the church. The New Testament Scriptures constitute an essential component of the apostolic deposit.

Notwithstanding all these similarities, we still have certain differences to which I have called attention in the preceding pages. As a Catholic I regard Bloesch's view of human nature and of reason as too pessimistic. He seems to me to be insufficiently open to the workings of grace beyond the visible limits of Christianity. Although I have not dealt with his ecclesiology in this essay, I believe that his doctrine of revelation suffers from traces of biblicism and is insufficiently ecclesial. While recognizing that the church is always under the Word of God, and that it struggles amid the ambiguities of history, I am convinced that it is trustworthy in its authoritative mediation of the revelation given once and for all in Christ.

Bloesch and I should not be conclusively divided on this point. He is a stalwart champion of the gospel, and I seek to be firmly loyal to the church. But the gospel and the church, according to the plan of God, belong together. As Catholics become more evangelical, and evangelicals more catholic, we should be able to advance toward that full unity for which Christ prayed.

Five

Donald Bloesch's Doctrine of Scripture

MILLARD J. ERICKSON

ONALD G. BLOESCH IS ONE OF THE MOST INFLUENTIAL THEOLOGIANS OF the latter half of the twentieth century. He has endeavored to reconstruct evangelical theology in such a way as to free it from what he considers to be its dangerous alliance with rationalism, which has resulted in distortion of the true biblical and Reformation tradition. To this end, he has drawn heavily upon the thought of Karl Barth. The vigor and creativity of his theology is nowhere more clearly seen than in his doctrine of Scripture. From the brief statement in his earlier writing,[1] he has now expounded it in much greater detail.

In understanding Bloesch's theology it is helpful to know something of his background and pilgrimage. The son of a pastor in the Evangelical and Reformed Church, he attended Elmhurst College and then Chicago Theological Seminary, which at that time was part of the Federated Theological Faculty of the University of Chicago. There he encountered a more liberal theology than he had expected or previously experienced, which was largely based on the philosophy of Alfred North Whitehead. It was what today is called process theology but at that time went by the title of naturalistic theism.

In seminary he read with considerable approval the writings of Kierkegaard, Barth, Brunner, Tillich and Bultmann but gradually narrowed his commitment more to Brunner and particularly Barth. It appears that these were the views that he believed presented the best alternative to the type of liberal theology he was exposed to. It did not appear to him that any of the leading American evangelical theologies of that time were able to answer adequately the type of problems for traditional theology created by modern philosophy and theology.[2]

His Theological Orientation

Bloesch helpfully begins his discussion of Scripture with a statement of the perspective from which he does his theology. Those whom he lists as his primary mentors in his volume on Scripture include Martin Luther, John Calvin, Karl Barth, P. T. Forsyth and Emil Brunner; others he lists who have had a major influence on his doctrine of Scripture include Augustine, Pascal and Kierkegaard.[3] He accepts certain designations of the position that he adopts, but rejects others. Those which he accepts, although always with qualification, are "evangelical," "catholic" and "Reformed." He summarily rejects the labels "Pelagian," "semi-Pelagian," "latitudinarian," "panentheist" and "fundamentalist."[4] Although he is not completely happy with the label "neo-orthodox," he prefers it to Thomas Oden's "paleo-orthodox," which he sees as too hasty a return to the orthodoxy of the past. Rather, his aim is "forging a new statement of orthodoxy that stands in continuity with the past but addresses issues and problems in the present."[5]

Many theologians, including some evangelicals, are seeking to create a postmodern theology. Bloesch does not accept the designation of postmodernism, because it has been associated with a neglect of metaphysical questions and a virtual equation of the gospel with narrative. He does, however, believe that we are living in an age in which Enlightenment modernity is being questioned, and consequently, it is necessary to speak to issues related to the new intellectual and cultural climate.[6] His policy is to retain the vocabulary of the past wherever possible, but to constantly reexamine and reinterpret each phrase and definition in light of "the Word of God and the continuing guidance of the Holy Spirit."[7] Thus this initial statement of aims anticipates something of the shape and direction of his entire doctrine of Scripture.

As Bloesch looks over the current Christian scene, he observes certain controversies raging both within Protestantism and Roman Catholicism. Examples of these are the politicizing of the church's mission, inclusive language for God and homosexual ordination. These are only symptoms, however, of a much deeper split between two views of Scripture.[8]

On the right is what Bloesch terms "evangelical rationalism." This approach virtually equates revelation with the Bible. It proceeds in two ways. In its deductive form it begins with first principles found in Scripture and draws conclusions from them. When it works inductively, it compiles the facts recorded in Scripture and derives principles from them. Bloesch labels the second option "religioethical experientialism." This measures theological truth by human moral experience. In this view, "The Bible is valued because it provides the insights that elucidate the universal experience of transcendence."[9]

Distinct from both of these views is Bloesch's position, which he calls "biblical evangelicalism." Here the Bible is not to be thought of as the revelation itself but the divinely prepared medium or channel of revelation. Biblical evangelicalism affirms the possibility of real knowledge of God, but not as a permanent intrinsic quality of Scripture. Rather, such knowledge is always "given anew by the Spirit of God in conjunction with the hearing and reading of the biblical message."[10]

It is apparent that Bloesch has more sympathy for evangelical rationalism than he does for experientialism, which tends to take either the form of an idealistic worldview or a naturalism. The major difference between his view and that of evangelical rationalism, however, is that "the latter regards the knowledge of God as a human possibility because of a universal divine revelation in nature and history."[11] By contrast "the biblical evangelical believes that real knowledge of God is not possible apart from faith, which is a gift of the Spirit."[12] This knowledge moves downward, as Christ descends to us, not upward to God through speculation, as posited by medieval scholasticism.[13]

Bloesch is trying to avoid either of two extremes. On the one hand, the experiential orientation of religious liberalism virtually eliminates any content from revelation. On the other hand, theological fundamentalism has frozen revelation into the Bible, so that the former is equated with the latter. Bloesch appears to be seeking to retain a real but dynamic relationship between revelation and the Bible, so that we can say that the Bible is the Word of God, but not intrinsically or inherently so. Here revelation remains with God, and the Bible comes alive when the Spirit of God illumines the mind of the reader. He desires to form a theology of Word *and* Spirit, not the one without the other. In this he claims the precedent of Calvin, and at least in terms of the formal terminology, this is correct. He says, "The biblical word stands in continuity with the living Word, but only faith can discern the measure of this continuity."[14] He adds that this Word of God is "living and dynamic."

By contrast the evangelical and conservative view has too often viewed the Word as "something static and frozen, waiting to be analyzed and dissected."[15] The ability to know the Word must not be thought of as a human possession, but as resting on the "prior action of the Word. The Word himself must take the initiative and break through the barrier of human sin and finitude if we are to know the truth that regenerates and redeems."[16] Repeatedly Bloesch emphasizes this dynamic relationship of the Word to the words. He indicates his agreement with Emil Brunner that God's revelation does not consist in a system of statements that are humanly accessible. "Rather," he says, "it is a transforming reality that can be known only through searching the Scriptures in the context of the fellowship of faith."[17]

In his interaction with evangelical theologian J. I. Packer's statement that "the Bible is the Word of God not only instrumentally but also instrinsically," this view becomes even more clearly focused. Bloesch says he can agree with this kind of affirmation because "the Bible constitutes a reliable testimony to God's self-revelation in Christ by virtue of its divine inspiration."[18] Yet, he says, "it is not divine revelation intrinsically, for its revelatory status does not reside in its wording as such but in the Spirit of God, who fills the words with meaning and power. It is the written Word of God because its authors were inspired by God; it becomes the revealed Word of God when God himself speaks through the prophetic and apostolic witness, sealing the truth of this witness in our hearts."[19]

Furthermore, Bloesch is willing to speak of the Bible as instrinsically the Word of God because it is included in Christ's redemptive act, as the Spirit works within the community of faith. However, he again states, "The Bible in and of itself is not the Word of God—divine revelation—but it is translucent to this revelation by virtue of the Spirit of God working within it and within the mind of the reader and hearer."[20] Logically, we are faced here with a difficult task of interpretation. To say that x is intrinsically y but that x is not in and of itself y seems to involve a different definition of intrinsic than that which it usually carries.

The Crisis in Biblical Authority

Bloesch sees the problem in theology in the last two decades as being the division of the theological scene between the two camps of the liberals and the evangelicals, with no real middle ground. He faults the liberals for losing sight of the divinity of the Bible, and for giving up the biblical teachings about personal morality while emphasizing the support of social causes. Conservatives, on the other hand, have defended traditional moral values, but have not spoken out against "weapons of mass extermination."[21]

One might assume that neo-orthodoxy would represent a suitable middle ground between these two groups. Unfortunately, however, if this movement is not in total eclipse, its particular emphases have faded. His specific criticism, more true of Brunner and the Niebuhrs than of Barth, is that "it was unable to hold together the divine and the human sides of Scripture. It can be faulted for fostering a Nestorian approach to the Bible in which the divine word and the human word are only loosely associated and never function in an indissoluble unity."[22]

The crisis can be seen quite clearly with respect to biblical criticism, which has had a continuing negative effect upon both theology and biblical studies. This methodology has come under considerable fire in recent years. While some conservative evangelical scholars have endeavored to assimilate the valuable elements within historical and literary criticism, others have rejected these elements, in toto, falling back upon the doctrine of biblical inerrancy. This he believes to be a result of some evangelicals' "epistemic bondage to Enlightenment rationalism."[23] The same phenomenon is found in Roman Catholicism, where some are retreating to the doctrine of papal authoritarianism, while many younger Catholic theologians are adopting such recent theological fashions as liberation, process, feminist and narrative theology. Bloesch sees narrative theology as "an attempt to evade both the question of the historicity of the events and miracles recorded in Scripture and the question of their metaphysical implications."[24]

There are several different possible responses to this crisis occasioned by biblical criticism, related to the three models of biblical authority: (1) the sacramental, (2) the scholastic and (3) the liberal, or modernist. These stem both from differing theological methodologies and from different philosophical conceptions of truth.

The sacramental model sees the Bible as an instrument or channel through which God works in relating to humans. It holds that there is an infinite qualitative distinction between divinity and humanity, but contends that the human can be used instrumentally by God. Bloesch cites as examples of this model Augustine, Calvin, Luther, Forsyth and Barth (at least in his middle period).[25] On this model the Bible is a channel or vessel of revelation. It is the sign of the thing signified (God's self-revelation in Christ). The relationship between the divine and human sides of the Bible is analogous to the mystery of the union of the divine and human natures of Jesus Christ. Revelation is actually God in action, making himself known to the eyes of faith. It is a complex phenomenon: "Revelation has a personal, a propositional and an experiential pole. What is revealed is a personal presence in conjunction with a spoken or written witness and received by a believing heart." God is hidden even in his revelation, not being directly available to human perception or conception. He is known only as he enables persons to know him.[26]

In the scholastic view the infinite is accessible to the finite. It also maintains that it is possible and even desirable to systematize the revealed knowledge found in Scripture. While partially present in some Catholic theologians like Peter Lombard and Thomas Aquinas, it is especially characteristic of Protestant orthodoxy.[27] On this view, the Bible is a collection of revealed truths or propositions. While suprarational, the knowledge given in revelation has such continuity with natural knowledge that human reason can understand it.[28]

The third model emphasizes divine immanence over divine transcendence, to the point of creating a unity between divine and human. Its orientation is more psychological than theological, emphasizing the effect of the divine on humanity, rather than the nature of divinity as such. While there is considerable variation among different adherents of this type of theology, in general they hold that revelation is more a matter of breaking through to new self-understanding than it is a matter of information about God or his plan of salvation.[29]

These three models of Scripture also involve differing views of infallibility. The sacramental view holds to a derivative infallibility. The Bible is not infallible in itself, but the one who uses it as an instrument of revelation is infallible, and the Bible is uniquely inspired, thus transmitting infallible truth. The scholastic model contends that the Bible has absolute infallibility or absolute inerrancy, resident within its very words. The liberal view considers the Bible a fallible record of human experiences.[30]

Each of these views of theology and of the Bible has its own distinctive and appropriate understanding of faith as well. In the sacramental view, faith is "an existential commitment to the personal God revealed in Jesus Christ."[31] Since scholastic theology considers the Bible to be a collection of divinely revealed propositions, it accordingly understands faith as intellectual assent to propositional truth.[32] For the liberal view, faith is either a discovery of our contact with the creative power within nature, or an insight into our connection with the divine. The relationship of faith and revelation is also significant: "In the first model faith is included in the event of revelation. In the second, revelation is prior to faith. In the third, revelation tends to be subordinated to faith."[33]

Finally, these three different models of biblical authority also involve different conceptions of the nature of theology, corresponding to their view of the Bible. On the sacramental model theology is "the systematic reflection on the mysteries of divine revelation for the purpose of presenting a viable and intelligible witness to this revelation in our time."[34] For scholastic theologians theology is seen as more directly knowledge and systematic: it "consists in harmonizing the axioms of Scripture in order to arrive at a comprehensive life- and worldview."[35] The liberal-modernist approach is quite different: "Theology is an interpretation of our experiences of God in the light of the modern historical consciousness. It signifies basically a reconstruction of the biblical witness."[36]

Revelation

The doctrine of revelation is basic to Bloesch's doctrine of Scripture. It underlies and affects his view of inspiration, inerrancy, interpretation and even his methodology. His definition of revelation occurs throughout his volume on Scripture, but the fullest statement comes in his chapter on revelation. He is, as one might expect from what we have already examined, sharply critical of the neo-Protestant and neo-Catholic views of revelation, which make it an experience of the divine or a discovery of one's own potential.[37] He is, however, equally clear about rejecting any type of view that simply equates revelation with the Bible.[38]

The heart of his doctrine of revelation is found in his discussion of revelation as truth and event. The truth of revelation is not to be thought of as static. Rather, it is "truth that happens, [or] truth that creates."[39] Revelation is a meeting between God and the believer. It involves two elements: personal encounter and the impartation of knowledge. This revelation is both direct and indirect, both divine presence and divine meaning. Thus Bloesch takes issue with Pannenberg, who contends that revelation is always indirect through historical actions. Bloesch's understanding of direct revelation includes dreams and visions. There are two poles or aspects to this revelation: the historical and the experiential. It is both God speaking and the human being responding, but this response is through the power of God's Spirit.[40]

There seems to be both an original and a repeated form of revelation in Bloesch's formulation of the doctrine. There is a once-for-all character to the original revelation: "Revelation happened in a final and definitive form in the apostolic encounter with Jesus Christ."[41] However, there is also a derivative or recurrent variety of revelation: "But revelation happens again and again in the experience of the Spirit of Christ."[42] While the central focus of revelation is Jesus Christ, this is not an isolated event. There is a sacred history which prepares for the coming of Christ, and within which it was received. Although Bloesch does not use the term "progressive revelation," he does speak of "cumulative revelation" and "levels of revelation." There has been a building of the revelation given to prophets and patriarchs of Israel, culminating in the historical Jesus.[43]

Although having great sympathy and affinity for the neo-orthodox view, in which revelation gives us personal knowledge but not theological propositions, Bloesch is not prepared to follow it entirely. He seeks to retain the conceptual dimension of revelation, even while subordinating it to the personal. This is because God's self-revelation comes through the instrumentality of the prophets and apostles, employing their writing. What God gives is not just his presence, "but also the imparting of the knowledge of his will and purpose for human-kind."[44] This knowledge is conceptual as well as existential and can be formulated but never possessed or mastered in propositions. Bloesch believes this places him in the tradition of Luther and Calvin.[45]

Bloesch insists that there is a conceptual content to revelation. Here he stands opposed to a powerful twentieth-century trend that makes revelation merely a confrontation of wills without any impartation of knowledge. While agreeing that revelation is indeed an act, he insists that it is also a truth, in fact, *the* truth about God and the world, and ourselves. While it takes place in an encounter, it includes "knowledge of the significance of this encounter."[46] He contends that there is "a built-in interpretation of the truth of faith within the Bible that is normative for us."[47] The nature of this truth must be correctly understood, however. It is "not a comprehension of the totality of things, as in idealism, but a concrete understanding of a unique and definite occurrence."[48] It is "an illumination that enables the mind to discern the specific truths revealed by God."[49]

Yet having said this, Bloesch wants to avoid the view that the propositions of Scripture *are* the revelation:

> Yet the law and the gospel cannot be equated with objective proposi-
> tions either in the creeds of the church or in Holy Scripture. They
> indicate the divinely given meaning of these propositions, a meaning
> that is never at the disposal of natural reason. To be sure, the divine
> promise and the divine command come to us through objective
> statements and words. But they always connote much more than a

surface understanding of the text in question. These objective statements are not themselves revelation but the vehicle and outcome of
revelation.[50]

This dialectical or, as Thomas Torrance puts it, "dialogical" relationship
between the revelation and the biblical propositions requires some expansion. These propositions are "the result of revelation, the concrete embodi-
ment of revelation."[51] Together with Bernard Ramm, Bloesch regards the
phrase *propositional revelation* as ambiguous, because there are many
different literary forms in which revelation comes. He subscribes to the intent
of the phrase, however, because it means that revelation is intelligible and
conceptual.[52] One reason the commandments and promises of God cannot
be limited to objective written material is that "their meaning-content includes
their significance for those who hear God's Word in every new situation."[53]
It is important to understand the nature of this knowledge. It is not merely
conceptual knowledge; it is also existential knowledge. With Calvin, Bloesch
insists that it is more a knowledge of the heart and the affection than of the
head and the intellect.[54]

This dialogical relationship of revelation to propositions also applies to
the relationship of revelation to history. Thus Pannenberg's virtual equation
of revelation with universal history is unsatisfactory, as is also the very
different *Heilsgeschichte* approach of G. Ernest Wright, in which revelation
is equated with God's mighty deeds in salvation history. The knowledge of
God in these views is indirect, for it results from reflection upon God's
working in history.[55]

As in Barth's view of revelation, Bloesch's also insists on God's sovereignty
and initiative in revelation. God is not under our control or generally available
to human understanding. God can, however, make himself an object for our
understanding, so that we can really know, even if we do not fully
comprehend.[56]

The absoluteness of God's Word must always be tempered by the relativity
introduced when humans appropriate and formulate it. Not only are all of
our attempted understandings merely approximations of the Word of God,
but "this is also true of the prophetic and apostolic interpretation in the
Bible."[57] This is apparently why the biblical propositions, although inspired,
are not to be equated with divine revelation. It is not so much that our
understanding is mistaken but rather is incomplete. We are never able to get
an absolute or all-inclusive perspective.

Bloesch has little time for natural theology or even for general revelation. He treats it in his volume on authority and method (*A Theology of Word & Spirit*), rather than in the volume on Scripture. After surveying a number of views of general revelation, and the biblical texts generally appealed to as support for the idea of general revelation, he concludes:

> I am coming to agree with Hendrikus Berkhof that "general revelation" is a term that should probably now be abandoned because of its ambiguity and imprecision. If revelation is essentially a personal encounter, general revelation would seem to contradict this essential dimension of revelation. If revelation is defined as God's effectual communication of his will and purpose to humanity, then we have no revelation in nature that can be positively conjoined with the biblical meanings of "unveiling" (*apokalupsis*) and "manifestation" (from *phanerŏ*).[58]

But if one follows this view of general revelation, how are we to regard God's work in nature and conscience? This, says Bloesch, should be understood as a display of these qualities of God, rather than a revelation, which would manifest his purposes. He says, "Through his general working in nature and conscience, we are *exposed* to the mercy of God as well as to his wrath and judgment, but God's light and truth are *disclosed* to us only in the encounter with Jesus Christ as presented in Holy Scripture."[59]

The Inspiration of Scripture

Much of Bloesch's treatment of inspiration is devoted to a discussion of others' views, but he does enunciate his own view at some length. His definition of inspiration is more inclusive than that generally found in evangelical theology: "the divine election and guidance of the biblical prophets and the ensuring of their writings as a compelling witness to revelation, the opening of the eyes of the people of that time to the truth of these writings, and the providential preservation of these writings as the unique channel of revelation."[60] Thus it includes not simply the writing of the documents, but the reception of those writings by people of that time, and the preservation of those writings down through history. It makes the Bible a witness to revelation and "guarantees that the biblical affirmations are divinely authorized and true." Beyond that, it "makes Scripture revelatory—open to divine truth." One must bear in mind that Bloesch does not restrict the term *revelation* to the original events reported in Scripture, but to God's reiterated use of them. Thus he can say, "Inspiration means that God sends forth his Spirit to prepare the way for his Word; revelation means that God speaks his Word in conjunction with the testimony of his inspired prophets and apostles."[61]

Bloesch can use the expression *verbal* to describe his view of inspiration, for it is both verbal and conceptual. By that he does not mean exact factual inerrancy or mechanical dictation but rather that God adopts the words of limited and fallible human to serve his purposes.[62] Yet it should be borne in mind that the revelation is not these particular words or letters. The mistake of fundamentalism has been to absolutize the words of the biblical writers, just as liberalism has erred by relativizing them.[63]

Bloesch also uses the term *plenary inspiration,* by which he means that all of Scripture is inspired rather than merely parts of it. He insists, however, with Bernard Ramm, that a "flat view" of Scripture must be rejected, since it makes no distinction between "what is essential and what is marginal, what is in the foreground and what is background material."[64]

Bloesch's statement that inspiration makes Scripture revelatory is one of the most significant differences between his view of the Bible and a more traditional evangelical view. In the latter, inspiration logically follows or perhaps accompanies revelation. In Bloesch's view it also precedes revelation, for revelation is not simply in the past, as noted above.

What was it that the biblical writers were given by inspiration? It was not a complete or literal grasp of the mystery of divine salvation. Rather, says, Bloesch, "they were given a reliable but incomplete knowledge of God's will and purpose" and their language about these is not univocal but symbolic or analogical. Because of the transcendence of God the writers' words are not identical with God's Word.[65]

Inerrancy

A key word in much evangelical discussion of the Bible in the latter half of the twentieth century has been *inerrancy.* While the exact meaning of this word has varied among different evangelical theologians, Bloesch states that in general the fundamentalist use of the term has been related to the idea of complete factual accuracy of the Bible in all its details. Because fundamentalism rests its basis for belief in the empirical references of a divine book, rather than the Spirit who speaks to us in that book, inerrancy is of great importance to it.[66]

Bloesch grants that many of the fathers of the church spoke of the Bible as free from error but contends that it is illegitimate to assume that they meant simply what some twentieth-century theologians mean when they use that term: Those fathers were operating with a view of truth that was quite different from the modern empiricist view.[67] In biblical religion, he would say, error meant "swerving from the truth or wandering from the right path, rather than defective information."[68] So he says, "Scriptural inerrancy can be affirmed if it means the conformity of what is written to the dictates of the Spirit regarding the will and purpose of God. But it cannot be held if it is taken to mean the conformity of everything that is written in Scripture to the facts of world history and science."[69]

He points out numerous historical inaccuracies and internal consistencies in the Scripture that would certainly appear to belie the idea of inerrancy as absolute factual inerrancy, interpreted in terms of a modern scientific view of truth. Claiming to be following Calvin's principle of accommodation, he grants that the form or mode in which Christ's teaching comes to us involves the writers believing the common conceptions of their day regarding scientific matters.[70]

There also are some theological discrepancies between the Old and the New Testaments. Of these he says, "I agree that the people of ancient Israel entertained numerous misconceptions of God as well as antiquated and even sub-Christian notions of human life and destiny. Yet such notions, which belong to a past time and culture, still have a place in the total biblical panorama, for they direct us to the center and apex of biblical history—the self-revelation of the living God in the person and work of Christ."[71]

Bloesch indicates that at the root of a view of inerrancy is the understanding of the nature of revelation: "I depart from some of my evangelical colleagues in that I understand the divine content of Scripture not as rationally comprehensible teachings but as the mystery of salvation declared in Jesus Christ (compare Rom 16:25; Eph 1:9; 6:19; Col 1:26; 2:2)."[72] Thus what we are given in the Bible is not "an absolutely accurate account of Israel's history, but we have a faithful rendition of God's action in the community of Israel."[73]

It appears that Bloesch's view of inerrancy is quite close to what is often referred to as "inerrancy of purpose." He says, "The Bible is imperfect in its form but not mistaken in its intent."[74] While the Scriptures are not fully adequate in the sense of giving a comprehensive explanation, it is also not appropriate to refer to them as in error. "They are adequate to the truth revealed in them."[75] He prefers terms like *truthfulness* or *veracity* to the word *inerrant,* probably because these are positive rather than negative in what they say. *Infallibility* is also preferable to *inerrancy*. Yet all of these terms must be qualified, for strictly speaking the qualities to which they refer derive from the one who reveals himself through the Bible. It is appropriate to apply terms like *infallibility* and *veracity* "to the whole Bible, to its overall message, to its revelatory meaning, not to any particular text or report of the Bible."[76]

Interpretation of the Bible

Hermeneutics is important to Bloesch, for in his judgment interpretation of the Bible presents a problem for the church today, just as does the question of its authority. Merely repeating what the Bible says will not be sufficient; it is necessary to interpret it to get at its true meaning.[77] In addition Bloesch recognizes that his view of the nature of the Bible complicates the hermeneutical task: "The task of interpretation would be much easier if the words of the Bible were identical with divine revelation. But because these words are related to revelation as form to content, interpretation is far more difficult."[78] Critical methods may be legitimately used with respect to the form but not the content of Scripture.[79]

As can be seen from the foregoing comments, Bloesch's understanding of biblical interpretation follows his view of revelation. His method, like that of classical evangelical hermeneutics, involves both exegesis (determining the author's intended meaning) and exposition (determining its significance both for that time and ours).[80] With James Packer he holds that a text may have a deeper meaning, of which the writer was not aware.[81] In Bloesch's case, however, there is a special reason for this:

> The truth of faith lodges not in the human interpreter nor in the community of faith but in the Word of God, whose presence encompasses the text of Holy Scripture. Understanding happens when God's Word speaks to us anew as we submit ourselves to his authority and direction mediated through Holy Scripture. We begin to know when the text becomes transparent to its transcendent meaning through the action of the Spirit in the biblical words and in the human heart.[82]

How do we come to know the Word of God? That is the critical question. Bloesch proposes a fourfold process:

1. The first stage is a reverent and humble coming to the text. Such seeking will be done only by someone who already is a believer.

2. The next stage is critical, involving the use of the tools of research; these apply primarily to the form, not the content, of revelation.

3. It is then necessary to let the text criticize us. We must criticize the very presuppositions we brought to the text.

4. Finally, in a state of prayerful receptivity we learn from the text and apply it to our lives.[83]

Bloesch's view of revelation reasserts itself in his discussion of the natural and the spiritual sense of Scripture. He says, "I believe that we must make a clear-cut distinction between the historical meaning of the text and its revelational or spiritual meaning."[84] By the former he is referring to the traditional idea of the author's intended meaning. By the latter, however, he means "the pneumatic or spiritual meaning that the text assumes when the Spirit acts on it in bringing home its significance to people of faith in every age."[85] Here again, this is a meaning not available to unbelievers, being "accessible only to those who participate existentially in the tradition of the faith, for only they are in experiential contact with the realities to which the text witnesses."[86]

The Role of Rationalism

A recurrent theme in Bloesch's writings is the role that rationalism has played in producing the fundamentalist view of Scripture or, indeed, the whole conception of propositional revelation. This appears in numerous places, with the most complete and systematic exposition of the topic coming in an appendix to the first chapter of the forthcoming fifth volume of his Christian Foundations. The prominence he gives to rationalism can be seen in the sheer number and size of references to it. In his volume on Scripture, for example, the index shows no fewer than twenty-six references to rationalism, a number exceeded only by the references to revelation, the Holy Spirit and faith. Some examples can be given of his statements on the subject:

> Against the rationalists who reduce faith to intellectual assent to verbal truth and the experientialists and spiritualists who appeal to private illuminations over the written Word of God, I affirm the paradoxical unity of Word and Spirit so that the reception of the Word is both a rational apprehension and a redeeming experience. I have considerable difficulty with the view, so appealing to those of a rationalist bent, that the Bible is impregnated with universal, unchanging truths that are waiting to be discovered and formulated.[87]

> I believe the hope of theology rests on a genuine evangelical renaissance, but such a renaissance will not happen until evangelicals break out of their epistemic bondage to Enlightenment rationalism.[88]

Rationalism is evident in many of the theological luminaries of the past, especially in those who would be classified as philosophical theologians or even Christian philosophers.[89]

Bloesch does not really define his usage of *rationalism*. This is unfortunate, since the term has borne a number of different meanings over the years. Indeed he appears to use it in a number of senses. Perhaps the inclusive definition that can be derived inductively from the several references to it in his writings would be something like "an excessive role assigned to the contribution and power of reason in the doctrine of revelation and in the doing of theology." What he considers to be the excessive role must be seen from what he says about rationalism:

1. Rationalism is allied with a belief that our language about God is univocal: that predications made about him are identical to predications made about ourselves or other objects of empirical observation.[90]

2. Biblical truth is immediately accessible to reason. It can be understood without dependence upon any illumining work by the Holy Spirit.[91]

3. There is a tendency to dissolve mystery into logic.[92]

4. In its empiricistic version rationalism tends to rely upon external evidences to establish the reality of revelation, or the truth of the doctrines.[93]

5. An insistence on ideas, including our knowledge of God, being clear and distinct.[94]

6. An exact correspondence between linguistic signs and their objects.[95]

7. Belief that by reason one may prove, even apart from grace, such fundamental doctrines as the existence of God and the resurrection of Christ.[96]

The thrust of his analysis of rationalism and propositional revelation is that the increasing influence of the Enlightenment on Reformed theologians gradually transformed their view from a more existential view that allowed room for mystery, into a view of revelation as the communication of propositions. With this went the increased emphasis upon theology as systematization of those propositions.[97]

Overall, Bloesch's view of Scripture, while combining elements of neo-orthodoxy and traditional evangelicalism, appears closer to the former than to the latter. Significant presuppositions are at work in Bloesch's doctrine of Scripture. One of these is important enough to warrant a separate extended treatment. This will help us understand why, at least in part, he feels so strongly about rationalism and its effects.

Bloesch's Presuppositions

It is commonly recognized that the early Barth, the Barth of the *Römerbrief* and for that matter the *Christliche Dogmatik*, was heavily influenced by the existentialism of Søren Kierkegaard. Indeed Barth himself recognized and acknowledged this dependence and resolved to purge his thought of the influence of this philosophy or any other. He believed he had succeeded in that endeavor and that what he was writing was now simply biblical, free from philosophy.[98] Yet that may be challenged. While more subtle than in his early writing, existentialist ideas were still present in his thought. Bloesch acknowledges as much.[99]

Bloesch, like Barth, seeks to avoid the corrupting influence of philosophy. His analysis of fundamentalism consists in large part in endeavoring to show how the true biblical tradition was distorted by the growing presence of rationalism, whether in what he calls the idealistic form or the empirical. The historical growth of this is part of his argument.

It appears, however, that Bloesch himself works from significant philosophical presuppositions. While these are complex and represent an intertwining of several strands, we will concern ourselves here with the existentialist presuppositions he displays. He acknowledges his indebtedness to Kierkegaard, Barth and even Bultmann. At a number of places one can detect significant resemblances between his thought and twentieth-century existentialism. While similarity does not establish derivation, it is one of the evidences of that.

1. His opposition to systematizing, or comprehensive statements of the truth. One of Kierkegaard's continuing outcries was against "the system," by which he meant Hegel's comprehensive philosophy, which explained everything, including all of the data of history. Over against that view he presented the idea of the existing individual, who can never be simply reduced to a universal or any collection of universals.[100]

2. His opposition to the idea of the static character of revelation. While Bloesch's insistence upon the dynamic nature of truth is held in common with much of twentieth-century thought, it has special affinity with Kierkegaard's famous distinction between objective and subjective truth. Objective truth is appropriate to science and history, where exact description of the object is important; however, real truth, religious truth, involves the infinite passion of the inward. Truth, said Kierkegaard, is truth for me.[101] Although Bloesch insists on both the objective and the subjective dimensions of revelation, his vehement rejection of any freezing of revelation in propositions reflects this presupposition.

3. His insistence on the recurrent nature of revelation, that it is not simply something that occurred but recurs, also reflects existentialism. Kierkegaard discussed at some length the impossibility of being a disciple at secondhand and maintained that we must become contemporaries of Christ, or more correctly, he of us.[102] This is strongly parallel to Bloesch's contention that the Bible is not so much revelation as revelatory, the means through which God manifests himself anew.

4. His opposition to the idea that God's truth can be captured within logic also reflects a major existentialist theme. He would not go so far as to maintain that this truth is contrary to logic, but his understanding of God's transcendence and of the paradoxical nature of the relationship of the words of the Scripture writers to the Word of God is reminiscent of Kierkegaard's discussion of the paradox that occurs when the eternal and infinite enters the realm of the temporal and finite.[103]

Bloesch does not believe that he is working from a particular philosophical perspective. He is working from the biblical view and from the correct understanding of the fathers and the reformers. The nature of presuppositions, however, is that they are brought unconsciously even to interpretation of the Bible or to the study of history. They represent the lenses through which we view reality. Although the insight is not new to the latter part of the twentieth century, postmodernism and the sociology of knowledge have in our time prosecuted the idea that every thought and writing proceeds from some historical setting. It appears that Bloesch's thought is no less indebted to twentieth-century existentialism than, according to Rogers and McKim, the Old Princeton school of biblical inspiration was to Scottish commonsense realism.[104]

Evaluation of Bloesch's View

It is helpful in evaluating Bloesch's theology to remember something of the path he has traveled in arriving at his present position. He has come to an evangelical theological position from the left. He was exposed to the naturalistic theism, or as it is now termed, process theology, at the University of Chicago. In this context, he was attracted to neo-orthodoxy and especially to the thought of Karl Barth. Thus those evangelicals who criticize him for his at least partial Barthianism need to realize that this does not represent a defection from a more traditional variety of evangelical theology.

Bloesch has sought to creatively fuse the insights of neo-orthodoxy and a more traditional orthodox view of Scripture. Whether he has successfully accomplished this, he has attempted to improve on the view of Karl Barth, avoiding some of the gaps and pitfalls of it. He has correctly seen that sometimes revelation has been made so much an object of intellectual belief that the relationship of the person to it is simply a passive matter.

Much of his criticism of conventional evangelicalism is clearly on target. For example, some theorists of hermeneutics, even some who proclaim themselves to be Calvinists, believe that the unregenerate person without any special reliance upon the illumining work of the Holy Spirit can correctly understand the Bible. Indeed some even insist that, all things being equal, unbelievers can better understand the Scripture, since they have no vested interest in what it may say.[105] And some have approached the issue of authorial intent with such a reliance upon secular hermeneutics, most notably that of E. D. Hirsch Jr., that the role of the Holy Spirit in the process of scriptural writing, and thus in authorial intent, is neglected. Further, some practitioners of an inductive approach to apologetics have contended that reason can establish at least the *notitia* and *assensus* elements of faith, although not *fiducia*.[106]

Bloesch has rightly seen the need for a theology cognizant of and related to the issues raised by current views. Without doing this, theology loses its ability to speak to a new generation. Additionally, however, following the insight of his mentor Barth, he has seen the danger of simply allowing the culture to set the agenda for theology and even of incorporating some of contemporary culture into the content of theology.[107] The history of the church, as seen in the endorsement by some German Christians of Kaiser Wilhelm in 1914[108] and of Adolf Hitler in the early 1930s[109] as well as at other times in its history, indicates that such an incorporation of culture into its ideology robs the church of its strength.[110]

Further, Bloesch has correctly apprehended and emphasized that the end of revelation is not simply to provide information. It is given for the purpose of establishing and strengthening the relationship between humans and their Creator and Redeemer. This is to be found in the testimony of the biblical writers themselves (Jn 20:31; 2 Tim 3:16; 1 Jn 1:4; 5:13). At the same time he has correctly noted that while narrative theology rightly acknowledges the narrative character of much of Scripture, it must not exclude the ontological reality that breaks into human discourse.[111]

Having said this, there are three areas where I believe Bloesch can assist his friends and followers, as well as those who are simply interested in his theology, in understanding it. This is not to say that these are inherent defects in his thought. It is likely that the shortcoming lies with my lack of perceptiveness rather than obscurity of his thought.

Revelation, in Bloesch's thought, is neither primarily informational nor, in the sense that evangelicals like J. I. Packer and Carl Henry use it, propositional. It is, however, cognitive. While it can be expressed in propositions, it is personal, not propositional. The problem, then, which in my judgment is never sufficiently clarified by Bloesch, is the exact nature of the connection between personal truth and the propositions of Scripture and of theology. He speaks of "truths of revelation," which he defines as "truths that rise out of revelation and therefore presuppose a conceptual content in revelation,"[112] but it is not clear just how these rise out of revelation.

Bloesch cites Brunner's use of the analogy of the phonograph record[113] and the distinction between "thought-in-encounter" and "thinking-about-it,"[114] but Brunner does not really explain the relationship between the nonpropositional encounter and the doctrine which is "indissolubly linked" with it "as instrument, as token, as framework."[115] This is but a label, not an explanation. This lack of clarity regarding the linkage is a difficulty which neo-orthodoxy never, in my judgment, adequately resolved,[116] and Bloesch could do us all an immense favor by expounding it more precisely. Bloesch quotes and cites specific Scriptures in setting forth his theology, although not as extensively as do some other evangelical theologies, but the exact basis of this use is not entirely evident.

Second, Bloesch should clarify and justify the presuppositions from which he works. Much of his criticism of traditional evangelicalism's view of the Bible is based upon what he perceives to be its underlying rationalistic presuppositions. He conveys the impression that this criticism comes from a philosophically neutral basis. However, as we have endeavored to show, this is not the case. It comes from his own position, which itself is based upon a major philosophical presupposition.

Although the insight that everyone works from some presuppositional basis is not new, it has been given special emphasis by the postmodern movement. One can, if that insight is correct, follow one of two courses. One can either retreat to a sort of epistemological pluralism, where differing positions are all equally true and adjudication between them is impossible because they rest on differing starting points. Or one can seek to argue for the superiority of one's own presuppositions over those of others. By their very nature presuppositions cannot be antecedently verified. They can, however, be justified or validated and compared with one another by making

given presuppositions, tracing out their implications and assessing which of
these lead to a set of conclusions which more adequately account for the
data they are intended to explain. This is what Bloesch needs to do if his
assertions are to be accepted.

There is another dimension to this matter of philosophical presuppositions. Bloesch seeks to show how orthodoxy or fundamentalism deviated
from the biblical view, or that of the early fathers, or the Reformers, by
adopting rationalism. The effect of this argument is to render the view in
question historically relative: it is the product of the intellectual milieu from
which it sprang. That type of argument is a two-edged sword, however, for
if applied to Bloesch's view, it would have similar effects. He must be
prepared to argue that either his view does not suffer from this type of
historical conditioning or that the historical setting that has contributed the
presuppositions with which he is working is somehow preferable to that
from which the competing theology issued. To fail to do this is to fall into
the argument, now increasingly recognized as the Enlightenment modernist
belief in progress, that what is current is superior to what has preceded.

There is one other area where I would appreciate additional clarification.
That is the question of the grounds for adopting a particular religious
perspective. This is the "warrant" issue now widely discussed by philosophers. Bloesch has basically adopted the position that receiving revelation is
essentially self-certifying. The experience itself removes all doubt of its
genuineness. This, however, is an increasingly problematic position in a
society characterized by empirical religious pluralism, that is, the presence
of adherents of differing religions. Many members of other religions, including the so-called New Age religion, find their religious experience to be
equally vivid and indubitable.

Bloesch cites with approval Brunner's use of the analogy of "His Master's
Voice." In that context Brunner faces the question of how to respond to the fact
of the Muslim who also hears his master's voice within the Koran. In effect, his
answer is, We are not Muslims.[117] This, however, seems like a very ethnocentric
response. It lends support to the contention that if you scratch a fideist, under
the skin you will find an authoritarian. It would be helpful if Bloesch clarified
in just what way his position avoids that problem. It is apparent from his
discussion of narrative theology that he is not a pluralist, and he believes that
the best response to competitive religious views is to confront them with the
gospel, not by relying upon human powers of persuasion.

Bloesch has indeed combined the traditional evangelical view of Scripture with a Barthian neo-orthodoxy. His statement that "the Spirit of God speaks to every person in a slightly different way"[118] and his emphasis on the illumining work of the Holy Spirit sound very much like the traditional evangelical doctrine of illumination, although such evangelicals would probably prefer to speak of God's applying the Word in different ways to different people. Yet his next statement, "God's Word is always new, always specific and concrete,"[119] reflects more the emphasis of Barth. Whether these two elements can be held together in a stable combination remains to be seen. Yet by his profound probing of the issues of the doctrine of Scripture, he has placed all of us in his debt and stimulated us to think more deeply upon them.

Six

Jesus Christ in Bloesch's Theology

GABRIEL FACKRE

IN THE EARLY 1950S DONALD BLOESCH AND I ENTERED THE ORDAINED MINISTRY of the Evangelical and Reformed Church, now part of the United Church of Christ.[1] In this half-century we have been in many of the same church struggles for christological integrity. Both of us played active roles in organizing neo-confessing movements in the United Church of Christ, each helping to draft their initial documents, looking on these movements as the last best hope of an acculturated Protestantism.[2] In 1978 we each launched long-term projects in systematics, concerned as we have been for the recovery of Christian foundations.[3]

The *kind* of theological renewal sought reflects both the similarities and the differences to be detailed in this chapter. The convergences and divergences are a showcase of how two kindred commitments—Donald Bloesch the "ecumenical evangelical" and his friend the "evangelical ecumenical"—strove to keep company with their "Savior, Redeemer and Lord."[4]

Editor Colyer's invitation to do the chapter on Christology poses a question of theological semantics. The rubric has a long association with the doctrine of the incarnation.[5] In this sense, Christology as the person of Christ—humanity, deity and unity—is distinguished from the atonement, the work of Christ as "objective soteriology." However, there is also a long tradition of Christology interpreted as both person and (objective) work.[6] In the latter case, it is succeeded by the locus of salvation-soteriology in its subjective sense or present tense, taking up the "application of the benefits of Christ."[7]

None of the above quite fits Bloesch's doctrine of Christ. As developed in the recent volume of his systematics series, *Jesus Christ: Savior & Lord,* and in earlier analyses in *The Christian Life and Salvation, Jesus Is Victor!* and *Essentials of Evangelical Theology,* Christology is both person and work *and* both objective and subjective soteriology. The inclusion of "application" in Christology puts Bloesch in continuity with other major works in the broadly evangelical tradition such as those of Charles Hodge and Augustus Strong. For example, in Hodge's *Systematic Theology,* "Soteriology" is the major locus that includes "The Person of Christ," "The Mediatorial Work of Christ" (past and present) and the application of the benefits of Christ described by the familiar *ordo salutis.* Hodge's soteriology also includes a long initial section on the "plan of salvation" and concluding sections on "the law" and "the means of grace," matters also dealt with in Bloesch's Christology but not in similar detail in this locus.[8]

The inclusion of the believer's appropriation process within Christology is also related to the influence of two of Bloesch's mentors, P. T. Forsyth (to whom he dedicates *Jesus Christ*) and Karl Barth who returns ever and again as Bloesch's interlocutor. Forsyth insists on the *moral* dimension of doctrine with the subjective work *in us* inseparable from the objective work of Christ on the cross. While the soteric weight of the subjective is quite different in Barth, volume four of his *Church Dogmatics* integrates the applicatory work of the Holy Spirit in faith, love and hope with his revised version of the natures, states and offices of Christ.

A case could be made that an even wider circle needs to be drawn to encompass Bloesch's Christology. In *Jesus Christ* "anthropology" is integral to the development of the doctrine of Christ, and election, ethics and eschatology are discussed. This larger web of doctrine also appears in *Christian Life, Jesus Is Victor!* and *Essentials.* In addition to these subjects a long investigation of Mariology is undertaken in *Jesus Christ.* While allusion will here be made to these matters, the limits of space and focus preclude detailed exploration. The discussion of Bloesch's Christology will, therefore, take up his view of the divine-human person and its entailments, and the work of that person, both objective and subjective. General reference to pertinent writings will be made throughout with supportive quotation at places where Bloesch is breaking new ground or entering hotly disputed terrain.

Formative Factors

Traditions. Bloesch's periodic self-descriptions and general orientation point to three theological traditions that inform his Christology: (1) evangelical,

(2) Reformed and (3) catholic. Their interaction contributes to the distinctive way in which the doctrine of Christ is interpreted, one, indeed, that varies from current treatments of Christology in each of these three traditions.[9]

Bloesch is one of North America's best-known evangelical theologians, *evangelical* understood as the interiorization and radicalization of the formal and material principles of the Reformation (the authority of Scripture and justification by faith).[10] For Bloesch, Scripture is read with an "infallibilist" hermeneutic,[11] and justification is seen as experiential appropriation of Christ's penal substitution evidenced in personal holiness and evangelistic intent. In Christology these evangelical stigmata are evident in Bloesch's insistence of the scriptural basis of all assertions with extensive biblical documentation, and as noted, in the inseparability of subjective soteriology from the doctrine of Christ.[12]

Bloesch is also a self-described Reformed theologian. This identity is borne out in the regular appearance of the characteristic Reformed emphases of *sovereignty* and *sanctification*.[13] His choice of Barth as conversation partner is a natural corollary. Formation in the Evangelical Synod wing of the Evangelical and Reformed Church contributes to the Reformed influence. However, the dual Reformed and Lutheran heritage of this "Prussian union" church helps Bloesch appreciate the Lutheran contributions to theology and sheds light on his interest in Reinhold Niebuhr whose roots also lie in the Reformed-Lutheran conjunctions of that same church.[14]

Asserted in Bloesch's early works[15] and gaining high visibility in *Jesus Christ* is the Great Tradition, the doctrinal heritage and sensibilities of pre-Reformation Christianity and current Roman Catholic and Eastern Orthodox thought. Thus the section on Mary in *Jesus Christ* engages the Marian dogmas and the role of saints in Christian faith. Critical appropriation of the Great Tradition reflects also an "evangelical catholicity" with affinities to the Mercersburg theology of John Williamson Nevin and Philip Schaff. Catholic identity in this sense has to do with the desire to honor all the theological charisms in the body of Christ, marking Bloesch as an *ecumenical* evangelical.

Polemics. The convergence of these three streams has caused a mighty Bloeschian wave to roll over the parched shores of contemporary theology. Over the years Bloesch has made an increasingly sharp contrast between his evangelical, Reformed and catholic perspective and the "neo-Protestantism" and "neo-Catholicism" in mainline churches and their ideological counterparts in the academy. The attack on the acculturated theologies of the day has been accompanied by institutional efforts in theological reform, with special reference to his own denomination, the United Church of Christ. In addition to drafting the Dubuque Declaration of the Biblical Witness Fellowship (a conservative evangelical group in the UCC), he continues as an important resource to that constituency.[16] Recently he has written sharp indictments of *The New Century Hymnal* published by an agency of the UCC.[17]

The polemic plays out in Bloesch's Christology. The development of any given aspect of the doctrine is prefaced by and permeated with analyses of present heterodoxies. In *Jesus Christ,* he views these deviations collectively as "a new theological paradigm," a capitulation to "Romanticism with its emphasis on individualism, pluralism and relativism."[18] The response to cultural captivity requires a Barmen-like *No!*

Christology and Its Contexts

Christology constitutes the heart of theology, since it focuses on God's work of salvation in the historical figure, Jesus of Nazareth, and the bearing it has on humankind. . . . To know the plan of God we must see the plan realized in the cross of Christ and fulfilled in his resurrection and second advent.[19]

Christology so understood is, as noted, conceived soteriologically, "God's work of salvation" as "realized" on Calvary and "fulfilled" at Easter and eschaton. Yet only the person ("God . . . in the historical figure, Jesus of Nazareth") can do the work. The soteriological exposition of Christology begins, accordingly, with the *context* (the problematic of *sin*) to which God's saving action is addressed, with anthropology playing an introductory role in a christological volume.

The prominence of harmatology appears in historical as well as theological context: the need to deal with Christology in a culture that must be asked, "Whatever became of sin?"[20] Context in this latter sense is reflected in *Christian Life, Essentials* and *Jesus Christ,* where the doctrine is expressed in the setting of modern debates about the meaning of Christ. The discussion of each facet (humanity and deity, preexistence, virgin birth, atonement, finality, *ordo salutis* and so on) entails a polemic mounted against current alternative views.

Chapter one of *Jesus Christ* illustrates this contextuality. The stage is set for the general christological inquiry by a rapid survey of deficient views, such as those of the Jesus Seminar and "Christology from below," as well as liberationist, feminist, pluralist, process and postmodern perspectives. Theologians and New Testament scholars questioned to one degree or another include John Dominic Crossan, Marcus Borg, Wolfhart Pannenberg, John Macquarrie, Hans Küng, Stanley Grenz, John Hick, Jürgen Moltmann, Jon Sobrino and Peter Hodgson.

On the other hand, twentieth-century theologians and traditions that have sought to maintain an "orthodox Christology" include "traditional Catholicism, Eastern Orthodoxy and conservative evangelicalism," and at least on Chalcedonian matters, "neo-orthodox theologians like Karl Barth and Dietrich Bonhoeffer." While their new interpretations go against the modernist stream, Emil Brunner and Reinhold Niebuhr are seen as less orthodox. Evangelical compatriots cited in the struggle for christological orthodoxy include Leon Morris, Howard Marshall, David Wells, Millard Erickson and David Parker.

This overall critique of the new theological paradigm in chapter one resurfaces in the analysis of each particular aspect of Christology in *Jesus Christ*. The discussion of "the finality of Christ" is representative. Current heterodoxies are traced historically to Schleiermacher, the History of Religions school (Troeltsch, H. Gunkel and J. Weiss) and William James. Bloesch then criticizes contemporary pluralist, historicist and immanentist views of Paul Knitter, John Hick, Gordon Kaufman, Langdon Gilkey, Marjorie Hewitt Suchocki, Edgar McKnight, David Griffin, John Cobb, Markus Borg, Matthew Fox and Rosemary Ruether.

Developing the doctrine of Christ in the context of a "battle for Christology"[21] entails institutional as well as theological warfare. Bloesch sees his work as undergirding a needed new confessional movement: "It is my hope that the Spirit of God will use my theology to prepare the way for a confessing church for our time."[22]

However, in both the theological and institutional struggles Bloesch distances himself from fundamentalists: political and apolitical, hyper-Calvinists and other defenders of the tradition whose own distortions and repristinations fail to honor properly the evangelical essentials, the *semper reformanda* of the Reformed tradition or the catholicity of the Great Tradition.

The Person of Christ
While soteriology is the framework for the doctrine of Christ, it is necessary to establish *who* is able do the work of reconciliation before investigating

what that work is. Thus, with Charles Hodge and Augustus Strong, Bloesch takes up the person before the work. Chalcedon sets the stage:

> Even when acknowledging that Greek philosophical categories were used to produce the Chalcedonian formula, I unashamedly stand by Chalcedon as an enduring expression of the faith once delivered to the saints. With the church fathers I affirm that Jesus was consubstantial with the Father, according to his divinity, and consubstantial with us mortals (except for sin) according to his humanity. . . . Chalcedon does not explain away the paradox of the incarnate Christ in human flesh but lets it stand as a depiction of mystery at the outer limits of human reason.[23]

Following Chalcedon, all three motifs (the divinity, humanity and unity of the person) are investigated in *Jesus Christ*, as in Bloesch's other christological analyses, with the struggle against human-scale reductionisms always to the fore.

In the general discussion of the person of Christ these refrains appear:

1. Jesus Christ is truly God, the unique incarnation of Deity as the second person of the Trinity, "an irreversible union between the Word as God and Jesus as man."[24]

2. Jesus Christ is truly human, sharing all our human characteristics (body, mind and spirit) sin excepted. The New Testament "insists on his true humanity . . . born of woman, born under the law (Gal 4:4)."[25]

3. Jesus Christ is truly one, the hypostatic union (not moral union) of the eternal Word with Jesus of Nazareth, the second person's assumption of an individual human nature constituting the unity, a "union . . . unique and incomparable."[26]

4. Jesus had no independent personal existence *(anhypostasia)* but had real human personality in God *(enhypostasia).*[27]

5. While "God is the acting subject" in Jesus, his human temptations and obedience were a genuine not an illusory struggle.[28]

6. Jesus Christ "became sin" in his identification with fallen humanity, but did not succumb to sin. The sinlessness of Jesus, a sign of his person, is related to the presence of the divine nature but is not predetermined by it.[29]

7. While the human nature of Christ did not literally precede the incarnation, it was integral to the divine plan of salvation; in that sense it is eternally inseparable from the person, constituting thereby "the preexistence of Jesus Christ."[30]

8. The person of Christ (as well as the work) expresses itself in the full

career of Jesus from preexistence through virginal conception, life, teaching, miracles, suffering, death, resurrection, ascension, session at the right hand of the Father to personal return.[31]

9. The virginal conception is a biblical teaching (an "essential truth of the catholic tradition") grounded in the historical core of "folkloric" biblical narratives, a necessary sign of the divine initiative which "safeguards" the central paradox of the Incarnation, but not an essential of faith indispensable for salvation.[32]

10. The Chalcedonian definition invites *exploration* ("faith seeking understanding") but does not attempt *explanation,* since the incarnation is a "paradox" impervious to human reason, accessed only by faith as it encounters Scripture through the work of the Holy Spirit.[33]

11. The "finality of Christ" is integral to the doctrine of the person with consequences in the work. Only in this man does God enter the world to redeem it from sin, suffering, death and the devil, the "scandal of particularity." Here is a radical exclusivity, albeit associated with an inclusivity that entails the relationship of everyone to Jesus Christ, whether that be unto salvation or damnation.[34]

12. To affirm the deity of Christ, the Council of Ephesus declared Mary to be the "Mother of God." The wider church's assertion of further privileges of Mary presses evangelicals to explore what "may well be the new frontier in ecumenicity."[35] While there is no solid biblical basis for the belief that Mary is free of original sin, or is queen of heaven or coredemptrix, she is

> an exemplar of faith . . . special covenant partner with Christ in making . . . salvation known and in communicating its fruits to both church and world . . . a means of grace . . . but never a necessary means of grace . . . an intercessor as are all the saints . . . and we may perhaps in our prayers ask for their intercession, but we do not go to them first in order to get to Christ or to God.[36]

13. A sound doctrine of the incarnation entails language commitments. Biblical authority supported by church tradition requires the retention of *Son* for the second person, signifying as it does a filial relation to the Father. The pronoun *he* for Christ signals a real flesh-and-blood incarnation, applicable to the unity of the divine-human person as well as the real humanity of Jesus. Because the privileged masculine images of Scripture and tradition can be misunderstood as human projection, their meaning can be clarified by usage

in personal piety of maternal images from Scripture, as for example the Wisdom figures that have been applied to Christ.[37]

The Work of Christ

Bloesch develops his own "biblical-evangelical" understanding of Christ's saving work in sympathetic-cum-critical conversation with "classical and Latin theories" and such theologians as Calvin, Barth, Forsyth, Anselm, Aquinas, Aulen, and in sharper exchange with current advocates of process, Bultmannian, liberal and neoliberal theologies of the left, and hyper-Calvinists on the right. He weaves together the following strands:

1. While there is "some truth" in varied theories of atonement that view Christ as saving from corruptibility or demonic powers, revealing God's love or reuniting the soul with God,[38] we must go to "the heart" of the matter:

> Evangelical theology affirms the vicarious, substitutionary atonement of Jesus Christ. It does not claim that this theory does justice to all aspects of Christ's atoning work, but it does see substitution as the heart of the atonement. The crucial point is that Jesus suffers in our stead, and he also conquers in our stead.[39]

Variously characterized as "satisfaction," "expiation" or "propitiation," substitutionary atonement has to do with the suffering and death of Christ as the fulfillment of the reconciling purpose of God "before history," accomplished on the cross by Christ receiving the divine wrath and judgment (the punishment as well as the penalty) we deserve, the result being removal "not simply of the sense of guilt but the very stain of guilt."[40]

2. The satisfaction of God and the forgiveness of sin achieved by the sacrifice of the God-Man is a "happy exchange" (Luther) of Christ's righteousness for our sin, a gift of both the divine holiness and mercy.[41]

3. The demands of divine holiness and the consequences of its violation are satisfied by God himself in the person of his Son, an atonement wrought in sovereign freedom by the divine initiative through the agency of the divine-human Mediator. This is God's own act, the "suffering of God" in the person of the Son, not the appeasement of God by Jesus.

4. In this turning point in God's history with the world, the varied biblical metaphors express one or another aspect of the fulfilled will of God: "reconciliation"—God is reconciled to the world, and the world to God; "expiation"—the human race's "stain of guilt" is removed; "propitia-

tion"—the divine anger is turned aside and God's righteous judgment is satisfied.

5. The life of Christ as well as his suffering and death are included in the objectivity of the atoning work, albeit in an "anticipatory" sense, for we are saved not "by the sacrifices in his life but the sacrifice on Calvary that purchased our redemption."[42]

6. The resurrection is essential to the atonement in that the victory over sin (1-5 above) is revealed, and the defeat of other foes (the devil, death and hell) is achieved.[43]

7. The work of atonement continues after Calvary and Easter, because Jesus Christ, at the right hand of the Father, intercedes for sinners and empowers believers.[44]

8. Christ's work also continues in the present kingdom of grace, "a hidden rule working as yeast and seed in church and world, a progressive lordship whereby the victory of Christ is carried forward into history through the outpouring of the Holy Spirit."[45]

9. Christ's atonement is universal but universalism is a heresy. Hell is real.

> God's election and predestination are realized in a different way for those who spurn the gospel; yet we can still hope and pray even for these condemned mortals, since we know they are in the hands of a God whose justice is evenhanded but whose mercy is boundless. I affirm no ultimate dualism (as in Augustinianism and Calvinism) but a duality within an ultimate unity, and this means that the pains of hell will be made to serve the glory of heaven.[46]

10. Again, atonement is universal in that all the race is included and no one will be unrelated to the love of God in Christ, but atonement is limited in that it is applied only in those who believe because of an efficacious grace that brings that faith to be:

> All people, irrespective of their moral and spiritual condition are claimed for the kingdom, but only some respond in faith and obedience. . . . All are heirs of the kingdom, but not all become members of the church of Christ. . . . The gates of the prison in which we find ourselves are now open but only those who rise up and walk through these gates are truly free.[47]

That the act of faith itself is integral to Christ's saving work leads to the third major aspect of Bloesch's Christology, its application.

The Application of the Benefits of Christ

The subjective is inseparable from the objective, for "His reconciliation needs to be fulfilled in the experience of redemption made possible by the Holy Spirit. . . . It is only in this subjective experience . . . that the Atonement becomes real.[48]

What has taken place *de jure* requires the *de facto* application of the benefits of Christ. Bloesch's evangelical encounter with Karl Barth, and entailed disagreements, helped to underscore for him the inseparability of objective and subjective soteriology.

In an early work Bloesch quotes Barth's assertion: "To *be* apprehended is enough. It requires no correlative on my side, and can have none."[49] Bloesch says that such a view

lends itself to misinterpretation. Indeed in the framework of Barthian theology it reinforces an objectivist as over against a paradoxical way of thinking. It is true that we are elected by virtue of the mercy of God and not because of deeds done by us in righteousness (Tit 3:5). Yet if this election is to benefit us we must believe in it.[50]

Thus Barth's delimitation of the status of faith to the noetic, excluding its ontic weight, must be challenged (although Bloesch acknowledges that Barth makes a place for the subjective in some sense, especially in his later writings). Contra Barth, the act of faith as a gift of grace has eternal import, as testified to by both Scripture and tradition.[51] Evangelicals who are drawn to Barth credit Bloesch with identifying "the Barthian error" at this point.[52]

Rationalism attempts to solve the problem of grace-faith (the divine initiative and our response) by erring in a hyper-Calvinist determinism or a Pelagian indeterminism, obscuring thereby the biblical paradox that cannot be penetrated by human reason. While faith is integral to salvation, it is not a "precondition": "We are not justified on the ground of our faith or works but on the grounds of God's free, unmerited mercy."[53] Inseparable from personal saving faith is "the Christian life," faith's obediential service. In the kind of pithy aphorism found throughout Bloesch's writings,[54] he declares, "We are justified by faith alone, but faith does not remain alone."[55] The work of the Holy Spirit in us generates a faith busy in love.

The insistence on sanctification is one of the gifts that the evangelical heritage brings to the Christian church and theology:

The German Pietists saw that salvation is not only something done for man but also something done in man. . . . Eighteenth century Evangelicalism in England and America shared a similar concern for the Christian life, with emphasis now being placed on the crisis experience of conversion.[56]

On occasion the emphasis on subjective soteriology in all its facets is summarized in the language of the *ordo salutis:*

Regeneration is the inward cleansing that is done by the Holy Spirit as he applies the fruits of Christ's redemption to the sinner. Justification is the act by which God imputes the perfect righteousness of Christ to the one who believes. Sanctification is the act by which God separates his people from the pollution of the world and remolds them in the image of Christ. Vocation or calling is the grace that equips the Christian for service in the world. Adoption is the privilege of being made a son or daughter in the family of God. Election and predestination refer to God's prior act of love that shapes human decision and commitment. Glorification is the final transformation of the sinner by the glory of God so that he or she becomes transparent to this glory.[57]

Bloesch notes that various Christian traditions have gravitated toward one or another of these dimensions of salvation. While there may be a *kairos* for bringing a given aspect to the fore (Luther on justification), all are needed to understand the application of the benefits of Christ's saving work.

Commentary on Bloesch's Christology

In the thirty years from *The Christian Life and Salvation* (1967) to *Jesus Christ* (1997), a remarkable consistency is apparent in the christological content of Bloesch's work, and with it the evidences of evangelical, Reformed and catholic characteristics. Indeed, many of the same formulations reappear in the five Bloesch volumes directly related to our topic.[58]

I share with Donald Bloesch the Reformed, catholic and evangelical markers, but the ordering is different as will be apparent in this commentary. The same overlap, with variations, can be seen in our critic-in-residence relationships to the United Church of Christ, differences that reflect "ecumenical evangelical" and "evangelical ecumenical" commitments. To the three major divisions of Bloesch's Christology we now turn.

Atonement. Atonement is the heart of the matter. But there are different ways to construe it, as is suggested by this encyclopedia entry:

> As the work of reconciliation wrought by God in Christ, atonement has been central in the Reformed tradition. Interpretations of the saving deed have ranged from an encompassing at-one-ment of God and the world accomplished by a manifold ministry of Christ (the three-fold office) to a delimited focus on a penal substitution carried out on Calvary to render the sinner acceptable to God. . . . Calvin's threefold office returns time and again to provide a vehicle for integrating the various accents of the Reformed tradition and for developing a more ecumenical framework for understanding the atonement.[59]

While Bloesch speaks from time to time of a many-faceted atonement, he is much closer to the "delimited focus" than to the "encompassing" view. Here the evangelical aspect of Bloesch's formation leaves its mark on Christology.

Given the Pelagian captivity of American culture and the temptation of the mainline churches to accede to it, and recognizing its weakening effects even in self-identified evangelical circles,[60] the emphasis placed by Bloesch on the priestly office is exactly right. So too is its underscoring by the incorporation of anthropology into his christological presentations, and Bloesch's frank, albeit nuanced, talk of total depravity. His dedication of *Jesus Christ* to P. T. Forsyth, with the latter's ardent witness to the "cruciality of the cross," is especially fitting.

In addition to bringing the cross to the center, Bloesch enriches the evangelical essential of penal substitution by relating it to the "classic motif," interpreting Calvary as through and through the work of God the Son, and sounding the note of Christus Victor. In contrast to the separation of the divine and human natures in piety and theology that view the cross as the appeasement of the wrathful God by the gentle Jesus, Bloesch sees the cross as a divine self-sacrifice made through the human nature of Jesus Christ on the cross. Here is a profound grasp of the suffering of God in the divine-human person of the Son. Again the salutary influence of both Barth and Forsyth is at work in acknowledging the divine passibility and rejecting the philosophically controlled concept of divine impassiblity.

Another enlargement and correction of the traditional penal substitutionary theory is at work in Bloesch's desire to honor the contribution of both mystics and moralists in holding up the Galilean ministry of Christ and its call for subjective response. Here is an expression of the catholicity to which

Bloesch is committed, the reach for a full-orbed understanding of Christ's work by including the varied theological charisms within the church, while at the same time challenging the reductionisms to which they are prey.

While substitution and the forgiveness of sin are central to the doctrine of atonement, there is a rich and crucial circumference to this center. It is developed in the Reformed tradition by the threefold office of Christ, as exemplified in major expositions by Calvin and Barth, two of Bloesch's chief mentors. While Bloesch makes random reference to the *munus triplex,* he does not use it as a framework for his Christology.[61] This is a puzzle to me, for it has functioned historically to express the full-orbed understanding of the atonement to which Bloesch points on occasion, and is a major accent in and contribution of Reformed theology.[62]

The "encompassing view" of atonement expressed in the *munus triplex* bears witness to Christ the Victim through the priestly office, Christ the Victor through the royal office and Christ the Revealer through the prophetic office. Each is often related to a phase of Christ's ministry (although not exclusively so, as each office permeates the others): prophetic—life, teachings, miracles; priestly—suffering and death; royal—resurrection and ascension. The work of Christ viewed as *only* one or another (either life or death or resurrection, or prophetic or priestly or royal) is exemplified in the historic reductionisms of the moral, penal and triumphal models of the atonement, all challenged by the holism, interrelationships and priorities of the *munus triplex.* When the incarnation is viewed as the presupposition of the atonement, both the contribution and the reductionist temptation of the Eastern tradition are recognized, for only the divine-human person can do the saving work of prophet, priest and king.[63]

This friendly critic wonders if the evangelical aspect of Bloesch's theology, with its tendency to give exclusive attention to penal substitution, obscures the fuller understanding of the atonement pointed to in the threefold office, a framework R. S. Franks asserts to be one of the lasting contributions of Reformation theology.[64]

The threefold ministry of Christ also has a history, past and present, in the wider church. The catholicity of its usage, albeit undeveloped, can be seen in such varied theologians as Eusebius of Caesarea and Thomas Aquinas. It also appears in a decree of the second Vatican Council, where the ministry of the laity is conceived as the outworking in the secular world of Christ's prophetic, priestly and royal offices, a concept anticipated by questions thirty-one and thirty-two of the Heidelberg Catechism.[65] Here Bloesch's catholic as well as his Reformed identity invite more consideration of the threefold office in articulating the work of Christ.

The linkage of Christology to the ministry of the laity in both Roman Catholic and Reformed traditions poses a related question: Has the influence of an evangelical pietism reduced the impact of the social-ethical concerns of the other two formative Bloesch traditions? Both Reformed and Roman Catholic theologies and histories are "world-formative,"[66] each holding that the church qua church must make a *systemic* witness. Bloesch also is concerned about the accountability to God of political, economic and social systems. However, he maintains

> the key to social transformation is wrought by the Spirit of God in the awakening to faith in Jesus Christ. A society can only advance toward greater justice when it contains within it a church that reminds it of a higher claim and a higher morality, a church that functions as an agent in bringing people a new life orientation and the spiritual gifts that enable them to realize this orientation in their thoughts, words and actions.[67]

Or again, the "cultural mandate" of the church is executed through the church's

> teaching and serving ministry. The church must never become a political lobby. . . . It is up to individual Christians as citizens of the state to apply the teachings of the church to the political arena. The church as church points directions but must take care not to propose political solutions, though there may be rare occasions when this is necessary.[68]

Personal transformation is surely a key to social transformation, but not the only key according to Reformed and Catholic perspectives. The church as church has a responsibility to challenge the "principalities and powers" directly in the public square, as well as indirectly through the conversion and nurture of individuals and their personal witness. Indeed, the political fundamentalists on the right and the "justice and peace" evangelicals on the left have raised legitimate questions about the apolitical tendencies of traditional evangelicalism, tendencies reflected in Bloesch's comments, albeit with his recognition that a systemic witness may also have to be made on "rare occasions."

We do need the *intra-institutional* witness of transformed persons to which Bloesch points. But partnership with the *counter-institutional* heritage of the Reformed and Catholic traditions is also required. Necessary as well is the *para-institutional* approach of the left-wing Reformation reflected in current "resident alien" ecclesiologies. All must be done concomitantly, and one or another to the fore as the "mind of the church" under the Word can best discern. Here, as elsewhere, catholicity strives to avoid the reduction of Christian mission to one organ of the body, for "there are varieties of gifts but the same Spirit; and there are varieties of service but the same Lord" (1 Cor 12:4-5).

Incarnation. Bloesch is a stalwart defender of the historic teaching on the person of Christ held by evangelical, Reformed and Catholic traditions. He sets it forth with biblical warrants, attention to learnings from the early christological controversies and respect for the Chalcedonian formula, which is still the standard belief of ecumenical Christianity. He is also right in his defense of the doctrine of Christ as a "paradox" that has been distorted by rationalist efforts on both left and right to explain what can only be explored. Further, he effectively challenges the many and varied current distortions of the person that continue either the early Ebionite or Docetist reductionisms.[69]

Along with the affirmations, however questions must be raised, initially, of a diagnostic sort: "The Christ of Chalcedonian orthodoxy is in palpable eclipse in most circles except those of the old Roman Catholicism, confessional evangelicalism and Eastern Orthodoxy."[70] This sweeping judgment does not take into account (a) the emerging centrist/confessional movements in mainline churches, (b) the "silent center" in clergy and congregations to which the former is seeking to give voice,[71] (c) the current vital bilateral and multilateral ecumenical ventures whose charter documents all assert classical Christian teaching, including the doctrine of the person of Christ[72] and (d) the reclamation in mainline seminary systematics departments of the Great Tradition.[73] The discernment of this wider circle of orthodoxy is not unrelated to participation in it. One of the sad consequences of evangelical-ecumenical polarization is the neglect of, and antagonism toward, outstanding evangelical theologians like Donald Bloesch by the ecumenical movement and the mainline churches and seminaries. This invites, in turn, lack of appreciation by evangelical theologians, including the best of them like Bloesch, for the theological ferment and recentering current in those places.

In a similar vein Bloesch is sometimes dismissive of the mainstream allies he has in the retrieval of Chalcedonian orthodoxy. Two cases in point are George Lindbeck and Wolfhart Pannenberg. Contrary to Bloesch's reading and rejection, Lindbeck does make ontological truth claims for his cultural-linguistic view of doctrine, as Bruce Marshall has shown in a study of *The Nature of Doctrine,* with an agreement expressed by Lindbeck.[74] For all the rationalist tendencies of Pannenberg's theology, with which both Bloesch and I disagree, Pannenberg is a strong advocate of classical Christianity and holds to both the deity and humanity of the one person, albeit interpreted within his unique eschatological framework.[75]

Mariology. On another point, by giving it the attention not often found among Protestant theologians, Bloesch makes an important evangelical contribution to a broadly conceived Mariology cum Christology. He rightly sees the virginal conception as a crucial sign of, though not proof of, the incarnation, an evangelical essential though one not indispensable for salvation. He is unashamed to speak of Mary as "the mother of God," affirming the christological rationale for the same. He gives respectful attention to Roman Catholic and Orthodox teaching on the privileges of Mary, but measures Mariological claims by Scripture, finding a place for Mary only "on this side" of the God-world divide. Mary, whom Scripture describes as "full of grace," is a unique model of holiness and companion in redemption, always an "exemplar of faith" but never an "object of faith."

The catholic sensibility, so well illustrated here by Bloesch's attention to Mary, could be pressed further, however, in the direction of much Catholic theology today by seeing through Mary's song (Lk 1:46-55) that God has "brought down the powerful from their thrones, and lifted up the lowly," giving thereby a mandate for solidarity with the lowly in their struggle for justice.

On the other hand, an *evangelical* catholicity and Reformed sensibility in the Mercersburg tradition would question Bloesch's proposal that we "may perhaps in our prayers" ask for the intercession of Mary and the saints, however that request for the intercession is surrounded by qualifications that "their prayers are effectual only when united with those of Jesus Christ."[76] The recovery of a biblical doctrine of the communion of saints in the Mercersburg tradition does not "go *to* them"[77] but rather prays *with* them. This is more faithful to Bloesch's own stated intention that Mary is "companion in redemption."

Inclusive language. Inclusive language has been a major question for Bloesch, current proposals illustrating the cultural captivity of modern theology. He is one of the first twentieth-century theologians to have given sustained attention to the subject and to have discerned its theological minefields. The topic with special reference to its bearing on Christology deserves, therefore, extended treatment.

Bloesch is right in challenging proposals that undercut basic Christian teaching about the Trinity and the person of Christ, ones which repeat the reductionisms rejected by the church in the ancient christological controversies. He sees (a) the docetic premise in the elimination of the maleness of Jesus both conceptually and pronominally, (b) the Nestorian separation of the natures by rejecting the language of "Son" and (c) the Arianism, subordinationism and reduction of the Trinity to a functional status in substituting "Creator, Redeemer and Sanctifier" or "God, Christ and the Spirit" for the universal trinitarian formula of Father, Son and Holy Spirit.

Along with his polemic against ideological feminism, but not often acknowledged by either his critics or his supporters, is the challenge he early mounted to "patriarchalism," his assertion that "God is not male" and his suggestion that "it might . . . be permissible on occasion to address the deity in terms such as 'Holy Mother, Wisdom of God' or 'Wisdom of God, our Mother,' since such usage has some biblical support."[78]

On the language for God as it pertains to the person of Christ, Bloesch draws on Barth's linkage of revelation with "the language of Zion."[79] Living and writing before the current inclusivist proposals, Barth's language practice is traditional in all respects, generically masculine for God as well as human beings. However, (1) Barth's teaching about "the preexistence of Jesus Christ" (which Bloesch appropriates and develops in his own way in *Jesus Christ*) and (2) Barth's view of the nonapplicability of our human understanding of "father" to God as Father (and son to Son) have import for the language issue, reflecting the Reformed accent on the divine sovereignty:

> No human father is the creator of his child, the controller of its destiny, or its savior from sin, guilt and death. No human father is by his word the source of its temporal life. In this proper, true and primary sense God—and He alone—is Father.[80]

Bloesch here quotes Barth, rightly commenting that "the prophets and apostles did not impose upon God a conception drawn from their patriarchal society, but they received from God through his revelation the true and original meaning of fatherhood."[81]

The christocentric-cum-sovereignty note appearing here means that only God will define what *Father* means and that we thereby look to Jesus Christ for that disclosure. Yet in the inclusive language dispute Bloesch contends that *Father* is used in Scripture and Christian faith to describe God because it conveys the masculine qualities of "power, initiative and superordination."[82] This argument for masculine usage is inconsistent with the Barth/Bloesch veto on attributing masculine human qualities to God the Father (or Son) instead of looking to Christ for definition of our analogies. It invites the Feuerbachian critique deployed by Barth against a liberal religion that projects into deity our values. Here Bloesch seems to be closer to *analogia entis* than Barth's *analogia fidei,* the catholic thereby edging aside the Reformed tradition.

A Barthian case, however, can be made for Bloesch's retention of "Son" trinitarian language and the use of the *he* pronoun for the person. The preexistence of Jesus means that a male figure is the Elect of God and thus, based on the unity of the human and divine natures, *only* "the Son" as well as "the only Son" in the trinitarian family. Based on that same unity *he* is the proper pronoun for the person of Christ in both natures.

Why God chose a male incarnation is quite another matter, one arguably related to the primal human sin of *hubris,* manifest in the history of human race in the abuse of power by history's dominant patriarchal societies. This masculine tendency toward the sin of *superbia* is radically challenged in the male Jesus. The meanings of *Son* and *he* have to do with the transvaluation of human values on the cross. Thus following Barth, we define *Son* as we do *Father,* not from the masculine attributes of power, initiative and superordination but from the victory won on Calvary by the divine vulnerability.

Ecclesial implications. With regard to the ecclesial implications of Christology, Bloesch's views on the sacraments have affinities with the Reformed Mercersburg theology, as in his affirmation of a baptismal grace that requires the response of faith in contrast to "catholic" views of baptismal regeneration.[83] However, Mercersburg's evangelical catholicity connects the doctrine of the incarnation to ecclesiology in such a manner (contra the too-simple "church as the continuation of the incarnation" as in the Oxford movement) that the sectarian tendencies of both frontier and latter-day evangelicalism are called into question. Here may lie the difference, institutionally, between an evangelical separatist tendency in the current church struggle based on an a sect-type ecclesiology, and an ecumenical strategy of internal reform based on a church-type ecclesiology.[84]

Application. In all his christological-cum-soteriological writings Bloesch makes a strong Reformation witness to the centrality of justification by grace through faith. He has faithfully resisted the pervasive works-righteousness of American culture and the accommodationist theologies of modernity and postmodernity. Evangelical and Reformed commitments are clearly at work here.

All three self-identifications (evangelical, Reformed and catholic) manifest themselves in Bloesch's stress on sanctification. From the beginning Bloesch has insisted that "the fruit is organically related to the root."[85] A biblical understanding of personal salvation views grace to be "imparted" as well as "imputed." Such is the insistence of the Reformed tradition in its long encounter with Lutheran theology.[86] Sanctification is *also* an evangelical emphasis and a Catholic accent. We are in Bloesch's debt for his stewardship of all three traditions.

Justification cum sanctification, further, is lodged within the *ordo salutis*. Here again Bloesch draws on his Reformed heritage to good purpose. While he has criticized most forms of narrative theology, a case could be made that the *ordo* itself is a version of it: a macro-story beginning with the protological electing love of God, proceeding into time through the general call to the application of the benefits of Christ to the believer who lives out the stages of a personal story (regeneration, justification, sanctification, adoption, perseverance) a narrative that moves finally to eschatological glorification.

While Bloesch gives sanctification its due, he understands also the persistence of sin in the pilgrimage of the believer. Reformed sobriety is here at work, but just as much so is the *simul iustus et peccator* of his Lutheran lineage and his debt to Reinhold Niebuhr. In this respect, the often too-exuberant expectations of the evangelical born-again experience are qualified by the realism of the magisterial Reformation.

A critical contribution Bloesch makes to contemporary theology in this soteriological locus emerges in his exchange with the views of Karl Barth and also in his debate with varieties of contemporary pluralist theology and some evangelical theologians similarly affected by today's religious pluralism. Bloesch gives a strong witness to the salvific weight of justifying faith. He is critical of Barth's construal of faith as *noetic* but not *ontic*. The hundreds of references in the New Testament to the inseparability of the act of faith from personal salvation call radically into question its delimitation to the status only of knowledge of a saving relationship previously established.

Barth's idiosyncratic view on this subject reflects a comparable refusal to associate God and/or grace unambiguously with one or another of the traditional media of the saving work of Christ to which they have been linked:

church, sacraments, Scripture, Christian ethics, the covenant with Noah and so on. In these latter cases, a Barthian actualism calculated to protect the divine sovereignty allows the medium to become ever and again only an *occasion* for grace as determined by the freedom of God, a discontinuity that disallows the promise of Christ to be always with the church: a continuing real presence in Word and sacraments, Scripture's trustworthiness a constant based on authorial inspiration, an ethics that affirms universally accessible moral norms and the reality of a general revelation.[87] In the matter of salvation by grace through faith, the freedom of God to be *for us* savingly in the once-happenedness of Jesus Christ and free *from* us otherwise precludes any lasting *state* of personal salvation by grace through faith. Bloesch, for all the influence of Barth, will not let go of this evangelical essential, and rightly takes Barth to task for his omission.

At another point, however, Barth is a corrective to Bloesch's view of the ultimate destiny of those without faith. Bloesch speaks in Barthian terms of a mercy that is boundless and our need and right to "hope and pray" for them. For Barth, reflecting here the Reformed accent on the divine sovereignty, this means the freedom of God to overturn even the most determined resistance (or ignorance) of those without faith. While a universal homecoming *cannot* be an *article of faith* (universalism)—given the freedom of God to determine what God will ultimately do—it *can* be an *article of hope*, for

> there is no good reason why we should forbid ourselves, or be forbidden, openness to the possibility that in the reality of God and man in Jesus Christ there is contained much more than we might expect and therefore the supremely unexpected withdrawal of that final threat. . . . If we are certainly forbidden to count on this as though we had a claim to it . . . we are surely commanded the more definitely to hope and pray for it . . . to hope and pray cautiously and yet distinctly that, in spite of everything which may seem quite conclusively to proclaim the opposite, his compassion should not fail, and that in accordance with his mercy which is "new every morning." He "will not cast off forever" (Lam 3:22, 31).[88]

This is a larger hope and a greater emphasis on the freedom of God than found in Bloesch's view, perhaps a reflection again of the need for the Reformed accent to be given its full due.[89]

There is another way to honor three of Bloesch's points in this discussion: the crucial role of the decision of faith, the reality of hell and the boundless mercy of God. (1) Following the Reformed traditions of the Mercersburg theology and the New England Congregationalist "Andover Theory" (each exegeting 1 Peter 3—4 and the descent to the place of the dead in the Apostles' Creed), the barrier of death is breached by the Hound of Heaven, who pursues those who have not heard or heard aright. (2) For those without faith and obedience, hell is real and lasting. (3) The boundless mercy of God through even the pains of hell is a rehabilitating love whose fires can purge our worst sin (1 Cor 3:13-15); hell is lasting but not everlasting. That such fires will cleanse all is, as Barth insists, not an article of faith but rather an article of hope that God "will not cast off forever."

Conclusion

Donald Bloesch has honed a Christology that could make a major contribution to the renewal of the church and the revitalization of Christian theology. Its uniqueness lies in the bringing together of evangelical, Reformed and catholic traditions. However differently they might be configured as indicated in the previous commentary, these are charisms integral to the body of Christ and to the body of Christian teaching about the person and work of Jesus Christ. Would that the church reformed and the church catholic receive the gifts so offered with the same welcome extended by the evangelical community! May the conversation carried on in this chapter, and in the book in which it appears, work to that end.

Seven

The Holy Spirit in the Theology of Donald G. Bloesch

CLARK H. PINNOCK

I T IS A PLEASURE TO WRITE ABOUT BLOESCH'S THEOLOGY, WHICH IS EXPANSIVELY
Reformed, ecumenical and evangelical and which almost never fails to
enrich readers. His work is one of the best expressions of modern
evangelical theology, if not the best to date. His scholarship is awesome, his
piety is transparent. I welcome this opportunity to touch upon highlights of
one of his doctrines and enter into dialogue with him. Let me pay tribute to
my friend who has led the way to a deeper appropriation of God's Word in
our time. The reader should know that the Spirit volume in the Christian
Foundations series (volume five) was not available to me at the time of writing
and that consequently I have had only earlier work to analyze. Nevertheless,
this has not imposed too great a burden because the lines of his thought
have been evident for some time (in *Essentials of Evangelical Theology*[1] and
elsewhere). The reader can enjoy comparing what I say here with volume
five to check on my discernment or the lack of it.

Spirit and the Word

The dialectic of Word and Spirit was a central issue at the Reformation, and
it is central for Bloesch. These leaders called for a return to the biblical
message, sealed in the believer's heart by the inner witness of the Spirit and
received by supernatural, God-given faith. As a Reformed theologian Bloesch
is in line with these convictions and entitles the first volume of his series *A
Theology of Word & Spirit.*[2]

One of the issues arising deals with the grounding of faith. The question is how believers are warranted in receiving the gospel as the Word of God. After all, many claims are made in the realm of religion; how does one sort them out? Is the decision to believe justified by any prior inquiry into evidence or not? Bloesch's position reflects the orientation of the Reformation. Luther, for example, reacted against the academic subtleties of scholasticism and stressed the priority of faith over reason. He even spoke contemptuously of apologetics and assumed that apart from the gift of faith, reason would be antagonistic to the gospel. Only after faith would the positive roles of reason come into to play.

Bloesch's dislike of rationalistic approaches in theology is well known and he is not sympathetic to children of the Reformation (including many evangelicals) who return to the older ways of thinking about reason as preparing the way for faith.[3] For him, believing precedes understanding, not the reverse. He much prefers the expression: "I believe in order to understand."[4] Faith is not born in the context of an intellectual quest. He writes: "Faith is simply the acknowledgment of the miracle of revelation in the chaos and darkness of human life."[5] He states: "The certainty of faith lies in the inward confirmation of the Spirit concerning the objective validity of the biblical revelation. We are given a spiritual, not a rational, certainty."[6] Elsewhere he adds that faith is "a venture of trust based on evidence that faith itself provides."[7]

I take Bloesch to be a fideist, that is, one holding the position that sees faith as self-authenticating and not the result of a process of thinking. I realize that it is not the term he prefers, knowing the value that most evangelicals place on a certain element of reasoning.[8] He does not want to reject apologetics altogether and therefore speaks of its servant role and of the need to be intelligible when we preach.[9] He even says that one does not believe without reason and that reason is involved in believing.[10] But Bloesch is always clear that reason becomes a positive factor only after it has been liberated from its bondage to sin. He does not say that apologetics can create a climate positive for faith. For him the evidence for faith can only be seen by believing eyes. Not that God's Word is not objective in the sense of being a real Word from God, but that it is not at the disposal of human reason.

The issue for him is more than political: issues of anthropology and the nature of faith enter in. Bloesch does not view faith as mental assent to something known to be rational by the mind but is the result of an encounter with divine grace which alone can bring sinners into contact with God. He is not opposed to reason so much as he is convinced of the power of sin to distort it and alienate whole persons from God.[11] Sinners are ill-disposed to acknowledge God's truth. It confronts what they believe and arouses hostility in them. A dark Reformed (Jansenist?) anthropology shapes his view of the role of apologetics. There are no reasons for faith that unbelievers are going to accept. Therefore the emphasis must fall on the power of the Spirit to bring about the conviction that apologetics cannot produce. Christianity cannot be shown to be true to sinners in their present orientation. One is led to believe that the image of God has been so damaged in sinners that they cannot even think straight, at least on ultimate questions. Evidence for the gospel (which Bloesch does believe exists) simply does not help them.

But there are difficulties here. Unfortunately it gives the impression that the gospel is not much of a truth claim if in fact nobody will find it impressive until they are already biased in its favor. It may even play into the hands of post-Kantians who contend that truth is constructed by the faith of the human mind and has no other foundation than that. Furthermore, it gives inquirers no help in sorting out the divergent claims to truth. It makes one wonder whether we might not be able to think of the Spirit using truth in moving sinners to faith. Why make the Spirit a fig leaf that covers the nakedness of the Christian claim? Is it necessary? The sinner's reluctance to accept it does not require Christians to cave in and not counter with solid arguments. The sinner's objections need not nullify the case for faith that is *not* "believing what you know ain't so" (Mark Twain).

I agree with Bloesch that faith comes about through the Spirit's work in us and that the road to faith is assisted at every stage by the grace of God. But I also see more room for rationality (and human freedom) in conversion. I believe that apologetics, though it cannot create faith, can create a good climate for faith. I realize that reason, though it cannot lead sinners to the full assurance of faith, can help them when synthesized with a grace-inspired desire to know God. I agree with him that we cannot argue people into faith, but at the same time I do not want to leave the impression that the decision to believe is a blind leap. While Bloesch would not call it that, the impression remains. The cognitive advantages of faith ought to be presented, even though the truth cannot be established within the present framework of the unconverted. I would like Bloesch to say that the decision to believe is a responsible exercise of human freedom that satisfies hungers of mind and spirit, hungers that cannot be satisfied apart from faith. I would like him to say that apologetics can facilitate the journey to faith by indicating values that cannot be achieved except through conversion.

Spirit of Inspiration and Interpretation

Another nuance in the relationship between Word and Spirit has to do with the Scriptures, the topic of *Holy Scripture* (volume two in Christian Foundations), in which Bloesch attributes to the Spirit's inspiration the existence of the Bible and even the possibility of its proper interpretation.[12]

As for the Bible's existence Bloesch insists that it is of divine origin and its composition has been supervised by God. He stands squarely in the conservative camp that identifies the words of Scripture with God's Word. The human dimension, though not ignored, is subordinated to God's control over the text. In this Bloesch stands closer to Calvin than to Barth, which endears him to evangelicals. He writes, "The paradox is that Scripture is the Word of God as well as the word of mortals. It is both a human witness to God and God's witness to himself. The Scriptures have a dual authorship."[13] He writes, "The Bible is divine in its ultimate origin and theological content but human in its mode of expression or literary form."[14] He says: "We can say with the catholic and evangelical tradition that God is the primary author of Scripture, and the prophets and apostles secondary authors," and "The Bible is God-breathed in the sense that it is a production of the creative breath of God."[15]

In saying that Scripture is "from above" Bloesch is not denying that Scripture is also "from below." Although normally this is a different model (one used more by liberals), he combines the two, affirming both divine authorship and recognizing the marks of true humanity in the text. He freely admits, for example, that the Bible depicts an ancient view of the world and that there are what appear to be historical inaccuracies and internal contradictions but that such do not matter because Scripture does not observe modern standards of accuracy.[16] The Bible is perfectly true but in ways in which it chooses to be true, not necessarily in ways we might wish. He writes: "The Bible contains the perfect Word of God in the imperfect words of human beings."[17] Bloesch thus rejects inerrancy in the sense of total accuracy but endorses his own view of biblical reliability. To put it in my words: in spite of human fragility the Word of God concerning Jesus Christ comes through effectively by means of these witnesses, thanks to the Holy Spirit.

This seems to imply that the Bible is given by inspiration without that inspiration signifying the kind of divine control ordinarily associated with the "from above" position. It involves more of a permissive guiding and approving than any dictating, which is less than has been typically asserted by that camp. Nevertheless, Bloesch stays closer to the evangelicals on this subject with his tension than Barth, who avoids tension by focusing on the encounter, not on the verbal side to inspiration at all.

More like Barth, though, Bloesch introduces the idea of pneumatic or christological exegesis.[18] Here his emphasis on the verbal character of inspiration is subordinated to a personalistic understanding of the revelation actually conveyed through it. He writes, "The text when taken only by itself, apart from its theological and spiritual context, is fallible and deficient. When the Bible is treated only academically or scientifically, it does not disclose the truth of salvation. But when the text is seen in its true context, then it becomes the vehicle of infallible truth. It becomes what it originally was and substantially is—the infallible Word of God."[19]

On this matter Bloesch seems evasive and unspecific but is not out of line with our normal practice. I believe he simply wants us to look for Christ in the whole of the Bible as the Spirit of God leads.[20] The Spirit knows how to bring us into contact with the theological meaning and center of Scripture, which is Jesus Christ, a meaning not available to ordinary historical-critical investigations of the text by the unsaved. It also fits well with his emphasis (already noted) that reason cannot attain the knowledge of God by itself. He writes, "We discover truth within Scripture after being confronted by the One who is the truth— Jesus Christ. We begin not with Scripture as a historical text but with the living Word of God—Jesus Christ—and then try to ascertain how Scripture bears witness to him."[21] We have to move beyond the confines of the text to discern the essential meaning that is given to human beings by the Spirit. We have to learn to read the Bible with the mind of Christ, because the text exists to witness to him and derives its authority from him. Christ presents himself to the church by means of the sacrament of Scripture as the Spirit helps us understand its true meaning. It is not the dead letter that Christians should care about but the living Christ, who speaks to us here and now through these inspired words. The Word of God is not just the text but the event in which readers encounter God, who is the Reality that the Bible exists to mediate.

Certainly the term "pneumatic exegesis" flirts with ideas of mystical and allegorical interpretations and a rejection of historical exegesis. But this would be to misunderstand Bloesch's position.[22] One must be a believer to understand the text, not because the text is gibberish otherwise, but because its central theme is Jesus Christ, who cannot be grasped by reason alone. It fits with his view of faith and reason and his insistence that the Word of God cannot be possessed apart from the activity of the Spirit. On a certain level, of course, anyone can understand the meaning of the biblical text and it can be a subject for discussion among everyone. But the saving encounter that the Bible exists to mediate cannot occur from just reading the Bible or doing anything else. One's eyes must be opened and one's heart strangely warmed. Bloesch always gives credit to the Spirit, even at risk of appearing to deny the objectivity of the Word. At the cost of rationality in relation to conversion and subjectivity in relation to interpretation, he persists in this course. Granted, there are less paradoxical paths to follow. One could place more emphasis on the truth present in the text and in history and view the Spirit more as commending the truth that is really there rather than giving an appearance of subjective constructivism. But Bloesch is a dialectical theologian not allergic to tension and mystery, and he thinks that he not only gives God greater glory by his way of viewing these themes but that he supplies the best response to the challenge of historical criticism. He believes (as Barth believed) that this frees theology from being dominated by modern influences and this is worth a little inconvenience.

Spirit and Trinity

The Trinity is an orthodox pillar of doctrine about which there is much discussion in contemporary theology and along with it conversation about the nature and mission of the Spirit. In authors like Colin Gunton, Catherine LaCugna, Jürgen Moltmann, Hans urs von Balthasar and Walter Kasper, one hears much about the dynamic relationality of God and the perichoretic dance among the persons of the Trinity. We hear about the Spirit, not only as the love between the Father and the Son (Augustine's *vinculum amoris*) but also as the overflowing surplus of that love pouring out into the world to create and vivify the world. The Spirit is seen by many today as the love by which the Trinity is oriented and is impelled outward. It is conceived of as the overflowing love of God in person in which God makes a gift of himself. Thus the Spirit plays a mediating role between the Father and his self-communication in history through Jesus Christ.[23]

Under the circumstances and given the importance of the doctrine of the Trinity to him, Bloesch says less than one might expect about it, at least in the volume *God the Almighty*. It makes me wonder how trinitarian his theology is. (Maybe we will find more than passing references to it in the Spirit volume.) I can think of a couple of reasons for the reticence. Much of the recent discussion emanates from social trinitarians, of whom Bloesch (I think) is not one. I think he (like Barth) would be reticent to reflect or speculate much on the mystery of the immanent Trinity. One recalls the Basel theologian referring to Father, Son and Spirit not as persons but as "three modes of being."[24] A theologian who cannot affirm three persons in God is not likely to rhapsodize about the triune relationality and its qualities of mutuality, reciprocity and cooperation. No, the emphasis is on God-for-us, not on God-in-himself. The focus rests on the event of revelation in which, by the Spirit, God in his freedom wills to be subjectively present to us. But to go beyond this is both to flirt with tritheism and fall into a kind of metaphysical speculation.[25]

Another reason Bloesch might not relish the new thinking emanating from the social trinitarians are the resonances of process theology in it which is such a bane to him. He is very opposed to this particular brand of radical liberal theology because he suffered under it in his student days at the University of Chicago. Therefore he always gives it a wide berth, and this extends to even its possible presence. The fact is that some process thinkers like Joseph Bracken and Norman Pittenger employ trinitarian language to do process work, and others (Pinnock and Boyd) appreciate the efforts of process thinking to attain a more dynamic (and scriptural) picture of God's nature. We appreciate all efforts to correct the one-sidedness of classical theism and project a model of God with real relations and real involvement with the world. Bloesch, however, is less appreciative of the efforts of process theology.

But let it be said, Bloesch wants to be seen as having a dynamic view of God himself.[26] He too wants to get away from the harmful effects of Greek philosophy on the classical synthesis and tries to express the truth that God enters the contingent realm and has new experiences. He speaks of "a dynamic biblical theism that does justice to both God's otherness and his personalness."[27] His model is of a God who becomes flesh and lovingly interacts with us, which is not exactly identical to the immutable and impassible God of conventional theism. At the same time, he is very cautious in this area (as one should be) and draws back from the give-and-take reciprocity of the openness view of God which implies risk for God.[28] He takes refuge at this point in an appeal to mystery regarding the relation between divine determination and human freedom and thereby gives up on coherence that lies beyond us. He chooses to find influences of process theology in the openness view, while I see the residual influences of Hellenism on his own view.[29]

On issues of gender and God-talk Bloesch generally takes a middle path.

On the one hand, he recognizes that God, though transcending gender, fashioned men and women in his image and is thus the ground of both the masculine and feminine. Therefore Bloesch is open to feminine God language and sympathetic to using it along with masculine language. He says, "I think we need to be alive to the concern of women for wider acknowledgment of the feminine dimension of the sacred. The God of the Bible is not exclusively masculine, nor is he exclusively monarchical. He is not only Lord but also Friend, not only Father and Brother but also Mother and Sister."[30] At the same time, he insists that God has chosen to relate to us in the form of the masculine as Father and Lord and that the Word also became incarnate as the Father's Son. These facts of revelation cannot be changed without changing revelation itself.

This is reasonable, but what about the Spirit? After all, it is possible to think of the Spirit in female terms: the breath and wisdom of God are both feminine in the Hebrew Bible, not just in grammar but in depiction. One recalls Count Zinzendorf speaking of the maternal office of the Spirit alongside Father and Son. Bloesch only refers to this possibility once and then states, "When we portray the Spirit of God or Christ as predominantly feminine, we are perilously close to polytheism, for we now have divinities that are basically unlike one another."[31] Of course, but that does not quite address the issue. The usage could be permitted without becoming predominant. Is it not all right to think of the Spirit as our Mother? Is there not an opportunity here for a theologian who wishes to overcome the masculinist bias in our speech about God? I wonder if the Spirit volume will have anything more to offer on this point or if Bloesch has gotten more traditional with age.

Spirit and Creation

The doctrine of creation is not prominent in Bloesch's work. It is only briefly discussed in connection to the doctrine of God.[32] This is odd in itself, given the importance of the doctrine in relation to ecology and science, and it explains the failure to say anything much about the cosmic functions of the Spirit. This lacuna is partly due to Bloesch's background in existentialism, where the focus is on the human search for meaning, not the realm of nature itself. Like Barth he discusses creation mostly in relation to anthropology.

However, this should not be misunderstood. Bloesch, like Calvin, affirms the Spirit's role in creation as the divine power creating and sustaining the universe. The Spirit is the Lord and giver of life, the power of creation and new creation. It is not an ornament of piety but the explosive life that hovered over the waters of creation and is at work in the whole world, in the evolution of life and in the cultures of humanity.

Though Bloesch accepts the universal operations of the Spirit, he does not attribute salvific value to them or see them as stepping stones to Christ. The fact that others would (like yours truly) helps to explain why he is hesitant. He does not endorse the formation of any natural philosophy (even though based in revelation) for apologetic purposes. He does say that one can only gain a knowledge of the creator Spirit in light of the redeemer Spirit and that the unbeliever cannot see truth in creation which is visible only through Christ. It is almost again as if he thinks of faith projecting itself onto the heavens rather than receiving a witness to God from them. He passes up the apologetic possibility of pointing to the divine wisdom displayed in nature, for example, the evidence of irreducible complexity in the biochemistry of life. Bloesch is not in the forefront of those who advocate a mutually enriching dialogue between theology and science or who are interested in rethinking the Christian message for people impressed by modern science. Again this is because of his believing that no aspect of the saving knowledge of God can arise from the sinner's rational reflections. To do these things is to invite contamination from modernity.

Second (along the same lines), Bloesch resists viewing the cosmic activities of the Spirit as providing a kind of stepping stone from a preliminary to a developed knowledge of God. He does not think of them as providing a platform for reflecting on God's saving activities outside the church among the nations. He does not appeal to the universality of the Spirit as balancing the particularity of Christ and as a biblical way of thinking of God at work among all peoples even in their religions and cultures. Although (with Calvin) Bloesch recognizes the universal cosmic activities of God, he does not (with Rahner) affirm a divine salvific activity co-extensive with world history. While acknowledging God's activity everywhere, he does not attribute salvific virtue to it. This activity falls under the category of "common grace" and can not be activity oriented toward salvation. He denies that divine activity is always saving activity and, even if it were, it would be nullified by human obtuseness. Bloesch does not think of creation leading us to redemption or recommend beginning with the Spirit's work in creation and moving to Christ's work of redemption. It works the other way around: it is in the light of redemption that we see signs of the goodness of creation. The experience of the Spirit outside of faith in Christ has only a negative meaning as far as salvation is concerned. Bloesch affirms (like Barth) that the hidden Christ is at work among all peoples but (also like Barth) does not develop the theme or its implications.

However, this does not make Bloesch a soteriological restrictivist, who deduces limited access to salvation from this and denies grace for the majority of the human race. For him the will of God proves to be salvifically universal finally only in the post-mortem situation. Contrary to the Reformed tradition, Bloesch believes God gives every person the opportunity for salvation, but not necessarily in this life. One may receive salvation on the other side of the grave, he says.[33] In this unusual way he squares his belief in the necessity of explicit faith in Christ for salvation with his belief in God's universal salvific will. With this eschatology he can be restrictivist with regard to salvation in history without being restrictivist with regard to heaven. In the end, God will make the salvific situation universal by granting a post-mortem evangelistic opportunity. Bloesch does not really need to consider the broad implications of the Spirit's cosmic functions or assign them a salvific function. There is no final price to be paid for the apparent niggardliness of God's activities in history. Unfortunately, among evangelicals at least, his solution will appear to be due more to wishful thinking than to any solid exegetical basis. For his part, however, Bloesch insists that the basis is there.[34]

Spirit and Jesus Christ

In *Jesus Christ* (volume four of Christian Foundations) the Spirit is not much discussed in relation to Christology, which is surprising since the Spirit is prominent in the gospel story of Jesus. If John the evangelist emphasizes Jesus as the man from heaven, Luke the physician emphasizes Jesus as Spirit-anointed. This is central to his vision. The Spirit is active in the conception of our Lord, in his communion with the Father and in his whole life and ministry. There is much discussion today about this in other books on Christology. People are seeing that Jesus as man of the Spirit, not Jesus as God incarnate, is historically the more original perspective on his identity. But Bloesch seems content with a one-sided Word Christology. Is there any reason why we cannot honor both Word and Spirit in this connection? Why does the virgin birth get a whole chapter in the book and the Spirit nothing? I can think of only one answer: the struggle with liberalism, not biblical interpretation *per se,* is calling the shots here.

But there may be more reasons than that. A Spirit Christology offers a long-term perspective on the Christ event. It stimulates us to think of the Spirit who brings to pass the divine indwelling in Jesus as the one who has always been at work in creation and in the history of Israel. It resists the idea that Jesus dropped out of heaven as an anomalous event and fosters thinking of the incarnation as the fulfillment of a long redemptive process coextensive with human history. But this is the dimension of universality that may explain why Bloesch steers clear of it, as we have already noted.

A Spirit Christology also stimulates reflection on the work of Christ. It challenges conventional thinking about atonement in terms of a legal transaction that comes more from Anselm than the New Testament. It puts the focus on the Spirit-empowered servant of God who proclaims good news to the poor and constitutes the supreme paradigm for the church's ministry. It lifts up the earliest thinking about atonement, namely, as a recapitulation of the human journey, and makes it a model for today. It is broader and more comprehensive than the juridical orientation of Western theology. It sees Christ's life, death and resurrection as a recapitulation of the whole Adamic history and a substitute on a much grander scale. But Bloesch seems on balance content to operate within the magisterial Protestant traditions and not to be looking (as I am) for fresh insights outside that stream. (For me this is simply too confining.) To be fair, though, I have to add that he is open to the participatory model as well as the Christus Victor motif and is not one-sidedly legal in his view of atonement. One sees that in his strong emphasis on new birth and the life of holiness, human transformation through participation in Christ.

Spirit Christology also highlights the nature of Christian mission. Isaiah 42:1-4, for example, promises that the Spirit will rest on God's servant and that there will be a universal spread of justice and mercy. It elicits the liberation dimension of salvation. On the surface this might seem to conflict with Bloesch's phrase "the spiritual mission of the church," but actually it does not. Bloesch's point in using this phrase is to oppose politicizing the gospel, but not to advocate disengagement from society. Again Bloesch's account is driven by the conflict with liberalism, and his love of pietism is a key to understanding that he too holds out a social and cultural mandate as part of the church's mission.[35]

In the early period of theology the deity of the Spirit was much discussed and in later centuries the relationship of the persons centering on the filioque controversy. This was a major and divisive issue for East and West, but I have not noticed Bloesch discuss it (unless in volume five). Is he negative or positive toward the inclusion of this phrase in the creed? I suspect he would be mildly in favor. I am negative (1) because the Western church acted arrogantly when it unilaterally inserted the term into Nicaea and (2) because it fosters a restrictivism of salvation. This phrase makes it sound as if the Spirit is restricted to zones where Christ is explicitly known and a gift, not to the whole creation but only to the church. The phrase thus diminishes the role of the Spirit and subordinates the Spirit to the Son, if not the church. This is the issue of universality again, and we know how Bloesch deals it with it in his eschatology of postmortem evangelization.

Spirit and Conversion

It is standard practice in Reformed theology to emphasize the sovereign or monergistic activity of the Spirit in effecting salvation in sinners. Faith, though a human response, is seen as a supernatural gift of God and not a human contribution to the salvation event. Faith is a fruit of the Spirit and an evidence that regeneration has already taken place. God effects conversion; it does not happen because a sinner wants it to. It happens because grace has already been thrust upon them triumphing over their obstinate wills. Salvation involves a radical new beginning before there can be any suggestion of human cooperation. In this connection remember how Luther spoke of God riding the sinner like a horse. Reformed theology normally has an unrelational doctrine of salvation that is manipulative of persons. Salvation is not seen as the healing of a broken relationship so much as the destruction of the old Adam. Grace is irresistible and there is no true reciprocity. Since the sinner needs a faith implant (as it were), there is little use calling upon her to trust God. The prodigal will not return home until he is forced to, an odd Reformed reading of the parable.

Is this Bloesch's view of the matter too? On the one hand, I believe that it is his view, but on the other hand, am sure that he will not admit it. But consider what he says: "Faith indeed is a decision of the will, but this is a will liberated by God's free grace. Faith is also a venture and pilgrimage, but it is one made possible and inevitable by the action of grace upon man and within him."[36] For Bloesch the decision rests not on free will but on a liberated will, a will emancipated from its downward proclivity by conquering, irresistible grace. Once our inward eyes are opened to the measure of God's love for us, once our will is liberated for service to this love, we will inevitably believe, decide and obey.

He writes, "Conversion signifies man's turning to the way of the cross, but he could not turn unless he had already been inwardly liberated by divine grace" and "Even his repentance and obedience testify to the work of the

Spirit within him, the grace that is drawing him irresistibly to Jesus Christ."[37] He says, "It is necessary to uphold the sovereignty of God the Holy Spirit who implants within man the principle of the new life."[38] He also writes, "It [justification] must be received by faith, but faith is not a work of man but a work of the Spirit of God within us" and "Man is impelled to respond voluntarily when his will is converted by the grace of God."[39] We read, "Not only faith but the very condition to receive faith is a work of the Spirit of God within us. Our redemption is wrought wholly by Christ—without our cooperation and aid."[40]

I was tempted not to read him in this way because I notice him struggling with it and because in discussing Barth, he counters the latter's view of faith. For Barth faith is mainly a response to salvation already accomplished, whereas Bloesch wants to say it is also a condition or qualification of salvation which "does not take effect except in and through man's decision of faith."[41] As non-Reformed I thought that sounded better but then noticed that he cites Luther and Edwards on his side, men who are certainly monergists. So I have to conclude that what he is saying to Barth is that experiential contact with Christ is essential, but not that it is a genuinely self-originating human contribution.

I conclude that Bloesch holds the standard paleo-Reformed view that God's grace liberates our will from its bondage to sin so that we are enabled to believe through the power of the Spirit. The will is not just assisted to respond as in Wesley but manipulated as in Calvin. Salvation is not truly personal and relational, because the human partner is subdued and not engaged. But let me add a proviso, because I sense Bloesch does not mean to say what he is actually saying. I suspect that his strong antipathy to semi-Pelagianism (which I do not share) prevents him from being as clear about the genuineness of the human response as he means to be.

Ordinarily this position (which I take to be his) would make one a double predestinarian for whom God manipulates the elect and lets the others perish for his strange "glory." But we know Bloesch believes that God gives every sinner the opportunity to be saved, if not necessarily in this life.[42] So he is not a particularist or predestinarian. The pertinent question becomes: How can he avoid being a universalist? He denies being one, of course, but how does he avoid it with coherence? He appears to avoid it by retaining the (nonmonergistic) belief that people are free to refuse grace on earth and in the postmortem situation. But by his own words he also seems to portray saving grace as irresistible against the background of human obtuseness.

What Bloesch says doesn't quite add up for me. I wish he would say what I sense he wants to say: God's grace assists but does not compel the response of faith. Love really wants to hear a yes from us.

More theologians accept the relational model, I think. They say that sinners are enabled to believe by God's prevenient grace but may decline it because God does not overpower them or compel their assent. They say that salvation requires the cooperation of two unequal but necessary forces: divine grace and the human will, in the spirit of the Greek fathers. Clement even coined the word *synergy* (cooperation) to express the idea of two powers at work: divine grace and the human will. Like Mary, mother of the faithful, saying yes to God, sinners are called upon to make a real response, assisted by the grace of God but not compelled and overcome.

For me Bloesch does justice to faith as an experience (versus Barth) but not to faith as a genuinely human response to God's offer through the Spirit (so Brummer). He accents the priority of grace so strongly that he does not leave room for an unforced personal encounter. The result is that conversion is not a personal event, not a relationship we choose to enter but rather the implantation in us of a reborn state for which there is no real choice.[43] God cannot effectually bring about faith without it ceasing to be our choice. For a personal relationship to be personal, it must be possible for a person to refuse it. At this point Bloesch succumbs to the paradox "which defies and eludes rational comprehension."[44]

Reformed people like Bloesch do not like the idea of genuine reciprocity for two reasons: (1) because they do not think of God in genuine give-and-take relationships where what God does depends on what human beings do and (2) they do not like to acknowledge an ember of the divine image still glowing in sinners.[45] In my opinion, Bloesch declares himself not to be monergist but fails to explain how and why he is not. He resorts to the language of mystery and claims to have a third position that is neither monergist or synergist. In my opinion the third position does not exist.

Spirit and Christian Existence

Looking at the nature of salvation from the standpoint of the Spirit could open up our thinking about it as mystical union with the triune God after the manner of Eastern Orthodoxy. The Spirit bears witness in our hearts to our adoption in the Son and leads us into intimacy with the Father, enabling us to share God's nature and love. We are united to Christ and caught up into the very life of the Trinity. John writes, "As you, Father, are in me and I am in you, may they also be in us" (Jn 17:21). This frees us from a narrow preoccupation with justification and even sanctification and lets us dwell on the everlasting relational aspects. As a historical theologian Bloesch is aware of this Orthodox move but does little with it explicitly; this is probably because of his Reformed loyalties, even though it represents a rich theme in Protestant traditions too and is ripe for recovery.[46] Perhaps, though, we should read his emphasis on union with Christ in this way and account for the absence of the theosis category in terms of the dangers he would see from the possible loss of the creature-Creator distinction if we used it, though this is not the way it is in Orthodoxy.[47]

On the issue of sacraments Bloesch helps free-church evangelicals (who predominate) to overcome the Spirit-matter dualism inherited from Zwingli. While making a real distinction, he makes no sharp dichotomy between water baptism and Spirit baptism. For him baptism and Eucharist are more than signs, but are means of grace by which the Spirit works in us. This puts him in line with the beliefs of the ancient church which sees it as normal for the physical and spiritual to coincide. In a nice balance, Bloesch avoids both formalism and spiritualism. Sacraments are the means of grace, but the human response matters; God works through signs but is not bound to them.[48]

It is safe to surmise even without the Spirit volume that Bloesch believes that Spirit baptism occurs at conversion to which (pedo-) baptism points, but that afterward there follows a lifetime of walking in the Spirit and what he calls continual conversion. He sees regeneration unfolding in stages and accepts the experience (commonly reported) of receiving an empowering of the Spirit later on in the Christian life. In an event of spiritual renewal, that which was given in conversion comes into fuller expression and deeper experience. He would not call it a second blessing, but it could be a second conversion. Bloesch will project a bridge over to the charismatic renewal by his openness to new works of the Spirit and to the experience of power for mission after conversion.

But I am unsure what he will do with the power dimension of pentecostalism in terms of ecclesiology. Clearly he is not a cessationist like most Reformed theologians who think that the signs and wonders that accredited the first proclaimers of the Word and (by extension) the Scriptures have passed away. I am sure that he believes that the kingdom of God is present in power, not word only.[49] On the other hand, I doubt if he will call for charismatic renewal in the mainline denominations even though his theology implies a need of that very thing. I think he expects tongues, healing and prophecies to happen in times of awakening, but not in the course of regular church life. The practical effects of cessationism tend to linger longer than the theory. On the other hand, it may be his worry that in such a renewal some might attempt to control and manipulate these unusual possibilities, which is not unheard of.

On the subject of Christian growth Bloesch shines out as a holiness theologian. As a pietist he simply loves these themes and enriches his Reformed theology with them. Believers are called to holiness, which means conformity to Jesus Christ, and they are expected to be active in realizing the fruits of righteousness. The goal is spiritual maturity and a perfection of their relationship with Jesus.[50]

On this subject even Reformed theologians gravitate to a relational model. They teach that God calls us to higher states of holiness and believe God is grieved when his summons are ignored. In this realm at least, they grant that God responds to what we do and lets himself be affected by it, even though when it comes to salvation they oppose these same ideas.

Bloesch, however, goes further than most. He takes the human response so seriously that he believes in the possibility of falling from grace. He writes, "Those who rely not on their own powers but on divine grace will persevere to the end; this indeed is the truth in the Calvinist doctrine of the perseverance of the saints."[51] Though I doubt myself that this is Calvinist doctrine, I do not doubt that it is Bloesch's view that Christians who do not rely on God's grace will not persevere. Evidently God does not exercise his manipulative control over the elect in this important matter. It appears that when it comes to salvation, Bloesch employs a nonrelational model, but when it comes to sanctification, he employs a relational model. I appreciate this and only wish he would go relational all the way. This takes us back to the question, is Bloesch conveying his view of conversion effectively?

Conclusion

In conclusion, I am impressed with Bloesch's broad awareness and understanding of both traditional and contemporary theology. He surely gives us one of the best contemporary expressions of an evangelical theology. He works within the Reformed tradition, where he polishes categories and occasionally changes them. To be "reformed" for him does not mean strict allegiance to the Westminster Confession, for example, but to situating himself within an evolving and adaptable tradition. Would that others were Reformed in this way!

If theology seeks a balance of continuity and innovation, then Bloesch gives more attention to continuity. Like most evangelicals, he is traditionally minded and antiliberal in his orientation and therefore largely suspicious of new ideas. One of the results of the impact of religious liberalism on evangelicalism sadly has been to shrink its imagination and curtail its liberty to think new thoughts and take chances. Although grace is supposed to liberate reason, there is all too little evidence of it here or elsewhere. Even Bloesch is slow to pursue fresh possibilities of interpretation readily available to him. It is not that he does not wish to speak in timely ways but only that the main way he exercises this liberty is by rearranging traditional Protestant ideas and not taking flights on his own. An exception might be the introduction of Barthian motifs (novel for evangelicals) which crop up in his theology and have now at long last become topics for discussion among them. Ramm wanted this to happen; Bloesch has made it happen.

I think he actually is free spirited in his thinking but he belongs to a liberal denomination in which free spiritedness has gotten out of hand. This alarms him. In this context, therefore, being faithful looms larger than being daring. A practical difficulty in reading Bloesch is a fair amount of ambiguity. He comes across to me as a cautious man, who loves to combine divergent positions and does not like to let good theological ideas go unless he really has to. Rather than taking bold steps, he prefers to run the risk of incoherence. And this is not a criticism, because we must remember that he is a dialectical theologian, the kind who works with apparent contradictions because he thinks they are intrinsic to the message and therefore does not want to resolve them. In some of my cases above, he might say that my insisting on coherence is wrong. Point well taken!

Eight

Bloesch's Doctrine of God

Thomas F. Torrance

ONALD BLOESCH'S WORK *GOD THE ALMIGHTY: POWER, WISDOM, HOLINESS, Love*,[1] in the Christian Foundation series, is surely one of the most significant books in American evangelical theology to appear in recent years. It is a particularly welcome contribution, for it helps to give evangelical Christianity a deeper theological foundation that is much needed today. As I see it, its far-reaching importance lies in the supreme place Bloesch gives to the doctrine of God.

It is more and more clear today that people's ultimate concept of God governs how they think of the faith, and even interpret the Bible, for our understanding of the nature of God and of the nature of divine revelation affect one another. That was something that became very clear at the Reformation in its shift away from logico-causal structure of medieval scholastic theology to a dynamic understanding of all God's ways and works governed by the incarnate centrality of the Lord Jesus Christ and his saving grace. As for Calvin and Barth, so for Bloesch the soundness of any theological position is finally measured by how it stands to Jesus Christ.

What Bloesch does in this book, then, is to cut through the morass of neognostic and neopagan spirituality and the naturalistic pluralism, relativism and pragmatism that have been threatening to swamp the mind of Christian people. That is why he directs supreme attention once again to the transcendence of the almighty living God and his unique self-revelation in Jesus Christ. He does it in such a way as to allow the power, wisdom, holiness and love of God, uniquely disclosed in Christ, to cut through all conceptualizing of God compromised by the so-called new theologies of imaging God in accordance with the spirit of the times and some subjective truth located in the depths of the human soul. Against all that, Bloesch affirms "the intractable reality of the living God," which constitutes the irrevocable foundation of the Judaeo-Christian faith that he understands from a "centrist evangelical" stance.

His book is significantly dedicated to the memory of Karl Barth and Emil Brunner, from whom he has learned much, for they have clearly helped him to reach a more faithful understanding of divine revelation and a deeper evangelical grasp of the faith once delivered to the saints. In these strange times there has been taking place a paradigmatic shift of immense proportions to a theology of radical immanence in which God, present in all creation, is indistinguishable from creation. Even evangelical Christians are often misled by false would-be apologetic rationalisms and sometimes even by premodern and postmodern notions of spirituality. This book directs people back to the biblical and creedal foundations on which the whole church rests.

In the book's introduction Bloesch is concerned to open up the way for a deeper evangelical theology today by cutting through the confusion that has resulted from a different understanding of God and his relation to the world, the new immanentalism displacing the transcendentalism of the classical creeds and the foundations of Reformed and evangelical theology. With a sharp theological scalpel he cuts into the dualist and relativist teaching put forward by opponents of classical theism today, separating the weeds from the corn. He directs readers to the holy and mighty living God of the Bible who is both wholly other and infinitely near, and who utterly transcends human sexuality and gender and the pagan ideas now being dredged up again from the murky depths of ancient fertility cults. That is what happens when recourse is made to "natural theology" which is inevitably infected by the sinful alienation of the human mind from God.

The theological task today is not that of a neoromantic imaginative reconstruction of the picture of God, not the logical systematizing of divinely revealed concepts (as in scholastic orthodoxy), nor the clarification of states of inner consciousness (as in romantic liberalism). Rather the task is the explication of the mystery of God's self-revelation in Jesus Christ; faithful reasoning, he adds, never exhausts this mystery but enhances it. And that is just what Donald Bloesch does in *God the Almighty*.

The task of theology is to articulate the message of faith in the conceptuality of the age while at the same time bringing this conceptuality under the searing critique of divine revelation. In the process, cultural concepts and images are transformed as they become bearers of transcendent meaning.[2]

In going on to discuss "theology's attempt to define God," Bloesch makes a point of showing that although theology must engage in the conceptual language of philosophy, it cannot ally itself with any philosophical system. Theology must respect the nature of God's self-revelation under the impact of which all our own conceptual modes of thought and speech are transformed. Even in making himself known to us in Jesus Christ, the incarnate Word, God does not surrender his transcendence, so that a faithful theology must always operate with open forms of thought and speech that point beyond themselves to the ultimate truth of God. *Deus semper maior* (God is always greater).

Of particular importance is the stress Bloesch lays on the "living God of the Bible who is not static being but act in being."[3] This is in line with the teaching of Athanasius and Barth, and also with Jüngel "who cautions that we should not speak of a God who becomes but of a God whose being is dynamic, not static. 'Becoming' indicates the manner in which God exists."[4] This leads Bloesch to offer a more dynamic and more evangelical (that is, controlled by the gospel) account of the attributes or rather "perfections" of God, which contrasts with the rather stereotyped accounts found in traditional Protestant scholastic theology.

What I like here and throughout his work is the studied fidelity of Bloesch to the gospel. Thus in relation to unevangelical notions of God's almightiness as some sort of omnipotent causality he writes:

> The gospel is not a proclamation that God necessarily wills both election and reprobation, and that all we can do is submit to our divinely appointed destiny. Rather it is an invitation to enter into the fellowship that God opens for all humanity. Grace sets us free to respond in decision and obedience to this offer of salvation.[5]

In a chapter devoted to the source of our knowledge of God, Bloesch maintains against both mystical and scholastic theology that while we cannot reach God by ourselves, God himself comes to us, addressing us in his Word, and enables us to think what was previously unthinkable. That is what happens in and through the Lord Jesus Christ, in whom the mystery and wisdom of God have become incarnate in human flesh. What God is in himself is identical with what he is in his incarnate revelation in Christ. The anthropomorphic character of the language used has to do with the fact that in revealing himself to us, God addresses us human beings personally in our littleness, need and human predicament, which is "singularly appropriate for theological discourse." At the same time God retains his transcendent mystery in the very heart of his self-revelation. This means that true knowing of God is inseparable from adoration and worship of the Father, the Son and the Holy Spirit.

This leads Bloesch to devote helpful discussion to so-called natural theology, which in a recent article ("The Finality of Christ and Religious Pluralism")[6] he has spoken of as "a dead end road." Here he declares, "There can be no bona fide natural theology because theology cannot rest on the universal human awareness of some higher power, an awareness that necessarily reflects a distorted and idolatrous picture of God."[7] Traditional proofs for the existence of God can be helpful, he maintains, in clarifying the relation of God to the world, but only faith can identify the God of rational demonstration with the God of divine revelation, as St. Anselm showed.

Of course, while real knowledge of God comes only through Jesus Christ, this does not mean that nature or history are bereft of the presence of God. He agrees with Moltmann: "Nature is not the revelation of God. Nor is it God's image. But it shows 'traces of God' everywhere, if we are able to perceive in it a mirror and reflection of God's beauty.' "[8] Revelation and redemption, however, belong together. It is in the light of God's redeeming act in Jesus Christ that we may learn to discern and appreciate the many signs of God's work and mercy in nature and in the cultures and religions outside the sphere of Christian faith. In his light we are enabled to see light (Ps 36:9), but these little lights do not generate light in and of themselves. They reflect the one great light, the Son of God, through whom the world was created and by whose work the world is redeemed.

All through this book Professor Bloesch, unlike many mainline professional theologians today, has his eye on the relevance of theology for the mission of the gospel. Thus in a helpful section, with a Calvinist emphasis on predestination in mind, he takes pains to show that the human subject is not entirely passive in the face of divine revelation. God enlightens our understanding and activates our will in understanding and articulating what he makes known to us. But Bloesch will have nothing to do with a theological determinism or with attempts to resolve the problem of the relation between human and divine acts in revelation and salvation by reducing mystery to logic. That has a baleful effect on preaching in a hyper-Calvinistic tradition, when the gospel is sometimes treated as a discourse on God's predestinating decrees instead of a proclamation of unconditional saving grace issuing from the free ground of God's own Being. The mystery of the gospel can be grasped neither by inductive reasoning (Warfield) nor by deductive logic (Gordon Clark) but only by the eyes of faith, a gift of the Holy Spirit.

The error in much "Barthian preaching," so Bloesch avers, is simply to announce what God has already done for us and that our task is to respond in loving service to our neighbor. However, as he goes on rightly to point out, that does not really figure in "mainstream Barthianism." He himself calls for "an expositional form of theology—one that expounds the abiding truths of God's Word in Holy Scripture and then relates it to the contemporary situation,"[9] all in accordance with the nature of the gospel of grace, and thus in an evangelical and indeed an evangelizing way.

Bloesch devotes the fourth chapter of his book to the transcendence and immanence of God, not in an abstract or merely philosophical way but as they have been revealed within biblical history culminating in the historical revelation of God in the Lord Jesus Christ. "The God of the Bible understood in the light of the incarnation of Jesus Christ is not a monochrome God but a fellowship of persons existing in dynamic unity. He radiates the splendor not of solitary majesty but of outgoing love."[10] God is portrayed not only as the supreme being, ruler of the world, but also as the incarnate Savior who identifies himself with the travail of the world. "The stance of Christian faith is a trinitarian monotheism that transcends the polarity between the Sky Father and the Earth Mother."[11] It is because he is a triune fellowship within himself that he relates himself to the world in a multitude of ways. Hence I could have wished that at this point Bloesch had given us his chapter seven on "The Mystery of the Trinity" and that in it he had given an account of the doctrine of the Holy Trinity not just "as the apex and goal of theology" but as *the ultimate ground and all-determining structure of Christian theology.* This would take Bloesch's account of God's attributes and perfections down to a deeper level, where their evangelical import would be more effectively apparent.

What is badly needed in evangelical theology today is a deep rethinking and reshaping of our fundamental grasp and account of all the doctrines of the faith, as well as of all evangelical worship and all evangelistic activity, from their ultimate ground in the doctrine of the triune God. This would have sharpened for me and made even more evangelically relevant Bloesch's account of the divine attributes as perfections and the dynamic nature of his supremely personal Being. This is especially true of Bloesch's elucidation of what is meant by speaking of God's immutability and impassibility and in his examination of the contention of "Orthodoxy" that while God did suffer in his human nature he did not suffer in his divine nature. Bloesch correctly sees that Jesus Christ suffers not only as human but above all as *God* become human; and was the sacrifice of Christ not grounded in the sacrifice of the Father in declining to spare his only begotten Son?[12]

This question is faced when Bloesch turns to discuss the infinity and spirituality of God, in which he draws help from Barth, Brunner and Kierkegaard, with some appeal to and criticism of Moltmann. Bloesch calls for a deeper and more biblical understanding of divine transcendence and immanence as essentially *dynamic* and of all the acts of God's creative and saving love as arising from *the free ground of his triune Being.* Bloesch admits that much of what he contends for is in accord with classical theism. Yet he differs from theism in his "envisaging God as a person who freely interacts with his creation rather than as a first cause or principle of being,"[13] when, as with H. P. Owen, this is presented in such a way as to leave out love.

Yet it is love that constitutes the biblical understanding of God as dynamic transcendence. As Bloesch notes, "It is love that gives meaning to the interaction of God with the world of his creatures. . . . God's transcendence is nowhere more graphically expressed than in his free decision to make his second dwelling place with the contrite and humble in spirit (Is 57:15). This decision is nowhere more powerfully revealed than in the incarnation of Jesus Christ, in which God makes himself weak and vulnerable for the sake of his people."[14] That the almighty ever-living God has freely entered into a relation with us in this way discloses the wonder and glory of his transcendence and immanence. This is the God whose perfections we may adore and the God to whom we may pray in unreserved confidence and trust. Bloesch is clear that "It is in Christ that we come to know God as dynamic transcendence, as the unbounded love that reaches out to us even in our sin and depravity in order to draw us toward himself so that we might share the glory of his eternity."[15]

Bloesch then turns to write of the attributes of God as he has been made known to us in the Holy Scriptures and as they are defined for us in his definitive revelation in the Lord Jesus in the incarnation of the power and wisdom of God and the glory of God, "his transcendent beauty." He is rightly critical of the kind of Reformed theology in which the idea of God as unrestrained power was carried over from medieval Latin theology. In this Reformed theology the divine decrees were regarded as eternal aspects of God's nature, and not as manifestations of God's freedom, as with Calvin.

Bloesch is indebted here again to Karl Barth who sought to correct classical and Reformed tradition by viewing God's power in the service of his love, and recovered the biblical focus on God's infinite readiness to redeem and heal. While we must keep in mind that the Scripture can describe God as having unbounded power, yet in the fuller biblical perspective God's unbounded power can be shown to be none other than the boundlessness of his love.

It is in this light that Bloesch writes about God as Creator (with emphasis upon *creatio ex nihilo*) and as Redeemer; biblical religion regards God as creating in order to redeem. What he writes here reminds me of the statement of H. R. Mackintosh that in the Scriptures creation is proleptically conditioned by redemption.

This provides the ground for an impressive account of the providential activity of God as Lord and Ruler. Far from being interpreted deterministically in accordance with some notion of omnicausality, providence is to be seen in close relationship to Jesus Christ, for all things are created for the sake of Christ and are directed to him as their goal:

> The theological task is to affirm both the inscrutable reality of divine providence whereby God unfailingly guides the world to its true destiny and the ineradicable reality of human freedom by which we cooperate with God's fulfilling the divine purposes. . . . Providence is the mysterious, hidden hand of God at work in all phenomena of nature and events in history, bringing into temporal reality what has already been envisaged and ordained by God from all eternity—but in cooperation with, and not in negation of, creaturely freedom.[16]

This brings Bloesch to the intractable problem of *evil*. In the history of philosophy the problem of evil has proved to be the most difficult to resolve, for it is rarely recognized that while terribly real, evil is utterly irrational and incomprehensible to reason. Here Bloesch finds himself nearer to the teaching of Luther than to Barth and is sharply opposed to the idea of process theology that evil is simply a fundamental obstruction, for at its core evil is ruthlessly destructive.

The Bible refers to it as "the mystery of iniquity" and does not offer a theodicy, but it does tell us that God himself has acted decisively in Jesus Christ and his atoning sacrifice to deal decisively with evil and save us from it:

> Theology cannot offer a fully satisfying explanation for evil, but it does offer a spiritual solution—the incarnation and atoning sacrifice of our Lord Jesus Christ. Something has gone radically wrong with creation, but God has acted to bring good out of evil. He has acted to reverse the work and powers of darkness and disorder by himself becoming human flesh and dying on the cross, taking upon himself the retribution that we deserve because of sin. That he rose again on the third day shows that the powers of sin, death and the devil could not defeat him. The cross proved to be the key to their undoing, for he rose from the dead and triumphed over them. The conflict between good and evil continues, but the future belongs irreversibly to Jesus Christ, for his victory over the powers of evil has already been secured.[17]

Following this, Bloesch turns in an impressive chapter on holiness and love as the two sides of God: "Holiness together with love is the quintessential attribute of God."[18] He will have nothing do with a current movement of thought, as with Sally McFague, that regards love as eros rather than agape or that subordinates holiness to love. The love of God precisely as the agape love of God is intrinsically holy. It is therefore always and implacably opposed to all that is unholy and unloving, even in God's overflowing concern and compassion that embraces unworthy sinners in the midst of their sin. Thus Bloesch takes the biblical teaching about the wrath of God seriously as a "real objective power," for as the wrath of the Lamb it is the power of the holy love which God eternally is as God.

This point badly needs restating today to evangelical Christians who become snared in the specious arguments often advanced by liberals in their proper concern for social justice. "I propose," asserts Bloesch, "an ethic of the divine command, which brings together the commandments and principles in Holy Scripture with the gospel of redeeming grace that created Scripture and forms its inner content. In this view the hope for a more just social order lies in the encounter with the God of holy love who alone gives meaning to life and direction in works of social amelioration."[19] Moreover, "the realization that we are sinners saved only by grace should prevent us from taking pride in our social achievements and ingloriously damning our opponents."[20] As majestic holiness and unquenchable love, God wills that his nature be reflected in all the life and activity of his people.

It is at this stage in his argument that Professor Bloesch turns to "The

Mystery of the Trinity"; this is understandable in the course of his argumentation, for it is the holy and loving relations between the persons of the Trinity that are the ultimate ground and source for the holy and loving life of God's people. Bloesch presents his doctrine of the Trinity at this late point as the culmination of biblical and apostolic reflection on the nature and activity of the living God. However, as Calvin showed, it is already given in the biblical witness. "Say there is a Trinity of Persons in the one Being of God," he said, and "you will have said in a word what the Scriptures say, and suppressed empty talk."[21] The Trinity is not to be regarded, therefore, as an appendix or as prolegomena to theology but, in Bloesch's words, as "the apex and goal of theology. . . . We do not deduce the doctrine of the Trinity from a general concept of God but draw out the idea of the Trinity from the total and biblical and apostolic witness concerning God. A commitment to the Trinity is already apparent in the early sections of this volume, but now it is the appropriate time to define the Trinity and ponder its implications."[22]

I have already questioned Bloesch's view of the doctrine of the Trinity as "the apex and goal of theology," for it is far more than that. Here, however, I have problems with his idea that the Trinity is both an analytical development of the central act of divine revelation (as Barth maintained) and a synthetic construction drawn from the church's reflection upon this revelation. His account of Barth's view here could have been supplemented with, and corrected by, closer attention to the great Greek fathers, especially Athanasius, Gregory Nazianzen and Cyril of Alexandria. They regarded the doctrine of "one God, three Persons" as giving decisive expression to the biblical revelation of God the Father, God the Son and God the Holy Spirit, and not as a second-order reflection of it. As far as I can see, the Trinity is fully implicit throughout the New Testament in God's historical manifestation in Jesus Christ as Father, Son and Holy Spirit, and is found in the worship of the church from the very beginning.

I miss here the all-significant doxological approach to the doctrine of the Trinity found in the early church in continuity with the very origins of the life and worship of the first Christians. And I do not regard the Trinity as a synthetic construction drawn from the church's reflection upon this revelation. Although they certainly unfolded and gave clear expression to the doctrine of the Holy Trinity disclosed in the apostolic witness, the great fathers of the evangelical theology in the ancient church regarded the Trinity as the saving mystery of salvation, the immediate and central truth of the gospel. The Trinity is not just a formal doctrine: for them it belonged to the inner core of the gospel, and that is surely how we must think of it also.

Bloesch, of course, is surely right in saying, "We do not project upon God the human experience of interpersonal relations, but find in God the perfection of personal interaction as this is mirrored in the self-revelation of the Father in the Son and through the power of the Spirit."[23] Does he not here lean too much to the notion that the doctrine of the Trinity is the product of theological reasoning? Rather, we must think of the triune God as himself the immediate content of his self-revelation.

An illuminating account, full of rich insights, is given by Bloesch in his examination of contemporary reassessments of the doctrine of the Trinity. Here I could have wished that he had taken into account the fact that the very concept of "person" originally derived from the doctrine of the Trinity, the consubstantial communion of Father, Son and Holy Spirit, three persons who mutually and eternally inexist and indwell one another. It would have been helpful, therefore, if Bloesch had taken into account the truth that the relations between persons belong to what persons are: in an uncreated way in the eternal communion of persons who are God, but in a created and derivative way in which we human beings are related to one another, such that our interpersonal relations belong to what we as persons are. That is the trinitarian source of the concept of person in human thought.

There was no definite *concept* of "person" in the ancient world, in the Jewish, Greek or Latin thought; however, there were forms of speech that, on looking back, might seem to us to adumbrate it. Introducing the fact that the concept of person was a creative innovation in human thought (a direct product of God's triune self-revelation as Father, Son and Holy Spirit) would have helped Bloesch in his interesting discussion of contemporary reassessments, where notions of personality derived from later reflection, philosophical and psychological, are projected into Deity.

Much depends, as Bloesch asserts in what he has to say of "Trinitarian monotheism," on how "person" is defined. But why as a Reformed theologian has he taken no account of the teaching of John Calvin, the Reformation vis-à-vis of Gregory Nazianzen in Greek patristic theology? Like Gregory, Calvin would have nothing do with the notion of *tropoi hyparxeos* or "modes of being," unfortunately taken over by Dorner, Barth and other modern theologians which has led them into difficulty. This applies to the critical question of subordinationism in the doctrine of the Trinity, to which Bloesch seems to have yielded in what he calls an "orthodox" and not a "heretical" form, albeit in a modified Augustinian way, reflected in his diagrammatic appendix. He is mistaken in saying that the Greeks vis-à-vis the Latins were inclined to explain the Trinity in terms of "causal relations." Gregory Nazianzen and Cyril of Alexandria, for example, denounced the introduction of causal relations into the doctrine of the Trinity as a monstrosity implying degrees of deity. Unfortunately both Latins and Greeks lapsed into the use of causal terms in seeking agreement on the doctrine of the Trinity in the ninth century (unlike the Reformed-Orthodox agreement concluded in 1992).

The Greek fathers rightly understood the word of our Lord, "The Father is greater than I" (Jn 14:28), to be understood not ontologically but soteriologically and "economically" of his incarnate life in the form of a servant, and so not of his divine person as such. In his failure to follow the Greek fathers and indeed Calvin at this point, Bloesch is misled into an unclear notion of the relation between the economic Trinity and the immanent Trinity. The subordination of Christ in his incarnate and saving economy cannot be read back into the eternal personal relations and distinctions subsisting in the Holy Trinity. So as Calvin argued, the mediatorial office of Christ does not detract in any way from his divine majesty. On the other hand, Bloesch insists very rightly that "the denial of the ontological Trinity is a potent indication that a religious movement is probably a cult or aberrant sect rather than a branch of the one holy, catholic and apostolic church."[24]

It is from his restatement of the doctrine of the Trinity that Bloesch cuts through not a little confusion in the teaching of some well-known contemporary theologians. Here he shows that a denial of the Trinity leads to deism, pantheism, polytheism or agnosticism and calls for fresh thinking about the bearing of trinitarian theology upon spirituality and prayer. This is a crucial point forcefully expounded in the recent book by James B. Torrance, *Worship, Community & the Triune God of Grace.*[25] In the chapter on "The Mystery of the Trinity" Bloesch makes an important contribution to Reformed theology and calls for a recovery of the central evangelical position which it was given in the teaching of John Calvin, but lost in the rather harsh doctrine of God so often put forward in Calvinist and Westminster Puritan federal theology. Its recovery in evangelical theology will mean much both for biblical preaching and evangelism, as is reinforced in the following chapter.

In the latter part of his book Bloesch offers a critical analysis and assessment of what he calls "The Biblical-Classical Synthesis" and "The Biblical-Modern Synthesis." Here the biblical and evangelical faith has in significant ways been compromised by would-be faithful theologians and clerics in their pragmatic accommodation to transient patterns of culture. This is evident not only in the classical synthesis of the Augustinian-Thomist tradition, but in the way in which committed Reformed thinkers have made use of non-Christian thought in seeking rational support for the faith. This is shown by Bloesch in relation to the way in which, for example, conceptions of providence and fate, revelation and reason, grace and merit, prayer and contemplation, reconciliation and reunion, have suffered in the exposition given by leading Protestant and Catholic thinkers alike in the past, in which the evangelical integrity of the faith has been damaged.

This is no less evident in accommodations of the truth of the gospel to modernity and so-called postmodernity. Bloesch spells this out in helpful discussion of the strands of vitalism, romanticism and naturalism rampant in modern times, which have given rise to new ideas of spirituality and theism in which divine transcendence is compromised or flatly repudiated. In this radically secularized outlook God is regarded as caught up in the ineluctable processes of nature and bereft of his almightiness, with devastating effect nowhere more than in belief in petitionary prayer and evangelical conversion.

Bloesch claims that the theology he upholds is "biblical-prophetic rather than modern, postmodern or premodern."[26] He thinks it is unwise, however, simply to attack or discard the signal contributions of either the mystical or rationalist traditions of the faith or dismiss altogether what moderns and postmoderns are saying about God, life and the world. "Their insights need to be integrated in a comprehensive vision of evangelical catholicity, which holds the Bible above both sacred tradition and the cultural ethos."[27] And so, in the face of all damaging accommodations of faith to transient cultural ideas that compromise the very evangelical heart of the Christian faith, Bloesch calls for

> a comprehensive vision of evangelical catholicity, which holds the Bible above both sacred tradition and the cultural ethos. A church that is truly catholic and evangelical will confront the world with the exclusive claims of the gospel, but it will also have a markedly inclusive thrust; its goal is to bring all peoples to a saving realization of what God has done for us and the whole world in Jesus Christ.[28]

God the Almighty is a very powerful and welcome contribution to contemporary theology, and not least to evangelical theology, for it is more and more clear that a distorted conception of God lies behind the problems of many Christian people and churches today. The loss of the transcendence of God and of the uniqueness of Jesus Christ is extremely disconcerting. What this book does is to reclaim for modern theology and evangelical Christians in particular the biblical message that Jesus Christ is God incarnate and that he came into the world to deliver a lost humanity from bondage to sin, death and the devil. The only God whom we may really know and trust is the triune God whose nature and being are revealed and defined for us in the Lord Jesus Christ. That is the great evangelical truth to which Bloesch's doctrine of God is dedicated.

Nine

Bloesch's Doctrine of the Christian Life

JOHN WEBORG &
ELMER M. COLYER

It is supposed that we shall all be saved, that we are Christians from birth—and instead of the fearful effort of having to make use of this life for an eternal decision it is supposed that everything is already settled, and at most it is a question of whether out of gratitude we live a reasonably decent life, which in any case from the purely earthly and worldly point of view is the most prudent thing to do.[1]
SØREN KIERKEGAARD

When I (Colyer) first decided to include an essay on Bloesch's doctrine of the Christian life in this book, I had no idea of the complexity of this particular theme in relation to Bloesch's theology, indeed his whole career. After talking with a number of potential authors who were familiar with Bloesch's theology, I quickly realized that I faced a serious problem. No one suggested anything other than laundry lists of various elements in Bloesch's doctrine of the Christian life that neither analyzed the place of this doctrine in his overall theological horizon nor sketched the architectonics of it. At this point I met John Weborg and after discussing the problem, he graciously agreed to write this essay with my collaboration.

Our work has convinced me of the utterly crucial place of the Christian life within Bloesch's theology and his career. It is the hermeneutical key to the interrelationship of Bloesch's early books and to the central Word-Spirit polarity characteristic not only of his theological method but also of his overall theology. Since Bloesch's doctrine of the Christian life is so interwoven in the entire fabric of his theology, it is impossible to give it adequate treatment within a single essay: someone ought to write a dissertation on the subject. The goal of our essay is more modest.

The first part (written by Colyer) discusses Bloesch's early publication in relation to his doctrine of the Christian life and then outlines the basic architectonic of that doctrine. The second half of the chapter (written primarily by Weborg) interprets many of the key themes of Bloesch's doctrine of the Christian life. It is a pleasure to pay tribute to our friend, Donald Bloesch, and we are grateful for his contribution in the area of theology explored in this essay.

Part One: The Autobiographic and Architectonic Dimensions of Bloesch's Doctrine of the Christian Life

An epigraph from Bonhoeffer in Bloesch's book *The Crisis of Piety* underscores *the* pivotal question that preoccupies Bloesch's attention throughout much of his early career: "The issue can no longer be evaded. It is becoming clearer every day that the most urgent problem besetting our Church is this: How can we live the Christian life in the modern world?"[2] All of Bloesch's early books are related to this question in one way or another. It is a theme that recurs in various forms throughout many of his later works as well.

In fact, it is possible to read Bloesch's early works, from his first book, *Centers of Christian Renewal*[3] (1964), through the enormously influential two-volume *Essentials of Evangelical Theology*[4] (1978, 1979), as an ongoing spiritual/theological autobiography in which Bloesch's central focus on the Christian life is developed in relation to a series of interconnected topics.

Bloesch's first book, *Centers of Christian Renewal* (1964), focused on "evangelical communities" in which people concerned with Christian revitalization "seek to contribute toward this renewal by living the common life under a common discipline."[5] Indeed "many religious communities provide an atmosphere in which the devotional life . . . can flourish."[6] Bloesch considered embracing communal life as an option for the nurture and expression of his own Christian life as an answer to Bonhoeffer's question of how to live this life in the modern world.

The Christian Life and Salvation (1967), Bloesch's second book, presents his most fully developed schematization of the Christian life. This is a carefully constructed work which not only thematizes Bloesch's doctrine of Christian life but develops the complex network of theological interrelations between the various elements of the divine and human poles of the *ordo salutis* and the Christian life. This is the pivotal text for understanding this theme in Bloesch's theology, though later publications append, expand and modify various components within it.

The Crisis of Piety (1968) is a collection of essays on related topics that brings Bloesch's discussion of the Christian life even more fully into dialogue with the American theological context of the 1960s. He argues for an interrelation of theology and life: "We therefore conclude that doctrinal theology (*theologia dogmatica*) should be held in balance with a theology of spiritual life or devotion (*theologia vitae spiritualis*)."[7] It was precisely this *theologia vitae spiritualis* that Bloesch found missing in so many of the theological proposals in the 1960s.

Thus the agenda of *The Crisis of Piety* (reflected in the title) was more controversial in character than his previous book (somewhat analogous to Barth's *Der Römerbrief*) placing Bloesch's theology of the Christian life in stark contrast to other theological programs of the day. The polemical character of *The Crisis of Piety* is evident in the author's note to the second edition, reissued in 1988, where Bloesch identifies death-of-God theology, secular theology and theology of revolution as some of the nemeses he sought to overturn by a reemphasis on piety, "fear and trust in the living God."[8] Whereas *The Christian Life and Salvation* was the more carefully developed theological statement, *The Crisis of Piety* was something of a battle cry and should be read in light of the former rather than vice versa.

This focus on the distinctive character of the Christian life raises pointed questions about the relationship between Christ and culture, particularly in light of the secularization of American culture in the sixties, and the reaction of the church and the theological community to it. Bloesch's fourth book, *The Christian Witness in a Secular Age* (1968), evaluates the proposals of nine contemporary theologians (Barth, Brunner, Bultmann, Reinhold Niebuhr, Tillich, Bonhoeffer, J. A. T. Robinson, Cox and Altizer).[9]

Bloesch also presents his own alternative. The church is to serve the world, but this inevitably means that the church has to call the world to repentance. The task is not to render the gospel relevant to the culture, but rather to bring the culture under the scrutiny of the gospel. The gospel is believed on the basis of its own power, not because theology can prove the superiority of the gospel over cultural ideologies.[10] Bloesch believed that this could not take place without a reformation of the church, "a reformation which will involve doctrinal restatement as well as new forms of witness and service."[11]

These are the themes Bloesch takes up in his next two books: *The Reform of the Church*[12] (1970) and *The Ground of Certainty*[13] (1971).

While some theologians claimed that the church was not sufficiently in the world, Bloesch's analysis was that there was too much of the world in the church. *The Reform of the Church* presents Bloesch's program for church renewal, covering everything from preaching, the sacraments, worship and ecumenicity to charismatic gifts, spiritual disciplines, evangelism and social relevance.

In *The Ground of Certainty: Toward an Evangelical Theology of Revelation* Bloesch begins to develop his own encompassing theological horizon. *The Ground of Certainty* deals with various issues of theological method. It represents Bloesch's sustained development of an evangelical theology of revelation, correlated with his doctrine of the Christian life as a more adequate alternative to the proposals discussed in *The Christian Witness in a Secular Age*.

From the publication of *The Ground of Certainty* onward throughout the 1970s, in his research and teaching, Bloesch was developing his brand of evangelical theology.[14] The fuller theological fruit of Bloesch's programmatic emphasis on the Christian renewal comes to expression in his highly acclaimed *Essentials of Evangelical Theology* (*Vol. 1, God, Authority and Salvation*—1978; *Vol. 2, Life, Ministry and Hope*—1979). There can be no reform of the church and no revitalized Christian life apart from theological renewal.

Throughout this period of Bloesch's career from the sixties through the publication of *Essentials* in the late seventies, his doctrine of the Christian life and the renewal of the church that it demands had been a central organizing theme around which his various publications revolve.[15] His writings chronicle the trajectory of his thinking which developed in a widening circle of related topics.

The Christian life is also one of the continuous threads in Bloesch's spiritual/theological trajectory from his family heritage in Lutheran and Reformed Pietism through his encounter with Christian existentialism and neo-orthodoxy to his mature catholic evangelicalism.[16] It is one of the central reasons why Bloesch has always been critical of Karl Barth's theology: Bloesch believes that Barth's objectivism undercuts the subjective pole of salvation realized in the Christian life.[17]

The doctrine of the Christian life is still central in Bloesch's mature (post-*Essentials*) theology and permeates his writings. The combining of theology and Christian life is one of the strengths of Bloesch's work and helps account for evangelicals and pastors finding his writings so formative.

We now turn to the architectonics of Bloesch's doctrine of the Christian life. In his book *The Christian Life and Salvation* Bloesch noted, "The paradox of salvation has many facets and thereby lends itself to diverse formulations."[18] The diverse thematizations of the Christian life in Bloesch's own voluminous writings on the subject bear witness to this complexity. Yet it is this very complexity that problematizes Bloesch's doctrine of the Christian life for his interpreters.

Anyone intent on writing about Bloesch's doctrine of the Christian life has to arrive at conceptual clarity regarding: (1) the relation of the Christian life to the wider horizon of Bloesch's theology (the easier task) and (2) Bloesch's schematization of the various facets of the doctrine and their interrelations.

The question thus becomes, does Bloesch provide a conceptually clear and comprehensive schematization of his doctrine of the Christian life anywhere in the vast corpus of his writings on the topic? His most fully developed architectonic of the Christian life appears in his early work, *The Christian Life and Salvation.*

Overview. In *The Christian Life and Salvation* Bloesch presents the following schematization of his doctrine of the Christian life and salvation:

1. There are two perspectives/poles that must be held in tension: theocentric-anthropocentric and objective-subjective.[19]

2. There are four basic categories: election, justification, sanctification and perfection or (glorification).[20]

3. There are three tenses/dimensions of time: past, present and future.[21]

The two perspectives or poles. The central theme throughout Bloesch's doctrine of Christian life (indeed, maybe *the* key motif of his entire theology) is the two perspectives (divine and human) or poles (objective and subjective) that have to be kept in paradoxical or dialectical tension.[22] Bloesch describes the two perspectives or poles of salvation in a variety of ways: salvation is a gift and a task; [23] God is the sole ground, but God completes his work in and through human agency; [24] Christ for us, but also Christ with and in us.[25]

Bloesch wants to keep divine agency and human agency in balance in Christian life and salvation, and in one's theologizing about it. This represents a synthesis of the Reformation emphasis on the divine initiative in the whole process of salvation with the resolve of Pietism, Christian existentialism and evangelicalism to fully affirm the importance of human participation and response in all aspects of Christian faith and life. Bloesch develops his position as a third alternative[26] to (1) monergism, in which God is the only agent in salvation and which separates the Christian life from salvation,[27] and (2) synergism, in which humanity works alongside of God and which makes the Christian life an additional foundation or ground of our salvation.[28]

This fundamental objective-subjective polarity becomes the organizing principle of Bloesch's systematic theology, Christian Foundations, as is evident in the title of the first volume: *A Theology of Word & Spirit.*[29] The Word is the objective pole and the Spirit is the subjective pole of revelation:

> When I speak of Word and Spirit, I am not thinking primarily of a book that receives its stamp of approval from the Spirit. . . . I am thinking mainly of the living Word in its inseparable unity with Scripture and church proclamation as this is brought home to us by the Spirit in the awakening of faith. It is not the Bible as such but the divine revelation that confronts us in the Bible that is the basis and source of spiritual authority. . . . Scripture is the Word of God to those with the eyes to see and ears to hear.[30]

It is the action of the Spirit that brings the Word of God (Jesus Christ) present, yet hidden, in Scripture to light so that people hear and respond in faith. This pervasive theme delimits Bloesch's position at every crucial point of theological method, as the authors of chapters three through five of this book point out.[31]

In addition, revelation and salvation are not two separate realities, rather they are two sides or facets of one reality. Therefore the Word-Spirit (objective-subjective, divine agency-human agency) motif thematizes all of Christian faith, life and theology. Knowledge of God and the reality of salvation are participatory in Bloesch's theology. This objective-subjective polarity is evident in the next dimension of Bloesch's schematization of the Christian life.

Four basic categories. Bloesch has a fairly traditional Reformed understanding of the four categories of his *ordo salutis* (election, justification, sanctification, glorification), except for the fact that he does not embrace double predestination. The crucial role of human agency along with divine agency is evident at every point and is schematized in the *ordo salutis* as follows:

Temporal Order/Human Agency	Eternal Order/Divine Agency
seeking for help	election
repentance and faith	justification
obedience in faith	sanctification
perfect love	perfection or glorification

The two orders are not parallel or independent processes but rather two ways of describing the outworking of human salvation. Also this is a series of interacting stages, and not a purely chronological process. While these are the dominant categories in Bloesch's schema, there are other facets that can be included (adoption, calling, sacraments and so on), though Bloesch says that all of them can be subsumed under one or more of the dominant categories.[32]

Here we see the way Bloesch understands the Christian life in relation to the wider horizon of his theology. By holding the divine and human in paradoxical tension Bloesch argues that the Christian life is not simply a pointer to a salvation already accomplished. Rather the Christian life is "the arena of salvation. It is the battlefield on which our salvation is fought for and secured. . . . The Christian life is . . . a vital contributing factor in our salvation."[33] Even in his most recent book, *Jesus Christ: Savior & Lord,* Bloesch argues that, "The Christian life is not simply the fruit and consequence of a past salvation accomplished in the cross and resurrection of Christ but the arena in which Christ's salvation is carried forward to fulfillment by his Spirit."[34]

Nevertheless Bloesch's position on this point has somewhat changed over time. He is concerned that the Christian life "is not to be seen as a means to gain additional merits."[35] One could say that the Christian life does not procure our salvation, but it manifests our salvation at every point of the *ordo salutis.*[36]

Three tenses or dimensions of time.[37] The past tense of salvation refers primarily to God's election of humanity in Jesus Christ and especially to Christ's life and death.[38] The present dimension signifies the realization of this salvation now in our lives through the Holy Spirit.[39] The future aspect is the eschatological element of salvation: "the kingdom beyond history . . . our final justification and eternal life with the saints in glory."[40]

Now this whole schema becomes extraordinarily complex, for Bloesch maintains that "Not only salvation itself, but every facet of salvation partici-pates in all three dimensions of time. Election, justification, sanctification, and perfection are all to be found in past, present, and future."[41] For example, "the seed of perfection is in the past, its germination occurs in the present, and the flower of perfection is in the future."[42] In addition, each of the four dominant categories (election, justification, sanctification, glorification) is organically related not only to every other one but also to many other important facets of the Christian life and salvation.[43] Thus the chapters of Bloesch's book unfold in a complex interweaving of these dominant categories with numerous other themes including sin, baptism, conversion, the Lord's Supper, prayer, love, ethics, assurance (not security) and reconceived notions of heaven and hell, among others.[44] Through it all, Bloesch rejects both monergism and synergism and asserts the central paradoxical polarity of Christian faith and life, "the coincidence of divine and human freedom."[45]

Questions concerning Bloesch's architectonics. I know of no place in all of Bloesch's writings other than *The Christian Life and Salvation* where he develops his doctrine of the Christian life in more depth, detail or careful architectonic. There are, however, significant discussions of other themes germane to the doctrine of the Christian life that are not developed or in some cases even mentioned in that book. For example, in *The Future of Evangelical Christianity,* under the section "A Biblical, Evangelical Spirituality," he identifies the gifts and fruits of the Spirit as integral to the Christian life, as well as various spiritual disciplines. Where do these fit within his architectonic?

The spiritual disciplines, of course, are means of grace within the pilgrimage of faith (Bloesch mentions some of them in *The Christian Life and Salvation*). I presume that the fruit of the Spirit is another way to speak of the Christian life in relation to sanctification where the salvation procured by Christ is carried forward to fulfillment by Christ's Spirit.

The issue of spiritual gifts is a bit more complex, since it underscores the crucial category of *vocation* which does not fit so easily within Bloesch's schema discussed above. Vocation, of course, was a pivotal theme for the Reformers but has recently received criticism by feminists and others.[46] This raises the question of a theology of work and leisure which I do not think Bloesch addresses indepth anywhere but which is utterly crucial, since work and leisure are integral to the Christian life. Bloesch is well aware of the issue of vocation, but he does not thematize and develop it within his doctrine of the Christian life.

The single most baffling point of Bloesch's architectonic (and for me, his overall theology) is the fact that in *The Christian Life and Salvation* he clearly sees and explicitly states the decidedly trinitarian ground of the *ordo salutis* and the Christian life:

> Our salvation takes place in Christ, but the sacrifice of Christ is made possible by the compassion of the Father, and it is made efficacious by the action of the Holy Spirit. Our salvation is *in* the Son, but it is *from* the Father and *through* the Holy Spirit.[47]

But if this is the case, then should not the Trinity play a more decisive role in the architectonics of both Bloesch's doctrine of the Christian life and his overall theology? For a number of years I have seen Bloesch's Word-Spirit motif leading quite naturally to a radically trinitarian, evangelical theology that does not seem to come to full fruition in the architectonics of Bloesch's theology thus far.[48]

Beyond these minor questions the architectonic depth, breadth and interrelation of Bloesch's doctrine of the Christian life is immensely helpful not only for thinking about the Christian life but for living it as well. This is, I believe, precisely what Bloesch intends, that his readers will hear the gospel in its full depth and breadth, take up the cross and follow Christ in Christian lives of radical and discerning discipleship.

Part Two: "A Pious Erudition" and an "Erudite Piety": Stewards and Safeguards of the Christian Life

The heading of the second half of this chapter underscores Bloesch's attempt to maintain a balance but not parity between the faith believed, which is primary, and the faith that believes, which is derivative. When that balance is maintained, it will be because of a "pious erudition" and an "erudite piety,"[49] terms that Eberhard Nestle used to describe the work of the Lutheran Pietist and exegete of Scripture, Johann Albrecht Bengel (1687-1752).

What Nestle recognized in the balance Bengel maintained between exegesis and piety, I (Weborg) want to identify in the balance Donald Bloesch seeks to preserve between dogmatics and devotion. A "pious erudition" and an "erudite piety" distinguishes but does not separate knowledge from wisdom. The function of piety is to keep erudition from becoming its own end, and the purpose of erudition is to keep piety from becoming its own end. Piety and erudition are the stewards and safeguards of each other lest either theology or the Christian life embrace an autonomy that is a caricature of the consistency and symmetry of the Christian faith-life.

For Bloesch the symmetry to which I refer is more than the internal consistency of the faith that is believed; it is the deeper resonance between the faith and faithfulness embodied in the Christian life. Therefore, in Bloesch's theology one cannot speak of the Christian faith without speaking of the Christian life, and one cannot speak of the Christian life without speaking of the Christian faith. The exploration of the inseparability of the two is the burden of part two of this chapter.

Theologia prima/theologia secunda. *Theologia prima,* or "primary theology," is speech to God. It may be formal or informal or both. When it is informal, *theologia prima* breaks out in protest, praise, petition or penitence. It emerges at times as an acclamation of God's power or fidelity and at other times as an argument with God more than as an argument about God or for God. Prayer, which plays such a pivotal role in Bloesch's theology and his doctrine of the Christian life,[50] is the common method of doing this form of theology.

In its more formal sense, *theologia prima* is expressed in the devotional life of Christians and the worship life of congregations. Here it utilizes liturgy, texts, creeds, confessions, psalms and/or written prayers as its vehicle.[51] When God is worshiped and God's deeds of help and deliverance are told and retold, the heart wells up with praise. The liturgy provides people with stories, texts and words when one's own words are hard to come by. People take heart in the assembly of the people of God; hope and grace often are more easily appropriated in common than alone. To hear and pray the testimonies of praise and lament of the ancestors in the faith is to open oneself to inner convincement by their witness to the plausibility of faith, hope and love. "And let us consider how to provoke one another to love and good deeds, not neglecting to meet together, as is the habit of some but encouraging one another, and all the more as you see the Day approaching" (Heb 10:24-25).

Theologia secunda, or "secondary theology," is speech about God. Speech about God is more studied than spontaneous, more dogmatic than doxological. Instead of direct address in the first person, this type of theology speaks of God in the third person, and when careless in doing so, risks portraying God as an object. If *theologia prima* relies mainly on prayer, *theologia secunda* uses propositions to develop arguments for the cogency of the Christian faith and its doctrines. The end product of *theologia secunda* is often a "system" like Karl Barth's *Church Dogmatics.*

Theologia prima resists systemization and will not settle for premature solutions. In like manner, *theologia prima* forestalls the intellectual security if not pride in *theologia secunda*. Even the most sophisticated propositional resolutions to theological problems have not made prayer obsolete.[52] Yet *theologia secunda* keeps *theologia prima* from being a prisoner to its own subjectivity and enriches the depth and breadth of its language and experience.

I would argue for a symbiosis between *theologia prima* and *theologia secunda*. When they mutually influence each other, we have the equivalent of a patristic axiom: the law of prayer is the law of believing, and sometimes the law of believing becomes the law of prayer. The result is a correlation between a pious erudition and an erudite piety.

Theologia dogmatica/theologia vitae spiritualis. At the heart of Bloesch's theological vision is a correlative distinction between *theologia dogmatica* (doctrinal theology) and *theologia vitae spiritualis* (theology of the spiritual life or devotion) and an equally passionate concern for a symbiosis between them.[53] *Theologia dogmatica* and *theologia vitae spiritualis* are not antithetical, and if they are left unrelated they become caricatures of themselves.[54] By itself *theologia vitae spiritualis (theologia prima)* can easily become zeal without any criteria for self-assessment, commitment without counting the cost, and an unhealthy fideism. A substantial *theologia dogmatica* has to be present to keep the Christian life from being reduced to moralism, formal orthodoxy, cultural norms, escapism or perfectionism.

By itself *theologia dogmatica (theologia secunda)* can easily be nothing more than lifeless intellectualism, a theological mind game cut off from a vital relationship with the living God and offering no theological discernment for one's devotion. Bloesch's rejection of all forms of theological rationalism has its genesis in his long-standing concern for *theologia vitae spiritualis*.

Bloesch seeks to maintain a balance but not a parity between *theologia dogmatica* and *theologia vitae spiritualis* (in my terms *theologia prima* and *theologia secunda*). In *Essentials of Evangelical Theology* he writes, "The act of believing *(fides qua creditur)*, though supremely important, must never prevail over the content of faith *(fides quae creditur)*."[55] Hence when I conjoin an "erudite piety" with a "pious erudition" in regard to Bloesch's understanding of the Christian life, I am identifying his concern that the faith exercised by persons does not become the object of their own believing. Faith in faith collapses of its own vacuity. No one is justified, consoled or called by such faith. The reason it collapses is that there is no genuine relationship involved. It is an individualism of a most deceptive and disappointing sort. It is the victim of a commitment without either content or course of life. But if such believing is erudite and informed, it has a critical principle by which to practice discernment and set a course for life.

Most of all, as Bloesch understands these matters, such a faith and life will not collapse into their own vacuity because they are formed by trust in the God of Jesus Christ whose fidelity is attested to by witnesses. The testimony of these witnesses became included in the church's canon of Scripture. When one becomes erudite in this text, the Bible, one comes to know both the faith testified to (*fides quae creditur, theologia secunda; theologia dogmatica*) and the faithful whose faith sometimes inspires the faith of contemporary believers, especially when the times compel believers to cry out, "I believe, help my unbelief" (*fides qua creditur, theologia prima; theologia vitae spiritualis*).

Theocentric and anthropocentric. In framing the *theologia dogmatica* of the *theologia vitae spiritualis,* Bloesch argues for a spirituality that is "radically but not exclusively theocentric since it also includes a concern for God's creatures who are made in his image."[56] In another place he calls for a piety that will be "at the same time fully theocentric and radically anthropocentric, since it is related to both the glory of God and the restoration and well-being of man."[57] The reader will notice that in the first quotation "radical" was applied to God and in the second, to anthropology.

Since for Bloesch's understanding of the Christian life all saving activity begins with God and ends with humans, how does a radically transcendent God establish a radical anthropocentricity?[58] First, let us recall that Bloesch argues that a catholic evangelical spirituality "is radically but not exclusively theocentric." The qualifier, "not exclusively," must maintain God's wholly otherness on the one hand, and on the other, guard against solipsism. The very use of the term *other* implies another, a human other in this case, whom we may term, using a favorite phrase of Barth, God's counterpart.

There is something about God that is basically unselfish. As Bloesch writes, "The glory of God does not reduce man to nothing but instead gives him hope and confidence."[59] Then he notes with approval Irenaeus's famous line, "The glory of God is man fully alive."[60] In this assertion Bloesch is consistent with himself. The piety he seeks must make room for the glory of God and the restoration of humans to a right relationship with their Creator. God does not endanger the individuality and dignity of any person. Creation established that.

Second, there is the matter of restoration, as Bloesch called it in the above quotation. Restoration implies a breakdown in relation and its repair. In

Bloesch's theology, sin is more than a privation of being.[61] It has an active side that shows itself as unbelief and hardness of heart.[62] As Bloesch has also written, sin is "positive rebellion" and an "attack upon the good."[63] The results of sin range from pride to cowardice, from envy to alienation, especially embracing a religiosity that seeks to control God for one's own ends.[64] The end result for the human is solipsism, the very thing that is uncharacteristic of God. Instead of being God's counterpart, the person has become God's counterpoint. God acts in the event of Jesus Christ.

Objective-subjective atonement. For Bloesch the supreme act of God's effort to transform the human as counterpoint into the human as counterpart is the atoning death of Jesus Christ. He writes, "The incarnation and the atonement are inseparable, but the gospel message focuses on the latter rather than the former."[65] And again: "The suffering of his life was also atoning but only in an anticipating sense. His atonement was not yet fulfilled until his cross and resurrection. It is not the sacrifices of his life but the sacrifice on Calvary that purchased our redemption."[66] God's justification of Jesus comes in the resurrection of Jesus which, as Bloesch says, keeps the cross from being a catastrophe, turning it instead into the place of victory. So the cross as the place of the execution of Jesus becomes, in the providence and power of God, the execution of death.[67]

Bloesch specifies the link between the objective atonement and its subjective pole in the Christian life this way:

> The atoning work of Christ is the basis of a biblical, evangelical spirituality. Here Christ is seen, not simply as the representative of fallen humanity nor as the model of the new humanity but as Mediator, Expiator, and Sin Bearer. Before he can be our example, he must be acknowledged as our Savior and Lord. True spirituality views the Christian life as primarily a sign and witness to the atoning work of Christ. The imitation of Christ is a token of our gratitude for his incomparable work of reconciliation and redemption on Calvary.[68]

In framing the doctrine of the atoning work of Christ, Bloesch strives for balance between these objective and subjective dimensions by eliminating the conjunction *and* and putting a hyphen in its place so that expression now reads objective-subjective. When this polarity is not maintained, erroneous accentuations of one pole or the other result. Examples of objectivism would include an absolutist form of predestination or an *ex opere operato* view of baptism. Examples of subjectivism would include any notion that treats experience as a source of salvation or faith as a human possibility sans the preaching of the cross in the power of the Holy Spirit.[69]

This balance between the objective and subjective carries over into all of the dimensions of Bloesch's soteriology, and it obviates the separation often noted between justification and sanctification, and between faith and love, while at the same time retaining a distinction between these elements.[70]

Bloesch's ordo salutis. This brings us to Bloesch's discussion of the *ordo salutis* in relation to the Christian life. Since the architectonics of Bloesch's position has already been outlined above, this section will discuss the detail of various elements of his *ordo salutis.*

Technically the distinction Bloesch draws between justification and sanctification goes like this. Justification is primarily a change in status for the believer who because of faith in Jesus Christ has a righteousness imputed to him or her. This changes the believer's status before God from that of the accused to the acquitted. The act of justification is complete and remains an enduring foundation. Sanctification, on the other hand, represents a change in being, imparts righteousness, but remains an incomplete process until it is completed at the consummation of the ages.[71]

When one repents and believes the gospel, one is justified before God. Bloesch wants to keep regeneration and conversion in a paradoxical unity, joining the divine work of regeneration and the human response as conversion.[72] Salvation is both from sin's guilt and power. Hence the response of conversion is grounded in the primal work of regeneration.

Since Bloesch calls this a paradox, I am trying to avoid an excessive temporal sequence between regeneration and conversion. As they occur, one might say that regeneration is the theologically prior event in the same way that preaching as a call to Christ is at least theologically prior (but not necessarily chronologically prior) to faith. It may be that with preaching faith simultaneously emerges.

Bloesch seeks to keep the temporal and eternal orders together in paradoxical unity giving primal priority to the Word of God (the objective) and a derivative but possibly simultaneous human response grounded in the work of the Holy Spirit (the subjective). This is the root of Bloesch's description of his theology as a "theology of Word and Spirit."[73] Thus the internal work of regeneration finds its counterpart in obedience and conformity to Christ on the part of the believer. Bloesch even calls regeneration the subjective pole of justification. In justification the believer is declared righteous and in regeneration he or she is engrafted into that righteousness as an active participant.[74]

While justification is a completed act, sanctification is only relatively achieved in one's mortal life. Bloesch avers that "our most lofty desires and virtues are tainted by sinful pretension. That is why we must repent of our virtues as well as our vices."[75] Only at the time of glorification when the believer faces Jesus Christ will the fullness of sanctification be realized and the process of purgation, fostered by responsible handling of what is illumined in one's life, be ended. Then the believer will be like Christ because he or she will see him as he is.

Bloesch does allow for a redefined Christian perfection in this life. Here "Christian perfection does not mean achieving moral rectitude but persevering in faith, remaining true to the gospel even in the midst of affliction and temptation."[76] What Bloesch has in mind is a perfection of spiritual maturity, but not an indefectible perfection.[77] Final purgation/glorification is the eschatological element in soteriology.

The Christian life as repentance. This means that for Bloesch, "The entire Christian life must be one of repentance, since we are summoned to fight against the sin within and around us, but we are assured of victory because of the presence and power of the Holy Spirit."[78] Again Bloesch writes,

> In much Protestant piety after the Reformation, sanctification follows regeneration: we are called to grow in the faith that becomes ours in the moment of decision. I hold that we must not only grow in faith but also return ever again to the Giver of faith. We need not only to repent of our sins when we are first confronted by the cross, but also to repent daily under the cross.[79]

Put this way, repentance is more of an initiating act of the Christian life than it is the initial act. By using the phrase "initial act" one is too tied to a temporal act, receding in significance as time moves on. By using the phrase "initiating act" one emphasizes the perduring quality of the initial repentance when one first responded in faith to the gospel message. The Word of the cross that created faith is the same Word that sustains faith. The Word of the cross that required repentance in the first place keeps repentance in place throughout one's Christian life.

The Christian life as means of grace. According to Bloesch, "We are not justified by a Christian life, but we are sanctified through a Christian life."[80] Again, Bloesch asks, "The Christian life is in one sense a fruit of conversion, but does not it also contribute to our conversion?"[81] In another context he suggests that the Christian life must also be seen as the subjective means of grace. The Word is given not only from faith but also to faith (Rom 1:17). The Word of God can be neither rightly perceived nor fully assimilated apart from seeking and believing. Nor can it be retained by those to whom it is given apart from their prayer, obedience and service.[82]

As I understand Bloesch, he does not attribute causality to the Christian life relative to sanctification. Yet what Christ has done for us "must be appropriated through the power of the Spirit in a life of obedience and piety."[83] Thus in Bloesch's mind, "The Christian life is not simply the fruit and consequence of a past salvation accomplished in the cross and resurrection of Christ but the arena in which Christ's salvation is carried forward to fulfillment by his Spirit."[84]

The Christian life as faith and love. When it comes to faith and love, faith is the subjective mode of justification and is the ground of love. Love is the subjective mode of sanctification and the fruit of faith. When faith and love are put together, Bloesch argues that believers are justified by faith alone and sanctified by faith and love.[85] Elsewhere Bloesch says,

We are justified by faith and sanctified by love. But even as faith is a gift of God, so love is also a gift, since this kind of love (agape) is not an element within our created nature. But just as faith is also a task calling for repentance and obedience, so love, too, is a task. Through the power of the Holy Spirit we can practice a love that is beyond natural human capacity—the self-sacrificing love of the cross.[86]

Bloesch's evangelical devotionism.[87] As I view Bloesch's argument, when a person hears the Word of the cross preached in the power of the Holy Spirit, a new freedom is granted enabling that person to repent and cling to Jesus Christ's mercy and grace.[88] Just as Bloesch does not want to separate the objective and subjective in the atonement, so he seeks to avoid a dualism in the act of being saved. He repudiates the separation of monergism from synergism by arguing that despite the free will of persons, they do not cooperate with God's grace but are liberated by God's grace in the power of the Spirit in order to believe and obey the gospel. This mystery or paradox of salvation is that God does all but wills to do it through human effort and decision.[89]

In earlier writings Bloesch cautioned against speaking of a natural human freedom, substituting instead the expression in Romans 8:21, namely "the glorious liberty of the children of God" (NKJV). He argued that "the paradox of salvation is that in the act of belief one is completely subjected to God and yet wholly free."[90] In advancing these paradoxical descriptions, both of the atonement and of soteriology, Bloesch is striving to maintain consistency with a spirituality that is radically theocentric and radically anthropocentric. God and humans in all of their distinctness are destined to be counterparts.

This implies the involvement of the whole person in the Christian life. Divine agency does not cancel human agency in Bloesch's soteriology. For this reason Bloesch prefers *evangelical devotionism* to either piety or devotionalism to characterize the Christian life. The term *piety* does not connote enough of commitment and will, whereas *devotionism* makes commitment and will paramount.[91]

Piety, for Bloesch, is too easily linked with multiple negatives. When piety and moralism are confused culturally, piety becomes an instrument of self-fulfillment. In reaction to this cultural phenomenon, the neo-orthodox emphasis on the objective act of God in Jesus Christ creates a separation between divine revelation and experience. Radical or secular theology makes the world rather than God the primary object of concern.[92] Moralism, as the attempt to make one worthy in God's sight, is a defeat of justification by grace through faith, robbing the believer of freedom in grace. Escapism from the world is the fruit of a piety that rejects servanthood as the mode of life in the world. For Bloesch this is often represented in the renunciation of relationships with the world in quest of mystical contemplation. Pharisaism lives by pretense to a spirituality one does not have and commits to disciplines that have only public acclaim. Perfectionism purports to believe that everything Christ demanded can be met, and thus the disciplines of the Christian life are turned into instruments of self-achievement rather than making the Christian more at the service of Christ and neighbor. Finally, rigorism almost makes adherence to the law a prerequisite for salvation.[93]

Over against all of these Bloesch argues for an evangelical devotionism (the passionate consecration of the whole person to God in repentance, faith, love and obedience) as the overarching thematization of the Christian life inclusive of the human response to divine grace at every point of the *ordo salutis*. Devotionism is a holy zeal, not a religious fanaticism:

> Fanaticism is the dedication of one's total life to the realization of one's dreams and desires. Holy zeal is the dedication of one's total life to him who is Lord and Judge of our dreams and desires. Fanaticism is

characterized by idolatrous enthusiasm and self-absorption. Holy zeal is characterized by self-emptying and self-giving love. Fanaticism is a fruit of the lust for power; holy zeal springs from the surrender of power to God.[94]

This kind of devotionism, or Christian freedom for obedience, as a response and witness to the grace of God, Bloesch claims,

is characterized not by exhibiting virtue but by radiating love. It is not do-goodism but generosity of spirit. It is compassionate daring on the basis of being loved by God. It is well doing on the basis of being well received by God. Our good works should be seen as the evidence of being blessed by God. What constitutes the Christian life is not morality (as the world understands this) but faith and its fruits.[95]

The impact of this quotation is that along with radiated love and generosity of spirit, Bloesch connects the Christian life more with faith and its fruit than with morality.

This is crucial. It often turns out that the more devoted people are, the more self-giving people are, the less they are acknowledged and appreciated. In a results-oriented culture—with its expectation of instant gratification—sacrificial service, especially when it is more taxing than triumphant, is hard to maintain over time. Believers often come to their death without knowing that their work has borne fruit. It is a loneliness with which Jesus was only too well acquainted. When this is the case, it is worth knowing that the earthly life of Jesus Christ, whom Christians call "Lord," also ended in what appeared to be defeat on the cross. The justification of Jesus' life and service came only after death in his resurrection by the God he called "Father."

Questions concerning Bloesch's evangelical devotionism. I would argue that Christians live not only by the justification that imputes an alien righteousness to them, but by the eschatological justification anticipated in the resurrection of the dead and the final judgment. According to Paul it is faith that acts in love and not love that acts in faith (Gal 5:6). Argued that way, faith sustains the acts of love because the believer knows that God will act in vindication, as God did in the resurrection of Jesus. Continued service to the gospel is not wasted effort. If love acted in faith, love would suffer and maybe even be terminated because love and vindication are not correlates. In the Christian faith, faith and vindication are correlative.

One of my concerns about Bloesch's doctrine of the Christian life is what appears to be his lack of treatment of the resurrection as a distinct locus of his theology in the published writings that I know. The believer's justification by grace through faith which is the perpetual link to the cross is, in my view, insufficient to give the believer the resources needed to maintain a healthy and hopeful evangelical devotionism when the service rendered seems to go for naught. True, Bloesch mentions the resurrection repeatedly, but I miss a specific link between the resurrection of Jesus Christ as vindication and the promised vindication of Jesus' followers who live and serve in light of Jesus' faith and love.

Bloesch rightfully stresses the regenerating work of the Holy Spirit and by implication, I think one could say, rejuvenating work of the same Spirit. But in order to keep the spirituality radically theocentric I think the vindicating act of God's resurrection as confirmation of Jesus Christ in spite of his humiliating and discrediting death is a work that requires equal billing along with the cross. In that way the believer is justified now even as a sinner and is justified eschatologically as a servant. Then faith can continue to act in love.

This eschatological element that ought to be present in evangelical devotionism cannot but raise the issue of faith and doubt. People who live devoted lives do not always sense that God reciprocates the fidelity. In the crucible of serving Christ and neighbor, people often feel that they spend more time in the Garden of Gethsemane than on the Mount of Transfiguration. Some people find the lament of Psalm 88 or the imprecations of Psalm 109 more true to life than the triumphal testimony of Psalm 107.

I use these psalms as a context for addressing Bloesch's assertion, "To be unfailingly effective prayer must be offered in the assurance of faith, for to doubt the ability or mercy of God is to sin against him. We should doubt ourselves, our own piety, our own worthiness, but we should never doubt the promises of God given in Holy Scripture."[96] In an earlier writing, Bloesch calls doubt "the intellectual form of sin."[97] Doubts of God's promises do occur but the source of them is the perduring sin, not the Holy Spirit's gift of faith.[98] In Bloesch's *Theological Notebook* doubt is attributed to a hardened heart.[99] Finally, "Questioning doubt is a sign of common grace; despairing doubt is the final fruit of original sin."[100]

My concern is that the experience of Christian life is more complex than these sentences seem to imply. Life tests the believer's faith and faithfulness both intensively as existential angst and extensively as unmitigated suffering over time. Bloesch's distinction between questioning doubt and despairing doubt is helpful, yet I am not sure that the author of Psalm 88 would separate the questioning doubt from despairing doubt. It is true that the sheer fact that he prayed and that in verse one he alludes to the hours of prayer indicates that neither total despair nor hardness of heart had taken over. Yet when crisis is deepest, one cannot separate emotional and intellectual doubt in any credible way. Tillich reports that what he learned from Martin Kähler was "the insight that the principle of justification through faith refers not only to the religious-ethical but also to the religious-intellectual life. Not only he who is in sin but also he who is in doubt is justified through faith."[101] Thus one can be both *simul justus et peccator* and *simul dubitur et creditur.*

Walter Brueggemann argues that in the psalms of anger there is a movement from owning the situation to yielding it and that prayer is the way one traverses the distance from owning to yielding.[102] Thus not all biblical prayer necessarily begins at a point of sincere trust or even purity of heart. Bloesch allows for defiant prayer and the struggle to change God's will. When he insists that our very prayers need to be redeemed, I think that relates to the issue of doubt. The very act of prayer itself is doubt's most effective combatant and is the act of one who is *simul dubitur et creditur.* In the act of prayer the theology of the cross proves its adequacy as much as in the daily combat against sin.

If the Christian life is a life of repentance, it is no less true in the practice of prayer than it is in the practice of Christian service. The same cross that redeems the life of a believer redeems his or her prayers as well, awaiting the final vindication of both a devoted life and a life of devotion. Then faith will pass away and love will remain (1 Cor 13:13).

To live a life of evangelical devotionism between the times requires a pious erudition and an erudite piety that (1) allows *theologia prima* both to question and learn from *theologia secunda* and (2) requires *theologia secunda* to learn how to love the questions that prayer raises, even willing at times to let the questions remain. An erudite *theologia secunda* knows that it needs pious *theologia prima* to keep it honest, and an erudite *theologia prima* knows that it needs a pious *theologia secunda* to keep it hopeful. Few theologians in the second half of the twentieth century have united the two as fully as Donald G. Bloesch. Where else can one find as erudite a piety and as pious an erudition as one discovers in his work?

Ten

Donald Bloesch as a Social Prophet

JAMES R. ROHRER

I feel that my vocation is to be a guide rather than a builder, a teacher rather than a confessor or martyr. But my hope is that I will be not merely a guide, but a herald as well; not merely a teacher, but also a prophet.[1]
DONALD G. BLOESCH

Throughout his long career Donald Bloesch has maintained a deep concern for the task of cultural analysis. Few developments of the post-World War II era have escaped his critical scrutiny. A dominant theme both of his classroom teaching and his theological writing has been the relationship between the kingdom of God and human culture. Repeatedly Bloesch has returned to this problem, challenging Christians to renounce the false gods of "culture religion" so that they might be free to speak an authentically prophetic word to humanity. The following essay probes this dimension of Bloesch's thinking, largely through the disciplinary lens of history.

Bloesch's Theology of Culture

Although Bloesch's theology of culture draws upon various theological strands, the influence of Karl Barth is clearly decisive. For Bloesch, as for Barth, the gulf between Creator and creature cannot be bridged by any means within human grasp. Humanity can know God only as God chooses to reveal himself, and this God has done uniquely and finally in Jesus Christ, as witnessed by Holy Scripture. Apart from this revelation there are no independent natural revelations, either historical or philosophical. While Bloesch acknowledges a sense in which God does reveal himself in nature and history, human sinfulness blinds us to this divine activity unless we have first been enlightened by Christ, who comes to us through the Holy Spirit in the proclamation of the gospel. Thus Christian theology, Bloesch asserts, rests solely upon divine self-disclosure rather than human speculation. "Whenever theology departs from its biblical foundations and appeals to a particular philosophy for validation of its truth-claims, it becomes another philosophy of religion and has thereby forfeited the right to speak on behalf of the church."[2]

Bloesch regards history as a field of cosmic conflict between Christ and Satan and has described the church as "a colony of heaven" in the midst of hostile territory.[3] The Christian community bears witness to the coming kingdom of God by faithfully proclaiming the gospel and working for social justice, but it does not fully embody the kingdom, nor can it build the kingdom by means of human exertion. The kingdom of God is an eschatological reality; its realization will signify the end of every human order. Whenever Christians forget this essential truth, Bloesch warns, they can no longer maintain their proper relationship to culture nor render effective service to their Lord. An obedient church will struggle ceaselessly against the forces of death in the social realm, and yet be inwardly detached from the transient values of this passing age and radically oriented toward the future dawning of a new heaven and earth.[4]

Throughout history, Bloesch asserts, the church has repeatedly failed to keep this eschatological horizon firmly in view. In every generation Christians have succumbed to the "ideological temptation," absolutizing the highest values of their culture and tailoring the gospel to fit the agenda of political and economic elites, secular ideologies or the reigning schools of philosophy. Repeatedly the church has been seduced by cultural values that are foreign to Scripture, readily surrendering the hard truths of biblical faith for the sake of political power, social influence or intellectual respectability.[5]

The German Christians of the 1930s and 1940s provide an excellent example of this deadly "ideological temptation," an illustration Bloesch often draws upon in his lectures and publications. The German church, he has frequently remarked, could be easily subverted because many of its leaders embraced natural theology, appealing to the political and cultural ethos of the German people as a source of revelation alongside Scripture. Reconceiving the gospel as a call to erect a new social order, German Christians came to understand discipleship in terms of "manly heroism." Some German theologians, Bloesch reminds us, reconceptualized God as the "Soul of the Germanic race" or the "Creative Spirit within the Volk." Having sacrificed biblical faith on the altar of nationalism, the doors of the church were left wide open to the entrance of fascist ideology and racial mysticism.[6]

The post-World War II era constitutes for Bloesch an age of barbarism unparalleled in history. Across the globe a host of idols compete for the allegiance of sin-blinded humanity: capitalism, communism, militarism, nationalism, technocracy, scientism, hedonistic individualism and an almost endless list of others. In the face of this demonic reality the modern church has too often chosen the path of accommodation rather than costly discipleship, proclaiming a lifeless "culture religion" in place of the gospel of Jesus Christ. This seduction of the church, Bloesch has warned, has not been limited to liberal Protestant circles, although its progress is perhaps most complete among mainline liberals. Evangelical Protestants as well as many Roman Catholics have likewise succumbed to the "ideological temptation," effectively "burying the gospel" beneath a trash heap of contending ideologies and causes, leaving only a remnant of biblically oriented Christians scattered among the various churches of the world.[7]

Since the early 1980s Bloesch has often called upon orthodox believers in every tradition to unite in a new Confessing Church movement, similar to that which challenged the distortions of German Christianity during the Nazi regime. The time is coming soon, he wrote in 1981, "when the church will have to define itself as the true church over against the false church."[8] This prophetic impulse has motivated much, if not all, of his theological efforts. The job of the modern theologian, Bloesch once asserted, is

> to demythologize not the biblical myth or saga, which is the divinely chosen vessel of the Word of God, but the secular myths of our time. We are also called to deideologize the cultural dogmatisms of the contemporary world, whether these be racism, nationalism, social determinism, naturalistic hedonism, humanism or scientism. Surely it is also incumbent upon Christian theologians to dereligionize an idolatrous culture, to expose and seek to overthrow the modern Molochs that beguile man in the secular city.[9]

This statement aptly captures one of the most characteristic features of Bloesch's theology: his effort to transcend ideological presuppositions. While acknowledging that people will inevitably have ideological preferences, he insists that Christians must self-consciously subject their own positions to judgment and correction by the holy Word of God.[10] This conviction has led Bloesch to refrain from wholehearted acceptance of contemporary social movements, even those which he most admires. Likewise it is difficult to place him squarely within any recent theological camp or intellectual school. While always insisting that Christians must be radically committed to acting out their faith within society, he has nonetheless maintained a certain critical distance from the successive causes and movements which have passed across the stage of modern history. He belongs to neither the left nor the right, and has been attacked by critics on all sides of the ideological spectrum.

Bloesch as a Social Prophet, 1950s-1980

A retrospective glance at Bloesch's theological career reveals the centrality of the prophetic note from the very beginning. During the 1950s he strongly criticized American Christianity for its idolatrous spirit, manifested most glaringly in the unquestioned support given to the West in the cold war. Regarding American "practical materialism" and Marxist dialectical materialism as equally alien to biblical faith, he called upon Christians to completely disassociate from the cold war and to take a firm stand against the use of nuclear weapons. "There is also a growing pathological obsession with our own security," Bloesch warned, which distorts the moral character of society. Christian support for the arms race could not advance the cause of human freedom, but only hasten civilization's "progression toward dictatorship or anarchy."[11]

Bloesch likewise saw in the postwar revival of religion the triumph of secularism within the American church. The upsurge in popular piety was not grounded upon faith in the holy God who speaks through Scripture, Bloesch observed, but instead reflected Christian captivity to the false gods of American culture. Many people, he argued, turned to the churches and eagerly embraced religion only because influential political and business interests "have found institutional religion to be useful and have therefore lent the church support." Church attendance signified little more than loyalty to the American way of life, and pastors encouraged this attachment by saying nothing to contradict the idolatrous "mores and folkways of the culture."[12]

Resurgent evangelicalism offered no alternative to mainline cultural complacency. Bloesch criticized Billy Graham, perhaps the most widely recognized leader of the postwar revival, for his reluctance to speak out against such social evils as racism and militarism. Despite Graham's admirable Christocentrism, he exhibited a "strange lack of prophetic insight . . . which would arouse certain opposition from vested interests." Graham's preaching, Bloesch argued, focused too much upon such cultural fixations as "happiness" and "contentment," while his image of the converted sinner looked suspiciously like the Victorian "bourgeois ideal of the respectable and cultivated citizen."[13]

Bloesch envisioned a church that would be radically committed to the conversion and transformation of the world, yet at the same time detached from the dominant values of society. To employ H. Richard Niebuhr's classic typology, he sought a blending of the "Christ transforming culture" and the "Christ against culture" models. Throughout the turbulent 1960s, as American churches became increasingly polarized over such issues as the civil rights revolution and the Vietnam War, he struggled to strike a balance that would preserve the paradoxical nature of Christian discipleship. On the one hand the church had to attack injustice; on the other hand it must not equate struggles for peace and social justice with the reconciliation accomplished in Jesus Christ. An authentically prophetic church, he insisted, could never sever the call for righteousness from the faithful proclamation of the gospel, the divine Word which stands in judgment over every human ideology and movement.

Thus Bloesch welcomed the increased commitment to social action exhibited by churches in the 1960s, even as he sharply rejected the radical turn in theology that helped to spark this commitment. The new secular and political theology, associated with such thinkers as Harvey Cox, Schubert Ogden, Paul Van Buren and John A. T. Robinson, represented an admirable attempt to relate the gospel to the pressing social issues of the age, yet failed to recognize the essential distinction between secular and sacred, Christ and culture, church and world. The new theological mood could be sustained, Bloesch charged, only at the expense of biblical authority. Thinkers like Ogden, Cox and Robinson had lost "sight of the transcendent holy God of the Bible who stands over against the world of His creatures and brings their fallacious and idolatrous dreams and plans to naught."[14]

These convictions conditioned his response to both the civil rights and Vietnam crises. As a long-time advocate of racial equality, Bloesch rejoiced that the church was at last addressing the pressing sin of racism in American society. For far too long many of the nation's churches had proclaimed a gospel divorced from "the agonizing turbulent world"; at last they were moving toward "concrete or incarnational witnessing." Yet, Bloesch pointed out, the liberation envisioned in such slogans as "We Shall Overcome" and

"Freedom Now" was qualitatively different from the liberation promised in the biblical message that "God was in Christ reconciling the world unto himself." Without denying the deeply biblical perspective of many civil rights advocates, Bloesch saw in the fundamental message of the movement "a type of folk religion" centered on the classical liberal conception of liberty and equality. There was a real danger, Bloesch warned, that many theologians and preachers failed to make this distinction and so confounded the beloved community sought by civil rights workers with the kingdom of God. Christians needed to demand both an end to racism and conversion to Christ. To promote racial justice without evangelism sacrificed that which is specifically unique in our Christian witness.[15]

Likewise Bloesch regarded the American war effort in Vietnam as "criminal" and "barbaric" and urged Christians to protest against the conflict. In a pamphlet entitled "This Immoral War: Why We Protest," which was distributed at the 1968 Iowa Republican Convention, he indicted the United States government for hypocrisy and murder. "The real heroes today," he concluded, "are not the soldiers who bomb villages or torture prisoners but rather the conscientious objectors."[16]

Yet Bloesch never called for unilateral withdrawal from Vietnam, and he distanced himself from the more militant expressions of antiwar activism. Opposition to the war, he insisted, must itself follow biblical models of righteousness. Amidst a national wave of campus violence, he wrote in 1970 that despite the criminal actions of the government, Christians are obligated to respect secular authority. "There is no place in the Christian strategy," he proclaimed, "for the burning of draft cards, the adulation of leaders of enemy nations, or the desecration of the national flag."[17]

As American churches became ever more polarized on social issues, Bloesch expressed concern that both conservative and liberal Christians had aligned themselves too closely to political ideologies that were distracting them from their primary call to proclaim the gospel. Where once he had denounced the apathetic acquiescence of Christians in the face of massive social evil, he now warned against uncritical support for political causes that had little biblical justification. Too many Christian leaders, he complained in 1970, lacked the ability to distinguish between spiritual and purely secular concerns. As a result, American churches were rushing to influence public policy on a host of issues in which the moral implications were ambiguous at best, such as the legal voting age, the status of China in the United Nations and trade relations with Cuba. In seeking to define a Christian position in such debates, Bloesch insisted, the church exceeded its competency and dangerously blurred the boundary between ecclesiastical and civil authority.[18]

Despite such criticism Bloesch certainly was not retreating to an apolitical stance. He has continued throughout his career to urge Christian involvement in social action whenever he has perceived a fundamental biblical principle to be at stake. Among the many issues he has addressed are the proliferation of nuclear arms and other weapons of mass destruction, the pollution of the environment, the new sexual morality, drug addiction, the population explosion, abortion, racial discrimination and factory farming and other forms of inhumane exploitation of animals.[19]

The problem, for Bloesch, has always been to keep ultimate and penultimate concerns in their proper relationship. "The great theologians of the past," he observed in a 1979 critique of liberation theology, demonstrated their faith in lives of witness and service, yet they "saw the primary purpose of the church as the saving of souls from divine judgment and hell rather than the improvement of the human lot here on earth." Works of love and justice, Bloesch insisted, are the necessary fruits of a living faith, but must not be identified with faith "or else we are once again in the morass of works-righteousness against which the Reformation directed its protest." Faithful Christians engage in the struggle for social justice in response to the love of God for humanity and as preparation for leading sinners to know Jesus Christ. But they will always remember that any justice obtainable here on earth is proximate justice that still falls far short of the kingdom of God. The church's ultimate concern, therefore, must ever be to point people to Christ, who alone can bring about an authentic revolution in human consciousness and society.[20]

Bloesch's Engagement with Feminism

Bloesch's ambivalent response to recent movements for social justice reflects his struggle to rise above ideological presuppositions. The essential freedom of theology from ideology has been a constant theme throughout his career. This concern, however, has emerged in his writings with ever greater urgency during the last two decades as overtly politicized theological movements have gained increasing influence within the postmodern church. Foremost among these movements is feminism, a phenomenon that Bloesch has critiqued in especially great depth.

At times calling himself a "biblical feminist," Bloesch has always fully supported the movement to achieve women's rights in society and has strongly insisted on "the dignity and equality of man and woman before God."[21] This includes support for the ordination of women to ecclesiastical office, which he believes to be upheld by biblical models of women who received gifts to exercise religious authority. Defining patriarchalism as a sin that treats women as property, he concedes that the church has historically been held captive by a patriarchal ideology that has tragically denied women their full stature in Christ. This conviction has led him repeatedly to challenge conservative Christian critics of feminism to understand the valid reasons for the feminist revolt. Opponents of feminist ideology, he has asserted, need to see in patriarchalism an equally dangerous and sinful idol and must be willing to subject it to the same degree of critical scrutiny.[22]

At the same time Bloesch has roundly criticized the ideological underpinnings of the feminist movement, especially those strands of ecofeminism that have aligned themselves with "deep ecology" and the neopagan mysticism associated with the Green social agenda. At the heart of much feminist social theory, he has rightly observed, lies an essentially panentheistic view of reality that fundamentally contradicts the biblical vision of God and the creation. According to this view both patriarchy and the environmental crisis stem from the Judeo-Christian conception of a transcendent God who has established a dualism between humankind and nature and who has given to humanity dominion over the creation. Regarding this as an inherently exploitative vision, many feminist theorists postulate instead a divinized cosmos in which all things exist as part of an interrelated, sacred whole.

Bloesch has stridently opposed the efforts of feminist theologians to reconceptualize God according to this mystical, neonatural worldview. Long before the furor sparked by the 1994 "Re-Imagining" Conference, Bloesch warned that feminist theology was drawing on sources more akin to Neo-Platonic mysticism and gnosticism than to biblical faith. Many feminist theologians aimed at nothing less than the creation of a new religion.

In *The Battle for the Trinity* (1985) he argued that the move toward inclusive God-language in the mainline churches threatened to replace the ontological Trinity with an essentially unitarian and impersonal conception of God. "The God of the Bible," Bloesch asserted, "is not a democracy. . . . It is important to understand that it is not we who name God, but it is God who names himself by showing us who he is." Alternative names for God proposed by feminist revisionists, such as "Primal Matrix," "God/ess," "Cosmic Benefactor" or "Womb of Being," invariably obscure essential dimensions of the biblical witness about the triune God and brazenly impose on the text thought patterns drawn from an ideology which is inimical to biblical revelation.[23]

In characteristic fashion Bloesch has sought to overcome the ideological polarization within the church by defining a biblical position that transcends both patriarchalism and feminism. He has called his own position, which he outlined in his book *Is the Bible Sexist?* (1982), "covenantalism." Bloesch begins with an acknowledgment that the biblical writers lived in a patriarchal culture, and that the biblical text clearly reflects this historical reality. Yet his sacramental understanding of scriptural authority, which makes a distinction between form and content, allows him to argue that the unconditioned divine Word that speaks through the culturally conditioned biblical text transcends and transforms the patriarchal context of the human authors. The revelation of God in Christ negates both patriarchalism and feminism by giving us a model of Christian marriage that is grounded upon a covenant of grace.

Within the covenant of marriage, Bloesch argues, the male has "representative headship," just as Christ is head of the church. But with Christ as his model, the Christian husband realizes this headship in a manner fundamentally different from headship in a patriarchal system. For as Christ emptied himself, taking the role of a servant who sacrificed himself for his church, so too the Christian husband must exercise headship by sacrificially dying to self. There is no room for patriarchal assertions of power; the husband must freely offer up his life for the welfare of his family and the kingdom of God. Likewise the subordination implied in the covenant model of male-female relations is not servile submission, but rather what John Howard Yoder has termed "revolutionary subordination," a freely chosen humbling of oneself in imitation of Christ. In short, while the Bible adheres to the form of the patriarchal marriage, the revelation of God in Christ has fundamentally transformed the content. The Christian marriage involves a mutual self-giving, a mutual surrender to Christ, whose grace unites the man and woman in partnership for service to the kingdom of God.[24]

Human language cannot fully capture the paradox involved in this transformation. We can speak, Bloesch argues, both of the headship of the male and of the full equality of male and female, just as we speak of the full equality of Father, Son and Spirit and yet acknowledge some primacy of the Father within the Godhead. What is clear is that the New Testament revelation precludes men and women from either seeking domination over the other or escaping into individual self-fulfillment. The Christian marriage is a covenant partnership with God, who seeks to bend both male and female to serve the kingdom. "The God of the Bible cannot be aligned with either patriarchalist or feminist ideology," Bloesch has written.

> Biblical teaching contradicts both subservience to earthly authority and emancipation from the strictures of tradition in order to realize personal goals. The God upheld in biblical religion cannot be reduced to either the Sky Father or the Earth Mother. He is not simply above or below but over, in, with, and around us. He is a King who overthrows all human conceptions of kingship and lordship. He is sole ruler of the world and sole Savior of humankind, but he desires to make us covenant partners with him in manifesting and demonstrating his work of reconciliation and redemption. He relates to us as Father, Son and Spirit, but he also acts in ways that sometimes permit us to describe him as mother, sister, and brother. His name is Father, Son and Spirit, but his ways with us call forth a myriad of images and metaphors that simply cannot be subsumed under either patriarchy or monarchy.[25]

I have quoted this entire lengthy passage because it touches on so many crucial dimensions of Bloesch's theology of culture. With God we deal not with an impersonal abstraction or a projection of our own subjective human experience, but with our sovereign Ruler and Savior who relates to us intimately as Father, Son and Spirit. These are not mere human metaphors but rather God's own self-designation that we are not at liberty to set aside. As finite creatures we are at all times utterly dependent upon God's sovereign action, but we are not passive. Graciously called to a life of obedient discipleship, we become "covenant partners," witnessing to the surrounding culture that God has reconciled and redeemed the world in Jesus Christ. Only in this life of revolutionary subordination to Christ can we find fulfillment; all attempts to shape history according to our own human conceptions of truth and justice will inevitably fail.

Critical Assessment of Bloesch's Accomplishment

In recent decades there has been an unmistakable shift in the theological center of gravity away from a biblical theology of transcendence toward an emphasis upon divine immanence within nature and human history. Donald Bloesch has firmly resisted this movement. In a postmodern age that champions toleration and glories in pluralism, he has unambiguously labeled the dominant drift in theology as apostasy. Perhaps no other theologian of our era has more consistently and perceptively identified the essential conflict between biblical faith and many of the political and intellectual fixations of our age. And perhaps no theologian has so pointedly and even-handedly challenged Christians of every ideological and theological orientation to recognize the full extent of our accommodation to the idols of our time. In the long view of history this prophetic insight may well prove to be Bloesch's most precious gift to the church.

Despite my basic agreement with his position I am troubled by several points where Bloesch seems to weaken or even undercut his own prophetic purpose. We have already mentioned his long-standing commitment to social justice and his belief that authentic faith will necessarily show forth in acts of love and mercy toward our neighbors. Yet in his desire to keep the eschatological horizon in view, to maintain the clear distinction between the kingdom of God and human culture he approaches concrete social movements with extreme caution and urges the church to avoid entanglement in causes that are "purely secular." This effort to differentiate between the sacred and secular is problematic. Can we say with integrity to the biblical witness that any issue is "purely secular"? Is there not a spiritual dimension to all of human existence, making every question before us at least potentially a theological question?

Moreover, even if we recognize an essential dichotomy between sacred and secular realms, how do we discern the boundary between them within the social sphere? By what criteria do we determine which contemporary issues clearly involve a biblical concern and thus demand Christian action, and which issues the church should refrain from addressing? Without a fuller delineation of his criteria, Bloesch opens himself to the charge of being arbitrary in his decisions. Can we, for example, confidently say that factory farming and the population explosion (a hotly debated concept) involve fundamental spiritual issues while the role of China in the United Nations does not? After all, from the perspective of many Christians in Taiwan (where I have until recently served as a missionary) the matter of nonrepresentation in the United Nations involves the most basic and vital questions of human dignity and justice, concerns that demand the attention of the Taiwanese church.

Likewise it would be helpful for Bloesch to delineate more carefully his conception of culture and the role of culture in the process of revelation. Throughout his career he has consistently (and properly) sought to balance a Christ-transforming-culture orientation with a more negative Christ-against-culture approach. Hence he can insist with Barth that Christians must live with a Bible in one hand and a newspaper in the other, seeking to relate the gospel to the real concerns of their cultural milieu. Yet at the same time he wishes to guard against the false notion that culture is a source of revelation. God is always distinct from the creation, and cultural values, no matter how noble, are always distorted by sin. Thus Christians must regard "the point of contact with the world as a point of conflict."[26]

Clearly Bloesch's theological method accords to culture a positive if ambiguous role in our spiritual journey. He has spoken of culture as "the arena God has appointed for humans to realize their destiny in service to his glory." Culture is the context in which "the people of God are tested and prepared for eternity." Although it cannot be identified with the kingdom of God, it can nonetheless be used by God as a "parable of the kingdom" that is to come.[27] In short, culture must be neither condemned nor absolutized. It is part of God's good creation and capable of reflecting the glory of God. At the same time it is tarnished by sin, and in need of redemption.

Although he assigns to culture a positive role in human life, when we survey the sweep of Bloesch's theological writings, the negative dimension of culture clearly emerges as the dominant theme. Despite his conviction that the gospel must be addressed to people in their concrete cultural milieu, he does not develop the point in any specificity nor explain the implications of this insight for the church's missionary mandate. At the same time, however, he frequently launches into strident criticism of those who seek to accommodate the gospel to culture. Thus Bloesch leaves his readers with the vague and perhaps unintended impression that the effort to contextualize the Christian message is a dangerous game, an undertaking that almost inevitably compromises biblical faith.

And contextualization *is*, of course, a risky enterprise, one that far too often is pursued uncritically to the detriment of our Christian witness. Nonetheless no task is more necessary if the church is going to fulfill its missionary and prophetic mandates. Although the term *contextualization* is relatively new, dating only to the 1970s, the Jerusalem Council clearly had the principle in mind when it decided that Gentiles could follow Christ without first becoming culturally Jewish (Acts 15). And the contextualization of the gospel has continued to occur ever since, whenever Christianity has crossed a new cultural frontier or Christianized societies have undergone cultural change. The growth of Christianity from a tiny sect in Palestine to a global religion that embraces people in thousands of discreet ethnolinguistic contexts has been possible only because the gospel message has been constantly re-represented in ever new cultural forms.

Surely then we must regard culture as more than an arena in which we are tested and prepared for eternity. Culture, while not a source of revelation, must nonetheless be regarded as an essential component of the very process of revelation itself. The incarnation suggests that we can hear the divine Word only when it becomes human, and human communication necessarily takes place within a culturally conditioned world of discourse. Unless the gospel is effectively contextualized, presented both in word and deed in a culturally appropriate fashion, those outside the Christian community of faith will have no genuine opportunity to hear and respond to the Word of God.

Contextualization need not compromise the integrity of the gospel or weaken the church's prophetic impact upon culture. Bloesch is surely correct that there is a demonic element within every society, and that the point of contact with the world is thus necessarily a point of spiritual conflict. I would contend, however, that it is only where the church has been organized along culturally appropriate lines that the true offense of the gospel will be felt and genuine repentance will be evident.

This criticism of Bloesch's position, of course, involves a question of emphasis more than principle. Bloesch's theological method so far as I can determine is completely commensurate with the contextualization task. It is indeed vitally relevant to that task, for we need always to remember that our message is not a matter of human speculation. Revealed truth must not be changed. As Donald McGavran has aptly observed, "The missionary is free to change the shape of the earthen vessel so that it may be more acceptable to men of another culture. He is not free in any way to change the treasure which the vessel carries."[28]

Bloesch's condemnation of "culture religion" seems to parallel Paul Hiebert's critique of "uncritical contextualization," the uncritical acceptance of existing cultural patterns in such a way that the gospel is emptied of its prophetic power and the original message is lost. Hiebert's distinction between critical and uncritical contextualization is most helpful, because it keeps in balance both the positive and the negative poles of culture and helps us to maintain our biblical focus even as we engage in the necessary task of adjusting our presentation of the gospel.[29] Precisely this sort of balance would make Bloesch's cultural critique even more effective.

Such criticism, however, does not diminish Bloesch's tremendous contribution. As Christianity prepares to enter its third millennium more deeply divided than at any point in history, his call to resist the "ideological temptation" assumes ever greater significance. The polarization of Christians on a host of intractable social and political issues has created an increasingly fragmented church, not only in the West but also throughout the non-Western world. Despite frequently heard rhetoric about unity within diversity, we increasingly lack even a minimal theological ground for dialogue. The reality of our sometimes virulent intramural feuding threatens to eclipse ecumenical hopes for a truly global catholic church, one that is diverse in language and culture yet unified in Spirit and mission.

It is sobering that at many Christian gatherings the rhetoric of the "culture wars" is more evident than the unique language of Scripture. In such a situation we need to hear the challenge that Bloesch's theology lays before us: to take our ideological preoccupations and political agendas to the cross, to truly die to ourselves in order that we might live exclusively for the Christ who stands in judgment over all our feeble human efforts to shape history. We desperately need to recover our sense of awe at standing in the presence of a holy and almighty God, a God whose righteousness and love both far transcend anything that we can humanly conceive, before whom all of our causes and stratagems are as nothing. Only then will the divisions that cripple us be healed. Only then will we recover the freedom to become, through the power of the Holy Spirit, the prophetic church of Jesus Christ.

Eleven

Donald Bloesch Responds

DONALD G. BLOESCH

I AM DEEPLY GRATEFUL TO ELMER COLYER FOR ARRANGING THIS TRIBUTE TO MY work by leading theologians today and for allowing me to respond to their comments and critiques. I am especially pleased that the contributors represent different positions within the theological spectrum, though with one or two exceptions all identify themselves as evangelical. The goal of my writing and teaching has been to build bridges between various evangelical positions in the search for evangelical and catholic unity in the church today. This book is a modest step toward overcoming the barriers that continue to divide biblical Christians, and I thank all the contributors as well as InterVarsity Press for making it possible.

On Olson

Roger Olson has given a helpful analysis of my theological pilgrimage. He is right that my spiritual roots lie in Germanic and Swiss Pietism. The fact that my maternal grandfather studied at the Basel Mission and my paternal grandfather at the St. Chrischona Pilgrim Mission (also in Basel) is revealing in this regard. I have nevertheless had significant exposure to the tradition of American evangelicalism as evidenced in my participation in InterVarsity Christian Fellowship while a student at the University of Chicago, my work with Young Life and my teaching at the Wheaton Graduate School of Theology and Ontario Theological Seminary (now Tyndale College and Seminary).

Concerning Olson's discomfiture with my reservations about narrative theology and open-view theism, I do not deny that there is much that is promising in both theological innovations. They manifest a growing uneasiness on the part of many evangelicals with both propositional revelation and decretal determinism, which subverts human responsibility and freedom. We need to recover the narrational form of revelation as well as the paradox of divine election through the instrumentality of human decision and obedience. My quarrel with narrative theology is that first it loses sight of the propositional dimension of biblical revelation, and second it tends to keep us within the confines of the biblical text rather than lead us out of the text to the living reality to which the text points. With regard to my critique of open-view theism, I fully share with all who espouse this position their concern for human responsibility in the working out of salvation. My only caveat is that we must continue to affirm the sovereignty of divine grace as well as human freedom. God allows us freedom, but he still maintains a considerable measure of control. To affirm pure contingency is to deny that God is guiding human history toward a predetermined goal. The need today, especially in evangelical circles, is to recover the element of paradox and mystery in our faith affirmations (I am not sure whether Olson would agree).

Olson is surely correct in perceiving the theological and historical roots of the evangelical movement in both the first Reformation (the magisterial Reformers and the Anabaptists) and the second Reformation (Puritanism, Pietism and evangelical revivalism). He might also have mentioned the third Reformation (the Pentecostal and charismatic awakening), which has left a lasting imprint on evangelicalism as a whole. This movement has not played a major role in my own spiritual pilgrimage, but it has definitely altered the landscape of modern evangelicalism. I have had some fruitful interaction with charismatics in both Catholic and mainline Protestant churches through participation in Allies for Faith and Renewal, which was based in Ann Arbor, Michigan. There has been a positive response to my writings in some Pentecostal circles, including the Pentecostal Bible College in Peterborough, Ontario.

On Grenz

I am truly grateful for the contribution of Stanley Grenz, since it helps pinpoint the areas of tension between myself and evangelical rationalists as well as postconservative evangelicals. His analysis of my theological method is perceptive and balanced.

Like Olson, Grenz sees me as a mediating theologian. This term is fully acceptable if it refers to my endeavor to bring together the various traditions that constitute Christian faith. But it is not accurate if it creates the impression that I seek to mediate between Christ and culture or between theology and current philosophy (neither Olson nor Grenz implies this). Mediation in this sense was the bane of culture-Protestantism or neo-Protestantism, which Barth rightly warned against. Part of my difficulty with the German Christian movement in the 1930s was that it elevated culture as a fundamental source of both revelation and theology and thereby denigrated the role of Scripture in shaping theology. It was recognition on the part of some church leaders and theologians of the peril of accommodation to the cultural ideology of National Socialism that led to the Barmen Declaration.

With Grenz I affirm the universal light of God's presence in all histories and cultures. The question is: How can we discern or understand this light? I stand with a formidable number of fathers and doctors of the church in contending that only in the light of God's self-revelation in Christ do we adequately grasp the full meaning and impact of these lesser lights in non-Christian culture and experience (compare Ps 36:9). I do affirm culture as a source for theologizing but not as a norm for determining theological truth. We need to utilize the language and concepts that culture and philosophy provide, but we must be adamant in refusing to allow these concepts to subvert the meaning of divine revelation. We do not reach divine wisdom by building upon cultural self-understanding, but we come to appreciate the broken lights that culture reflects when we are fully anchored in the divine revelation that transcends every culture, even that which is reflected in holy Scripture.

Grenz raises the question of whether there are points of contact between faith and unbelief. I believe that we are obliged to search for sociological and psychological points of contact with our listeners. How can we communicate effectively unless we speak in the language of our hearers? Yet we must resist creating theological points of contact, because divine revelation signifies a structure of meaning that overturns rather than crowns or completes the human quest for meaning and purpose in life.

Grenz also argues that my theology is too individualistic and that the idea of community needs to be more clearly articulated. I believe that I address this issue in some of my earlier works (for example, *Centers of Christian Renewal*,[1] *Wellsprings of Renewal*[2] and *The Reform of the Church*[3]) and have continued this reflection in the first two volumes of my Christian Foundations where I discuss the role of the church mainly in relation to theological authority and revelation. The church's role in salvation history will be a major theme in the sixth volume of the Christian Foundations series. Grenz and I may have differences in this area, but I don't think they are substantial. I see the basis of revelation not in human community but in the eternal decision of God to communicate his will and purpose to his people. When God speaks community is created, not only between God and the individual human subject but also among believers. Community is a sign of the reality of the presence of God with his people. Faith gives rise to community, and community is the seedbed in which faith flourishes.

On the relation between human culture and the kingdom of God, I give an in-depth treatment of this subject in the chapter "God the Civilizer" in my *Freedom for Obedience*[4] and in *Jesus Christ: Savior & Lord*[5] (chapter nine), which was not available to Grenz at the time of his writing. My position then and now is that the kingdom of God represents both the fulfillment of the longings and aspirations of human culture and the negation of the hubris that inevitably corrupts human culture because of sin. Both Augustine and John Calvin had a clear-cut vision for culture as well as for the church, but they saw human culture standing in need of reformation and redemption in the light of God's revelation in Jesus Christ. I think Grenz would agree that we do not want a Christ domesticated by culture but a Christ who is himself a transformer of culture. My problem with Grenz is that he tends to see mainly promise in cultural achievements and not also deception and self-aggrandizement. As Christians we are free to enjoy and appreciate the achievements of culture without placing our trust in any cultural ideology or social program that claims to be a panacea for the human condition. In a viable biblical, evangelical theology culture is neither deified nor demonized but relativized. It points us to some truths about the human predicament, but it does not of itself provide saving truth—the truth that redeems from sin, death and hell. This is found only in Jesus Christ, who enters human culture from the beyond and at the same time guides culture toward a transcendental goal.

On the allegation that my theology shows the imprint of Reformed pessimism, I retort that this describes only one side of my faith vision. I see myself as a provisional pessimist, because I am alert to the human proclivity to sin, but as an ultimate optimist because I affirm the sovereignty and invincibility of God's grace. Nations may fall, churches may compromise and falter, but the kingdom of God irreversibly advances in human history and is destined to overcome all obstacles. I believe that both John Calvin and Karl Barth were fundamentally optimists because of their faith in divine providence and predestination. Mark Noll, in his foreword to the second edition of my book *The Future of Evangelical Christianity*,[6] comments that he is struck by what he calls my "surprising optimism." We need to affirm both human depravity and divine grace, but grace is greater than our sin, God's *yes* is more powerful than our *no*, God's kingdom will triumph even when our faith is weak and uncertain. I hope that Grenz will join me in embracing this biblical, grace-centered optimism, which will always be tempered by a biblical realism that is not surprised by human failings while recognizing that the outcome of history is already assured through God's intervention in our space and time in Jesus Christ.

I have one final comment on Grenz's provocative essay. I would not say that a theologian will never "get it right," since on occasion the Spirit may grant the believer a true grasp of God's will and purpose, even of God's being and of human being. Yet our apprehension of God and his gospel will always be imperfect: adequate for salvation but not for a final system of truth. We can construct a worldview on the basis of the biblical story, but we must never identify this worldview with revelation itself. An articulation of a metaphysical vision will always be open-ended and subject to further elucidation. I want to avoid both a metaphysical skepticism that refrains from even raising metaphysical questions and a theological hubris that claims to have the full picture of ultimate reality.

On Dulles

I am very pleased that Avery Dulles has been included in this symposium, since he is trying to recover the indisputable evangelical heritage of Roman Catholicism without compromising basic Catholic convictions. He rightly notes that he and I have much in common, since we are both working to renew our respective churches from within.

The problem is whether the evangelical and biblical witness that Catholicism builds upon can be fully harmonized with all of the teachings of that communion. I believe the church needs again and again to be reformed and corrected in the light of the infallible and abiding Word of God, which is not simply Scripture in and of itself but the gospel of God, which we come to know through the preaching and reading of Scripture and the interior illumination of the Spirit. I think it can be shown that the Catholic Church itself has been too open to the rationalistic temptation to clarify mysteries that would be better left as mysteries. I here have in mind such doctrines as transubstantiation and the immaculate conception of Mary. At the same time

I heartily agree with Dulles that church and Scripture should ideally complement one another and that Scripture remains lifeless unless its teachings are lived out in the community of the faithful.

On the enigmatic relation of theology and philosophy, I contend that philosophy can indeed be helpful to theologians by providing us with the conceptual tools by which we articulate the claims of faith for our time. The danger arises when philosophy claims too much and thereby makes divine revelation irrelevant or illusory. Dulles errs when he accuses me of rejecting "the very idea of philosophic thought." I reject only the conclusions that philosophy (the creative thought of the natural person) comes to concerning God, humanity and the world. Philosophy can be celebrated as the pinnacle of natural human reasoning, but human wisdom must never be identified with the transcendent wisdom of God (compare Is 55:8-9). My approach to philosophy is utilitarian rather than complementarian. The theologian should be free to use philosophical insights and concepts to elucidate the meaning of faith but should not see philosophical claims as complementary to the claims of the gospel. Philosophy is not a salvific preparation for theology but a useful tool in the hands of discerning theologians. I confess that I have learned much from such philosophical luminaries as Plato, Kant and Kierkegaard, even Nietzsche and Whitehead. (Kierkegaard was actually a theologian who wrote in the guise of a philosopher.) What I reject is a synthesis of philosophy and Christian faith so that the idea of God advanced by the philosophers becomes identical with the idea of God given in biblical revelation. I think I have both Augustine and Thomas Aquinas on my side, since both of them made clear that the God of philosophic thought is definitely not the God of revelation.

While I have on rare occasions referred to my position as a revelational fideism, I have made clear in Word & Spirit[7] and elsewhere that this is a very qualified fideism and that the dialectical interplay between Word and Spirit is more representative of my position. I reject what is generally thought of as fideism, since I do not anchor theological reflection in a leap of faith but instead see this reflection as belonging to the response of faith to an objective revelation given by God in holy Scripture. Faith moreover involves rational assent as well as trust and surrender. Dulles would indeed agree with these asseverations, but he questions my reluctance to assign a creative role to reason before faith or in preparation for faith. I hold that the Spirit of God may indeed be working through natural means in pointing people to the gospel, but this is always in contradiction to the way people prefer to think and act.

When I say that revelation overthrows reason, I mean the sinful direction of our reasoning, not the structures of reason itself. Reason needs to be placed on a new foundation if it is to apprehend and serve the truth of divine revelation. I am not certain whether Dulles would concur in this judgment.

On the question of dialogue with the world religions, I am most certainly in favor of the principle of dialogue. It is the purpose of dialogue that is the source of contention. From my theological perspective dialogue should be carried out not in order to arrive at a synthesis that encompasses the truth in both positions but in order to clarify the positions of both parties and to provide an occasion for making a credible witness to the truth of Jesus Christ. In the light of Christ we can perceive glimmers of light in the great world religions, but these little lights are not of themselves salvific, because they are invariably misunderstood by people whose minds are darkened by sin. This statement need not be an illustration of theological hubris, since we as Christians must confess that the problem of sin belongs to us as well and distorts our vision of the truth whenever we diverge from faith in the gospel. In interreligious dialogue we must maintain that the hope of the world does not lie in any religion or belief system, not even in Christianity, but in the living God himself who breaks into human religion with a transforming and purifying word that is both grace and judgment. At the same time, there can be a true religion, one that is constantly purified and reformed by the gospel of Jesus Christ. I think here Father Dulles and I would be very close.

On Erickson

I greatly appreciate Millard Erickson for bringing to light the areas of tension between my theological position and traditional evangelicalism. I speak as a chastened evangelical, one who has been thoroughly exposed to higher or historical criticism of Scripture and to the relativism of late modernity and postmodernity as reflected in historicism, religious pluralism and the sociology of knowledge. Is it possible to be orthodox or evangelical if one accepts the legitimacy of the probing of modern philosophers and sociologists? Erickson would undoubtedly agree with me that one can still be evangelical and engaged in conversation with modernity from which we learn positively as well as negatively. I believe that modern evangelicalism is hampered by being precritical, pre-Kantian and pre-Barthian. Helmut Thielicke refers to a Cartesian way of doing theology, in which the credibility of theology is made to rest on rational consistency and clarity of ideas rather than fidelity to biblical revelation.

Erickson has trenchantly raised the question whether I have sufficient awareness of the philosophical presuppositions that I bring to Scripture and to theological discussion. He rightly points out my indebtedness to existentialism, including Kierkegaard and the early Barth. While freely drawing on Kierkegaard and his disciples in articulating my theology, I have acknowledged where I have learned from these sources and where I have broken with them.[8] On the subject of interaction with the world of philosophy, one must always differentiate between philosophers who speak out of a living faith (and who are therefore more theologians than philosophers) and those who appeal exclusively or primarily to their own experience and powers of cognition. Kierkegaard was one whose Christian commitment was unassailable and whose purpose in writing was to show that reason cannot lead us to the truth about God and ourselves. This position resonates with the seminal insights of the scriptural writers, notwithstanding Paul's address at Athens which produced very few converts. I continue to adhere to Kierkegaard's contention that the infinite must never be confounded with the finite, that God always remains wholly different from what we can know and experience on our own. Where I take issue with both Kierkegaard and the early Barth is in their thesis that the negation of reason can open the door to faith. In my view, which I believe to be in accord with the deepest insights of Scripture, faith opens its own door through the preaching of the gospel, not through an encounter with despair.

All of us come to the Bible with certain presuppositions, some of which are derived from philosophy. Unlike the philosophical theologian, the biblical theologian will not try to build upon these presuppositions but will subject them to critical scrutiny by the living Word of God, Jesus Christ, who meets us in the scriptural proclamation. We will not necessarily abandon our presuppositions but allow them to be corrected and reformed in the light of divine revelation. For example, Kierkegaard needs to be corrected when he posits a complete disjunction between time and eternity; he thereby fails to do justice to the biblical notion that time has its basis in God, for God created time. Moreover, the Bible seems to indicate that God experiences temporality within himself, and here we need to engage process philosophy and theology without succumbing to the dubious belief in a finite God. To sum up, we can never think creatively without presuppositions, but the mark of the biblical, evangelical theologian is to be constantly aware of the presence of these presuppositions and be willing to modify them or even set them aside if they conflict with the new light that breaks forth from God's holy Word.

Erickson questions whether I have offered adequate grounds for adopting a particular religious perspective. This may show a trace of rationalism in Erickson, for it seems that he is asking for rational and experiential corroboration of the claims of faith. If faith rests upon rational corroboration, then reason, not faith, becomes the ground of religious certainty. Yet I wish to affirm the rationality of faith, and this means that faithful reasoning has a role in elucidating the claims of faith. I have real reservations about justifying the claims of faith in the light of extrabiblical rational criteria. Faith justifies itself when God reveals the truth about himself and ourselves to us in the event of decision and surrender. This does not mean that the claims of faith are not confirmed in daily experience.

Reinhold Niebuhr was assuredly right when he contended that the Christian doctrine of original sin has more experiential confirmation than any philosophical claim. Yet I would maintain that only those whose inward eyes are open to the Holy Spirit can really discern the wickedness and depravity of humanity through the centuries as evidence of original sin. The evangelical way of doing theology is to justify the claims of theology by appealing to the written Word of God, but even here our appeal is not to some criterion external to faith but to faith's own criterion: the illumination of the Spirit through the encounter with the written Word.

Erickson notes that I nowhere seem to give a comprehensive definition of *rationalism.* I recognize that this is a slippery term, but I have defined it in various ways in all my writings. For our purpose here I would define *rationalism* as the attempt to arrive at ultimate truth through cognitive powers resident within the human person. From my perspective the claims of faith cannot be established by human reason, but they can be clarified and sharpened by faithful reasoning. When I propose a theology of Word and Spirit I am trying to counter not only rationalism but also experientialism or illuminism. At the same time, I wish to acknowledge a rational element in revelation as well as a mystical element. Faith invites us to both deeper understanding and mystical participation in the living Christ, and I vigorously affirm this against both an existentialism that reduces faith to the will to believe and a rationalistic idealism that empties faith of its mystery and transcendence (as in Hegel).

On the question of whether the Bible is intrinsically the Word of God, I contend that the answer lies in what meaning we assign to the Word of God. If Word of God is taken to mean written testimony to what transpired in sacred history, then the Bible is intrinsically the Word of God. But if Word of God refers to the transcendent meaning of divine revelation, then the Bible is a pointer or witness to the Word but not in and of itself the Word. I think Barth is biblically sound in his judgment that Christ alone is the living or revealed Word of God, yet the Bible can become transparent to this Word by the interior action of the Holy Spirit.

On the subject of biblical inerrancy Erickson may be right in his suggestion that I am propounding an inerrancy in purpose. Yet I also want to affirm that the Bible is without error in all of its teaching and doctrine, but this divine teaching is not self-evident in the Bible. It must be revealed or disclosed anew as we wrestle with the scriptural text to find its meaning for the life of the church today. What is truly inerrant and infallible is the transcendent gospel of God, but this is hidden in the scriptural text and can only be brought out by the Spirit in the moment of decision and surrender. The Word of God is not a truth waiting to be discovered in the Bible but a truth that breaks into our consciousness through our reading of the Bible and hearing the message of the Bible proclaimed and interpreted. Does my position reflect a philosophical presupposition at work in my thought, or is the interpretation that controls my thinking the actual teaching of the Bible that reason can elucidate but not establish?

On Fackre

Gabriel Fackre has been a stalwart defender of the historic faith in the United Church of Christ. He has worked both within and outside denominational structures in order to keep the UCC in continuity with the tradition of the church universal. I am more pessimistic than Fackre concerning the possibility of evangelical renewal in the UCC. He believes that heterodox trends in the UCC can be reversed, whereas I am not so sure. We both discern pockets of evangelical and Reformed faith in the UCC, and this is probably one reason why we have both remained in this denomination. From my perspective the new wine of the gospel calls for new wineskins. The old structures in all the denominations are crumbling, and we need to be alert to the work of the Holy Spirit in creating new structures that can carry the truth of the gospel. Like Philip Schaff we should strive to be transdenominational, pinning our hopes not on the refurbishing of denominational structures but on the inbreaking kingdom of God that may well leave denominational structures behind.

Fackre has made a real contribution to this discussion by pinpointing the various places where I take issue with Karl Barth. One of the problems is that Barth himself altered his position on some important questions. It could be argued that Barth's theology went through various stages: the liberal, the existentialist, the sacramental, the Christomonistic (or more properly, the theology of the Word of God) and finally a developing evangelical catholicity. I am close to Barth in his third stage, which reflects a neo-Calvinistic sacramentalism that affirms the truth that God deigns to meet us in the visible signs and forms of churchly life: preaching, baptism and the Lord's Supper. In his later stages Barth no longer speaks of the three forms of the Word (Christ, preaching and Scripture) but now sees Jesus Christ as the only sacrament and preaching and Scripture as witnesses to this transcendent reality.

With regard to language about God, Fackre and I are fairly close. We both resist current pressures to reimage God in egalitarian and panentheistic terms. Both of us defend the trinitarian name of God (Father, Son and Holy Spirit) because we see this rooted in biblical revelation. I contend that the right understanding of masculinity and femininity also has its basis in biblical revelation. Christ is the bridegroom and his church the bride, and this sets the pattern for the marital relationship as well as the wider relationship between the sexes (compare Mt 9:14-15; 25:1-13; Lk 5:34; Jn 3:27-29; 1 Cor 11:3-16; Eph 5:21-33). Cultural understandings of masculinity and femininity brokenly reflect the biblical vision, and we are free to make use of these understandings in the light of this transcendent vision. We should do so with care, however, because the biblical revelation sharply challenges cultural notions of lordship and hierarchy as well as of masculinity and femininity (as Fackre rightly reminds us). While Fackre defends the pronominal *he* for the second person of the Trinity, he is strangely silent on the appropriate pronouns for the first and third persons, and this may indicate a divergence in our positions. For my latest discussion on this issue see my *Jesus Christ: Savior & Lord* (1997), pages 75-79.

On the subject of the saints Fackre shares my deep reservations with the Catholic practice of the veneration of Mary and the saints, but Protestants need to give much more attention to the role of Mary and the saints in the plan of salvation. What does the communion of saints mean in the context of an ecumenical theology? Do we simply pray *with* the saints, or can we hope that the saints will pray *for* us and for the whole church? Can the saints be upheld in the life of the church as models of devotion and holiness, or do we point to Jesus Christ alone as the one model for all Christians? A careful examination of the New Testament will reveal that not only Jesus Christ but also his devoted followers can be celebrated as models or signs of holiness in the life of the church. Paul exhorts the Christian community to imitate himself as a person of faith (1 Cor 4:16; 11:1; Phil 3:17; 2 Thess 3:7-9; compare Heb 6:12). It is well to note that the Apology of the Augsburg Confession, one of the founding documents of the Protestant Reformation, was willing to acknowledge the saints as *intercessors* but not as *mediators* of salvation (article 21).

I salute Gabriel Fackre as a friend and colleague in the church committed to churchly reform and spiritual renewal in our time. His work and witness should be given serious consideration by all denominations because he is calling us to the coming great church that will transcend the parameters of narrow denominational loyalty.

On Pinnock

I have always appreciated Clark Pinnock's way of confronting the issues that matter most in theology, since he speaks candidly and with integrity. He does not try to cover up genuine differences but is ready to acknowledge where these exist and then try to overcome them if at all possible.

One of the principal areas of contention between Pinnock and myself is the role of faith in appropriating the treasure of salvation. Pinnock holds that our hearers are free to make a positive response to the offer of salvation. I can also speak in this way, but I maintain that this response is evoked by the power of grace working within us. In and of ourselves we are not free moral agents because of the imprint of original sin on the human race. As Jonathan Edwards expressed it, the person in sin is naturally but not morally free. Our wills do not simply need to be assisted: they need to be turned around by grace. Once grace descends upon us, we then become free to believe and obey. Genuine freedom is finding one's true master rather than deciding between conflicting claims. But we can find our true master only when the master has first found us. As Pascal put it, "I would not be seeking thee unless I had already been found by thee." Pinnock sees faith as "a responsible exercise of human freedom," whereas I see faith as the liberating act of God within us that sets us free to ratify and confirm our election in Jesus Christ.

Pinnock in a rationalistic style posits only two alternatives: monergism, in which God does all, and synergism, in which we do part and God does part. I contend that there is a third alternative: the paradox of divine grace realizing itself through a human willing that is itself propelled by grace. When grace first works on us we are passive; we are then made active when grace empowers our will and moves us to respond in faith and obedience. All the credit for our salvation goes to God, but the responsibility for continuing in salvation hinges on us. We cannot claim merit even for continuing in salvation, since we are kept by grace even as we work out the implications of our salvation in fear and trembling. The mysteries of faith cannot be simply resolved by choosing between logical alternatives. Pinnock is right that a dialectic approach does not resolve the issues rationally; yet it expresses these mysteries in such a way as to do justice to both sides of the paradox. It is not my purpose here to engage in biblical exegesis, but I think it can be shown that the biblical testimony in both testaments supports a paradoxical over both a monergistic and a synergistic resolution of this issue. Pinnock attributes my seeming reticence to affirm the free exercise of human freedom to my horror of semi-Pelagianism. I would counter that his downplaying of divine grace could be attributed to his horror of Augustinianism and Calvinism. Because I acknowledge the need for personal decision and obedience, I cannot embrace a full-orbed monergism. Because I believe in the sovereignty of grace, I cannot support an unqualified synergism. In this debate I seek to mediate between Calvin and Wesley rather than promote a hyper-Calvinism that often takes the form of decretal determinism in which everything is determined by the eternal decrees of God.

Pinnock suggests that I am not really a predestinarian. I am willing to describe myself as such but not in the sense of a determinist who believes everything has been arranged beforehand. Predestination must not be reduced to an action in the past that is fully resolved in the counsels of God. It is better conceived of as a dynamic process that unfolds through divine-human interaction in history and that is still to be completed in the future.

Interestingly Pinnock points to Mary as the model of faith, for the incarnation was supposedly dependent on her free cooperation with grace. Can Pinnock avoid coming to the Roman Catholic conclusion that Mary is our coredemptrix, since salvation then resides not only in Christ's work of atonement but also in Mary's obedience? Does not this irrevocably compromise the Reformation dictum that we are saved by Christ alone *(solus Christus)*?

Another area of tension between Pinnock and me concerns the work of the Holy Spirit outside the parameters of faith and the church. I strongly resist the caricature of my position as Jesus or the gospel simply dropping from heaven as an anomalous event in human history. I envisage a sacred history that commences already in the Old Testament and provides the sociohistorical and theological context for the incarnation and the atonement of Christ. This sacred history encompasses the revelation of God to the people of ancient Israel and the continuing illumination of the Spirit of God to the church through the ages. The Holy Spirit works redemptively in this sacred history moving people to accept Christ as Lord and Savior of their lives. But does the Spirit also work redemptively in universal history outside the nexus of faith and obedience? Pinnock says yes, whereas I in a more dialectical fashion have to answer yes and no. The Spirit works among non-Christian peoples in order to sustain them in the trials of life, yet also to preserve them for the time when they will be confronted and challenged by the redeeming Christ. Common grace is in the service of saving grace. Yet to imply as does Pinnock that the Spirit brings redemption to non-Christian peoples apart from the knowledge of Christ or the gospel is to deny that Christ alone is the way of salvation, that no other name is given by which we may be saved (Acts 4:12). I agree with Calvin that the church already existed in the Old Testament in the form of a preparatory fellowship of faith, but both Calvin and I would recoil from the Tillichian conclusion that the church exists even in anticipatory form in the other great world religions. I can accept the doctrine of the hidden Christ, for wherever the Spirit is at work there also is Christ. Yet I reject the idea that we can enter the redemptive fellowship of the kingdom of God through committing ourselves to a name other than Jesus or to a gospel other than the Pauline gospel of justification by faith. The Spirit is at work throughout human history converting universal history into sacred history, but he does this through the missionary proclamation of salvation through grace alone and through Christ alone.

Pinnock raises some important questions in my treatment of the Trinity. He is right that I am not entirely comfortable with the doctrine of the social Trinity, and I intend to clarify my position on this issue in volume five of Christian Foundations. I do not affirm three separate persons in the Trinity, because this implies tritheism. I do affirm three modes of relationship by which God exists within himself, or three agencies of personhood by which God communes with himself and with created humanity. Are there *three* suns conjoined in such a way as to produce a single stream of light, or is there *one* sun that exists in three different dimensions: light, heat and ionizing radiation?

I see dynamic interaction by God within himself rather than interaction among three selves. I do not reject the depiction of the Trinity as a perpetual dance involving Father, Son and Spirit so long as this is understood metaphorically. Pinnock is right that the Trinity does involve community within God himself. I wish to affirm a trinitarian monotheism rather than a trinitarian panentheism (as in Moltmann) which borders on tritheism and even polytheism. We need to do justice to both the unity of God and the diversity within God. But this does not mean that there is a divine family composed of three individuals. Instead it means that God has fellowship within himself because he exists in three states of being in relatedness (or "persons" in the original sense). Here again we are dealing with a mystery in which metaphor and poetry are much more appropriate than univocal predication.

One final response on the subject of Pietism. Pinnock rightly perceives my roots in evangelical Pietism, but he needs also to take into account my reticence to define my position as pietistic. While learning from Pietism I also recognize with Karl Barth how easily Pietism slides into liberalism and modernism. When the source of theological authority is reduced to the experience of faith, it opens the possibility of allowing reason to interpret this experience. The University of Halle founded by Pietists in the eighteenth century became within two generations a bastion of rationalism.

We also need to differentiate among pietists. I acknowledge the positive influence of Philip Spener, the Blumhardts, Zinzendorf and Kierkegaard on my theological development. I am much more reluctant to embrace Charles Finney, for example, who argued that we can convert ourselves with the assistance of grace and that revival can be effected through the right use of techniques and methods. I am much closer to Jonathan Edwards, who described revival as "the surprising work of God." Yet Finney must not be categorically dismissed, as he is by thoroughgoing Calvinists, since he tried to do justice to one side of the soteriological paradox: that human decision is necessary for the full realization of salvation in human life.

I regard Pinnock, John Sanders and other so-called Arminians as brothers in the faith who sometimes err by striving too sedulously for logical consistency and coherence with the whole of experience; yet their lives often mirror an abiding trust in the Lord Jesus Christ. Christian fellowship rests not on theological uniformity but on the willingness to allow our words and actions to be informed and corrected by the Spirit of God speaking to us in holy Scripture. This is the key to church renewal and church unity in our time. Could not we all agree on this point?

On Torrance

It is a joy to find someone so close to my theological position and concerns as Thomas Torrance. Torrance has been one of my mentors in the task of reformulating theology. We stand together in our defense of the transcendence of the God of biblical revelation against current attempts to reconceive God as essentially immanental (the way of panentheism). We are also agreed on the baleful effects of the biblical-classical synthesis in which the biblical conception of a dynamic interpersonal God has been compromised by an accommodation to philosophical ideas that depict God as immobile and static. I have learned much from Torrance's important work *The Doctrine of Grace in the Apostolic Fathers* in which he persuasively shows how the biblical notion of grace was eclipsed by philosophical conceptions in the thought of some of the church fathers.[9] Torrance has helped me see that the witness of the early church cannot be deemed final or infallible but must be subjected to the still higher criterion of holy Scripture.

Torrance has done much creative thinking on the mystery of the Trinity, and the church as a whole remains indebted to him in this area. I am in substantial agreement with him on the doctrine of the Trinity; yet there are places where our views tend to diverge rather than converge. I see the Trinity as well as the other salvific mysteries of the faith as having two sides: divine and human. I am reluctant to identify the church's dogmatic articulation of the Trinity with the self-revelation of God as triune. The language that the church uses corresponds with the transcendent reality and points to it, but is this language itself divine revelation? Cannot we say that the dogma of the Trinity is the product of *both* supernatural guidance by the Spirit and faithful human reflection that involves synthetic as well as analytic reasoning? Is the Trinity as a doctrine "the immediate and central truth of the Gospel," as Torrance alleges, or is it not an unfolding of the implications of the gospel for the worship and service of the church? Does the Trinity belong to the original kerygma of the church, or does it not belong to the doctrinal elucidation that follows the kerygma?

I believe the church was guided toward the doctrine of the Trinity through continuous reflection on its faith that lasted several centuries. The Trinity is an integral element in the church's confession of faith, but is it the core element in the evangelical proclamation? We should preach the Trinity not as an abstract dogma but as the good news of how God condescends to save us through Jesus Christ in the power of the Spirit. Is the Trinity itself "the saving mystery of salvation," or does not this accolade belong to the incarnation of Jesus Christ? Is the condition for salvation the acknowledgment of God as one being in three persons or the confession that Jesus Christ is Lord and Savior? I contend that the doctrine of the Trinity indeed safeguards and secures the faith of the church through the centuries, but is it the object of faith? While resolutely standing by the early church's creedal formulation of the Trinity, I hold that our faith rests on the redeeming action of the triune God in the life history of Jesus Christ.

I have no compunction in affirming that the mystery or the reality of the Trinity is an object of faith, but the Trinity as doctrine or dogma is better described as the outcome of the church's reflection on the message of faith than as the ground or basis of faith. While the trinitarian mystery is indeed an immediate implication of the fact, form and content of revelation, the doctrine of the Trinity represents a later development and is not part of the original testimony of faith. I am not sure whether our positions are reconcilable on this important question, but there may be a convergence if a clear differentiation is made between the reality of the Trinity and the conceptualization of this reality.

On the subject of subordinationism I concur with the faith of the church catholic that the three persons are equal and that the idea of subordination belongs to the economic Trinity, the way in which God relates himself to the world. At the same time I affirm a priority of the Father over both Son and Spirit in the inner life of the Trinity. There is no ontological superiority of the Father as the first person, but there is an order of succession in the Trinity. I think here I have both the Greek and Latin fathers on my side.

Torrance's remarks on how the idea of person in Western culture has its basis in the Trinity are innovative and insightful, deserving serious consideration. If this position can be sustained by historical research, it would be yet another blow to natural theology, which begins with concepts from below in order to explain transcendent realities.

On Colyer

Elmer Colyer is probably the most reliable interpreter of my theology, since he has been both a student and a friend and is now a colleague in the University of Dubuque Theological Seminary. Our positions are very close, though by no means identical.

He rightly discerns the crucial role of the doctrine of the Trinity in my theology, but he raises the valid question whether my theology is thoroughly trinitarian, since I do not spell out the trinitarian implications of my thought at the very beginning of my systematic endeavors. My answer is that I see the Trinity as integrally related to the concrete issues of the Christian life and religious experience, and I therefore discuss the Trinity mainly in relation to the self-revelation of God in Jesus Christ and the lordship of Christ in the task of daily living. Rather than a prolegomenon to theology, the Trinity is an ongoing mystery that impinges on every aspect of theology. As a doctrine it does not belong to the gospel itself, but it is a necessary implication of the gospel. I try to guard against a trinitarian objectivism in which we remain with the ontological Trinity and fail to relate the inner movements in the being of God to the concrete ways by which God relates himself to the world. I fully affirm the ontological Trinity but always in relation to the economic Trinity. The doctrine of the Trinity will be treated in more depth in volume five of the Christian Foundations series in the section "The Role of the Holy Spirit in the Trinity." For a further discussion see my comments on Torrance's critique of my theology above.

Professor Colyer points to an undeveloped area in my theology: the doctrine of vocation. Thus far in my theology I have stated that all people are called by God to the vocation of being witnesses and ambassadors of Jesus Christ, though this theme is not developed in any systematic way. I intend to explore this concept in volume six, which concerns the doctrine of the church. I also plan to write a book on sainthood after the Christian Foundations series, and I will contend that all people, especially those who believe, are called to be saints: imitators of God and Jesus Christ.

Colyer rightly perceives the crucial role I assign to the Christian life in salvation. The Christian life is not simply a byproduct but a concrete sign and witness of Christ's passion and victory in his struggle against the powers of darkness. But it is more than that: it is the arena in which the implications of our salvation are unfolded as we strive to appropriate the fruits of Christ's cross and resurrection victory. In my early writings I sometimes gave the impression that the Christian life is a contributory agent in the effecting of our salvation. I would now contend that our works of obedience mirror and proclaim Christ's work of obedience unto death, but they do not render his death and resurrection efficacious.

We do not help Christ in procuring our redemption, but through the power of the Spirit we manifest and demonstrate to the world the reality of this redemption. We are not coredeemers with Christ in winning salvation, but we are coworkers with Christ in proclaiming the good news of his salvation. The Christian life can be used by the Spirit to turn others toward the gospel, but it is not a means by which we realize the redemption promised in the gospel. It is not a means that effects redemption, but it is a means that brings the impact of redemption to bear in daily life and existence. The Christian life does not create much less earn salvation; however, the absence of a Christian life can imperil salvation, since God is not bound to extend his grace to those who continually rebel against it and thereby make a mockery of it.

On Weborg

John Weborg and I have much in common, since we share a pietistic heritage and we both draw on this heritage (Weborg more than myself) in the task of fashioning a viable theology for today's world.

I find some merit in Weborg's distinction between *theologia prima* and *theologia secunda,* which has its source in the church's liturgical tradition. Weborg rightly sees an affinity in his typology to my distinction between a dogmatic theology *(theologia dogmatica)* and a theology of devotion or spiritual life *(theologia vitae spiritualis).* Weborg would join me in affirming that a theology of the spiritual life will ipso facto include the practice of the spiritual life. I would also differentiate between existential and theoretical theology, and this manner of speaking is very close to Weborg's typology. While existential theology is born out of the conviction of the heart, it nevertheless involves ongoing reflection, for otherwise it becomes incapable of addressing the critical themes and issues of Christian thought and life. Unless it has a perduring experiential ingredient, theoretical theology becomes unnervingly abstract and speculative. Weborg calls for a symbiosis of the two types, which I fully endorse. This means that the theological task can be carried out only by believers and that the only right theology is a theology done by regenerate persons (*theologia regenitorum*).

The danger in elevating these kinds of typology into hermeneutical keys is that they tend to make religious experience rather than the gospel itself the source and norm of theology. The right order is not from experience to reflection but from divine revelation to human appropriation in experience, life and thought. Experience is not the regulatory norm or enduring basis of theology, but it is a vital and necessary element in theology. The transcendent source of a biblical, evangelical theology is the living Word of God who breaks into our experience from the beyond and remolds and transforms our experience and understanding. *Theologia prima* is not the foundation of *theologia secunda* but its correlative. Neither experience nor liturgy can contain divine revelation, but both can powerfully witness to this revelation through the action of the Holy Spirit.

Both Weborg and I would be quite comfortable with the Puritan distinction between notional or conceptual knowledge of God and affectional knowledge. If we have only the first, we are not in touch with the realities to which faith directs us. If we have affectional knowledge or the knowledge of acquaintance, we are then in experiential contact with the mysteries of divine revelation. But we should strive to articulate these mysteries as best we can, and this means that we will not remain content with feelings or states of consciousness but go on to understanding. I think Weborg would concur with this analysis of divine and human interaction.

This kind of approach resonates with certain themes in neo-orthodoxy (though both Weborg and I understandably maintain a certain distance from this school of thought). With Calvin and Luther, Karl Barth vigorously contended that theology cannot bear fruit unless it is solidly grounded in prayer. Emil Brunner made a helpful distinction between "thought-in-encounter" and "thinking-about-it" and in this way subordinated theological reflection to the interior illumination of the Holy Spirit.[10]

To Weborg's question on the absence of an in-depth discussion of the resurrection of Christ, my reply is that this subject will be dealt with more adequately in the volume on eschatology. For our purposes here I have seen the cross and resurrection as a unified action that dethrones the powers of darkness and brings life and liberation to people of faith. In my latest volume, *Jesus Christ: Savior & Lord,* I have stated that the resurrection both reveals and fulfills the victory of Christ on the cross. Karl Barth sees the resurrection together with Pentecost and the second advent of Christ as stages in the parousia, and I think this approach is fully in accord with the biblical exposition.[11]

Weborg gives a more positive role to doubt in the Christian life than is evident in my writings. From my perspective doubt has its origin in sin, though it may be used by the Spirit to promote the deepening of faith. We are justified even while we are still in sin and tormented by doubt, but Christ gives us the power to combat both sin and doubt. In the Christian walk we can make progress against both of these maladies. Doubt is not something to be celebrated but something to be overcome. Weborg might be uncomfortable with this phraseology.

Weborg is more supportive of patterned or liturgical prayer than I am, but I do not oppose this kind of prayer so long as it is not a substitute for free prayer. When we pour meaning into the prescribed words and rituals, these words and signs become conduits of faith and hope. The danger is that prayer in a prescribed form can easily degenerate into formalism in which we have the letter without the spirit. I acknowledge, however, that free or spontaneous prayer can also take prescribed forms and is then closer to a *theologia secunda* than to a *theologia prima*. Weborg and I are not as far apart on this issue as may first appear.

On Rohrer

It is indeed a source of satisfaction to know that a former student of mine, especially one with such brilliance, has arrived at a position similar to my own. Both of us object to reducing the gospel to a political program, but we both discern in the gospel a political thrust that can decisively alter the social landscape. Rohrer rightly concurs in my plea for responsible social involvement but with biblical and theological grounding. He might have mentioned the immense influence of Jacques Ellul on my theological ethics, for it was Ellul who best showed me how to be socially relevant without compromising the proclamation of the kingdom of God. A number of other prominent theologians, including John Calvin, Reinhold Niebuhr and Karl Barth, have helped me resist the politicizing of the church's mission without succumbing to the beguiling temptation to withdraw from the political fray.

Rohrer is surely right that every social issue has a spiritual dimension. It is the task of the church to discern this spiritual dimension as it grapples with the issues that bedevil society. When the church speaks, it will bring the sacred to bear upon the secular so that we are dealing no longer with a purely secular or political issue but with a spiritual issue. We are now focusing not simply on our responsibility as citizens of the state but on our obedience as disciples of Jesus Christ.

I greatly appreciate Rohrer's keen analysis of my debate with feminism. On the relationship between the sexes I affirm a complementarity in roles and an equality in worth in the sight of God. I also hold that the gospel relativizes though it does not negate our biological differences. It relativizes these differences because it calls both sexes to the high vocation of being witnesses and ambassadors of the Lord Jesus Christ. Where I take exception to radical feminists is their propensity to uphold androgyny and bisexuality as sexual ideals and their reimaging of God as bisexual rather than as essentially masculine in his relation to created humanity. To make God inclusive in their sense means to make God identical with the creation, and this I must firmly reject. Rohrer correctly notes my contention that the current debate parallels the conflict of the German church with National Socialism in the 1930s.

One possible point of divergence between our positions is Rohrer's strong endorsement of contextual theology, which makes the communication of the

Evangelical Theology in Transition

gospel rest on the ability of the preacher to translate the gospel into the cultural context of the hearer. Rohrer is firm in his conviction, however, that we must carry on this work without diluting or altering the basic message of faith. My question is whether he is prone to make the gospel depend on the expertise of the church in contextualizing rather than on the power of the Holy Spirit. The Spirit may speak his Word through a proclamation that is only partly contextualized or may withdraw his Word from a fully contextualized message because of disobedience, lack of piety or fear of the Lord or any number of other reasons. Is the gospel known only when it is "effectively contextualized" or when God wills to speak his Word in the power of the Spirit?

It is interesting to note that the apostle Paul tried to contextualize in his sermon at Athens (Acts 17:22-33), but it was not until he bore witness to the cross and resurrection of Christ that he began to make an impression on his hearers. Scripture indicates that he had very few converts from this engagement. When he went to Corinth he resolved to preach only Jesus Christ and him crucified (1 Cor 2:1-5).

Rohrer raises the pertinent question of how one can ascertain when the church is entering a confessional situation. When should the church speak, and when should it remain silent? A growing number of theologians, including myself, believe that a large part of the church today has become captive to cultural ideology and that the message of the church has thereby been irremediably compromised. Ideological infiltration is evident not only in our preaching but also in our services of worship, and this holds true for both liberal and conservative churches. "Seeker" services in which we appeal to the general human quest for meaning are beginning to supplant services based on the Word and sacraments.

The church is obliged to speak to the great moral issues that are presently tearing society apart, but what it speaks should be something other than what the world expects to hear. A confessing church in our time would certainly address the issues of the sanctity of life, human sexuality and environmental pollution, but it must not speak without probing the theological undergirdings and implications of these and other issues. In my opinion the church must engage in concerted theological reflection before it endorses any social agenda that arises out of the conflicts that engulf our culture. Yet it must not use this time of waiting to avoid coming to concrete conclusions and then acting upon them. We are living in critical times in which the church may have to battle for its Christian identity in a post-Christian and postmodern world.

Epilogue

In a climate that fosters an evangelical triumphalism, I want to make it very clear that my aim is to be a *self-critical* evangelical theologian. We should not simply defend what has been handed down to us by our own spiritual tradition but subject everything to a higher criterion: the gospel of God revealed by the Spirit in holy Scripture. Evangelicalism as a movement is being compromised by worldliness, which takes various forms.

One of the most beguiling temptations is the penchant to translate the biblical message into an ontology or philosophy of religion. The logic of faith is then supplanted by the logic of propositions. A theology of revelation is usurped by an evangelical rationalism that subordinates revelation to reason. In rationalism the primary loyalty is to the unity and consistency of reason, whereas faith's concern is submission to the revealed mystery of God becoming man in Jesus Christ, a mystery that confounds reason. Christian rationalism assumes that reason can establish or validate the claims of faith. In my theology reason can serve faith but cannot of itself move one toward faith. Yet against some of those who are fascinated with postmodernism and relish the breakdown of Enlightenment rationalism, I contend that faith does not overthrow rationality. Instead it employs reason to sharpen and clarify the demands of the gospel. Faith is not irrational but suprarational, leading one beyond the parameters of human reasoning and experience without abrogating the created structures of reason. Faith's paradoxes constitute not a fundamental logical contradiction but a picture of reality that cannot be contained in either human reason or imagination and appears contradictory because only a part of the picture is available.

Another temptation that evangelicals should be encouraged to resist is biblicism, which I define as an appeal to Scripture that disregards the ongoing commentary on Scripture through the ages, that is, the history of theology. Luther once remarked that we can gain help in spiritual and moral matters not only from holy Scripture but also from the lives of the saints. I stand by the Reformation principle of scriptural primacy, but this does not imply scriptural exclusivity. For the Reformers the final court of appeal is the paradoxical unity of Spirit and Word, and the role of the Spirit is to apply the truth of Scripture to the church in every generation. This means that we can learn not only from the written testimony of Scripture but also from the insights of the blessed through the ages who are guided by the Spirit to appropriate this testimony in the task of living out their faith. We need to be thoroughly biblical without being biblicistic in the sense of making the written word our sole or exclusive authority and thereby drawing a bifurcation between the revelatory witness of Scripture and the living voice of the Spirit speaking through the church. Scripture always stands over the church, but it comes alive in the church, the community where people are gathered to hear and celebrate the Word of God.

A bona fide evangelical theology will always take the biblical text with the utmost seriousness but will at the same time strive to get beyond the text into the reality to which the text points. This kind of theology will discriminate between the cultural or mythopoetic form in which Scripture comes to us and the transcendent content of the gospel, which brings to both prophetic and apostolic writers and the readers a new spiritual vision and horizon. Evangelicals who subscribe to a flat view of Scripture, which identifies the surface meaning of the text with the truth of divine revelation, are in effect secularizing the Bible by losing contact with its revealed mysteries.

Every authentic evangelical theology will necessarily contain a moderate dose of biblicism in that the biblical texts will be normative in the task of explicating the faith. Such a theology will be anchored in the Bible, but in the communication of the gospel it will not remain within the confines of the Bible. It will strive to avoid both an insular biblicism that reduces faith to historical facticity and a corrosive latitudinarianism that separates faith from the historical particularity of revelation.

Finally, I wish to break through the confusion that results from interpreting Scripture through the lens of cultural ideology. One of these ideologies has been patriarchalism, and patriarchalism still casts its shadow over the greater part of the evangelical community. Patriarchalism teaches the authority of man over woman and woman as the virtual property of man. In the present many people, including evangelical Christians, fearful of incurring the wrath and disdain of the cultural elites, are tempted to confound the scriptural message with the agenda of feminism, which preaches the essential autonomy of the sexes. What I call biblical covenantalism must be sharply distinguished from both patriarchalism and feminism. In this perspective man and woman agree to work together as a team in the apostolic mission of winning souls and raising families for the Lord. Jesus Christ is the ultimate head of the family, but the husband reflects this headship in his role as provider and spiritual director, and the woman also reflects this headship in her role of shoring up her husband to keep the family economically viable and in nurturing their children in the Lord. The man is not over the woman as in patriarchy, nor do man and woman have separate agendas as in feminism.

To be sure, the Bible uses the language of patriarchy to clarify the relation between the sexes as well as between God and his subjects. We are bound to use this same language, for content cannot be separated from form; however, we must always make clear that the Spirit pours new meaning into this language so that lordship as practiced by both Christ and the heads of families means no longer domination and unilateral decision making but now sacrificial service in which those who are called to lead place the interests of those in their charge before their own. They still lead, but indirectly and always in the spirit of love.

The appropriate symbol for patriarchalism is the *march* in which the husband leads and the wife duly follows. In feminism the guiding symbol is the *race* in which man and woman become rivals in the quest for self-fulfillment and worldly success. In biblical covenantalism the guiding symbol is the *dance* in which the man leads and the woman follows, but both act in such a way as to produce an enduring harmony. On occasion the man will invite the woman to lead, but the woman will not try to usurp the man's role in this regard.

In the biblical view the relationship between the sexes in the covenant of holy marriage is not simply one of partnership but one of unity, for in Christ we are now one flesh, and the subordination of woman to man is complemented by mutual subordination. It is also incumbent on single persons not to lead autonomous lives but to work out their destinies in collaboration with their sisters and brothers in faith, and this will involve loving submission (what John Howard Yoder calls "revolutionary subordination") as well as the responsible exercise of leadership.

Evangelicalism, especially in its American guise, must also confront individualism, an ideology rooted in the Enlightenment of the late seventeenth and eighteenth centuries. This ethos is reflected in the tendency to envisage revelation as a solitary encounter between God and the person of faith, a "moment of decision" in which the individual receives interior illumination and peace. This phraseology is indeed descriptive of one side of divine revelation, but it fails to do justice to its historical and communal dimensions. We must come to see that decision and obedience normally take place in relation to a faith community, leading to vital participation in such a community.

No one can believe for us, but others can lead us to faith and help us grow in faith. The church is not simply a place where we hear the Word of God proclaimed but a fellowship of faith and love (koinonia) that sustains us in the trials of daily living. The church cannot infuse faith into us through sacramental rites, but the believing community can strengthen us in our faith and provide the norms that keep our witness consonant with the faith once delivered to the saints.

While the ethos of American culture has been individualistic, there is now a noticeable trend toward collectivism that sacrifices individual freedom to the demands of collective security. The kingdom of God stands in judgment over both a rampant individualism and an imperialistic collectivism (as in modern nationalisms and tribalisms). The church should bring to the contemporary scene a socially redeeming message that safeguards individuality as well as creates a sense of responsibility for the welfare of others.

I am calling for a Christianity free from bondage to any cultural or political ideology as well as from alignment with any philosophy or metaphysics that transforms the content of revelation into eternal ideas or reduces revelation to experiences of self-transcendence. If we as evangelicals forge such an understanding, we will grow closer to Christians of other traditions, and we will begin to discover a unity in spirit that will gain the attention of the world and again make our message credible in the wider secular arena.

Selected Bibliography of Donald G. Bloesch's Major Publications

The following selected bibliography, arranged chronologically within each category, includes nearly all of Donald G. Bloesch's books and a sampling of his most important essays that have appeared in other works and in periodicals. Complete bibliographies of Bloesch's publications are found in the following works:

Adams, Daniel J., ed. *From East to West: Essays in Honor of Donald G. Bloesch*, pp. 233-49. Lanham, Md.: University of America Press, 1997.

Bloesch, Donald G. *The Battle for the Trinity*, pp. 121-34. Ann Arbor, Mich.: Servant, 1985.

———. *Theological Notebook*, 2:181-97. Colorado Springs: Helmers & Howard, 1991.

Hasel, Frank M. *Scripture in the Theologies of W. Pannenberg and D. G. Bloesch: An Investigation and Assessment of Its Origin, Nature and Use.* Frankfurt am Main: Peter Lang, 1995. Hasel provides an extensive list of doctoral dissertations on Bloesch's theology.

The Papers of Donald G. Bloesch collection in the archives at the University of Dubuque Theological Seminary contains most of Bloesch's books and periodical publications, numerous reviews of Bloesch's books, unpublished volumes of Bloesch's Theological Notebooks, unpublished papers from Bloesch's seminary and college years, and unpublished correspondence of Bloesch and others.

Books

Centers of Christian Renewal. Philadelphia: United Church Press, 1964.

The Christian Life and Salvation. Grand Rapids: Eerdmans, 1967. Reprint, Colorado Springs: Helmers & Howard, 1991.

The Crisis of Piety. Grand Rapids: Eerdmans, 1968. 2nd ed. Colorado Springs: Helmers & Howard, 1988.

Christian Spirituality East and West. Chicago: Priory, 1968 (coauthored with Jordan Auman and Thomas Hopko).

The Christian Witness in a Secular Age. Minneapolis: Augsburg, 1968.

The Reform of the Church. Grand Rapids: Eerdmans, 1970. Reprint, Eugene, Ore.: Wipf & Stock, 1998.

The Ground of Certainty: Toward an Evangelical Theology of Revelation. Grand Rapids: Eerdmans, 1971.

The Evangelical Renaissance. Grand Rapids: Eerdmans, 1973.

Wellsprings of Renewal: Promise in Christian Communal Life. Grand Rapids: Eerdmans, 1974.

The Invaded Church. Waco, Tex.: Word, 1975.

Jesus Is Victor! Karl Barth's Doctrine of Salvation. Nashville: Abingdon, 1976.

Essentials of Evangelical Theology. 2 vols. San Francisco: Harper & Row, 1978-1979. Reprint, Peabody, Mass.: Prince Press, 1998.

The Struggle of Prayer. San Francisco: Harper & Row, 1980. Reprint Colorado Springs: Helmers & Howard, 1988.

Faith and its Counterfeits. Downers Grove, Ill.: InterVarsity Press, 1981.

Is the Bible Sexist? Westchester, Ill.: Crossway, 1982.

The Future of Evangelical Christianity. New York: Doubleday, 1983. Reprint, with a foreword by Mark A. Noll, Colorado Springs: Helmers & Howard, 1988.

Crumbling Foundations. Grand Rapids: Zondervan, 1984.

The Battle for the Trinity. Ann Arbor, Mich.: Servant, 1985.

Freedom for Obedience. San Francisco: Harper & Row, 1987.

Theological Notebook. 2 vols. Colorado Springs: Helmers & Howard, 1989-1991.

A Theology of Word & Spirit: Authority & Method in Theology. Christian Foundations 1. Downers
  Grove, Ill.: InterVarsity Press, 1992.
Holy Scripture: Revelation, Inspiration & Interpretation. Christian Foundations 2. Downers Grove,
  Ill.: InterVarsity Press, 1994.
God the Almighty: Power, Wisdom, Holiness, Love. Christian Foundations 3. Downers Grove, Ill.:
  InterVarsity Press, 1995.
Jesus Christ: Savior & Lord. Christian Foundations 4. Downers Grove, Ill.: InterVarsity Press, 1997.

Contributions to Edited Works

"A Christological Hermeneutic." In *The Use of the Bible in Theology: Evangelical Options.* Edited
  by Robert Johnston. Atlanta: John Knox Press, 1985.
"Process Theology and Reformed Theology." In *Process Theology.* Edited by Ronald H. Nash,
  pp. 31-56. Grand Rapids: Baker, 1987. Republished in *Major Themes in the Reformed
  Tradition.* Edited by Donald K. McKim, pp. 386-99. Grand Rapids: Eerdmans, 1992.
"No Other Gospel: 'One Lord, One Faith, One Baptism.' " In *Courage in Leadership.* Edited by
  Kevin Perrotta and John C. Blattner, pp. 83-94. Ann Arbor, Mich.: Servant, 1988.
"Evangelicalism." In *A New Handbook of Christian Theology.* Edited by Donald W. Musser and
  Joseph L. Price, pp. 168-73. Nashville: Abingdon, 1992.
"Is Spirituality Enough?" In *Roman Catholicism.* Edited by John Armstrong, pp. 142-60. Chicago:
  Moody Press, 1994.

Selected Articles

"True and False Ecumenism." *Christianity Today* 14, no. 21 (1970): 3-5.
"Burying the Gospel, Part I." *Christianity Today* 15, no. 25 (1971): 8-11.
"Burying the Gospel, Part II." *Christianity Today* 16, no. 1 (1971): 12-14.
"The New Evangelicalism." *Religion in Life* 41, no. 3 (1972): 327-39.
"Whatever Became of Neo-orthodoxy?" *Christianity Today* 19, no. 5 (1974): 7-12.
"An Evangelical Views the New Catholicism." *Communio* 3, no. 3 (1976): 215-30.
"Toward a Catholic Evangelical Understanding of the Lord's Supper." *Spirituality Today* 30, no.
  3 (1978): 236-49.
"Crisis in Biblical Authority." *Theology Today* 35, no. 4 (1979): 455-62.
"Soteriology in Contemporary Christian Thought." *Interpretation* 35, no. 2 (1981): 132-44.
"The Catholic Bishops on War and Peace." *Center Journal* 3, no. 1 (1983): 163-76.
"The Need for a Confessing Church Today." *The Reformed Journal* 34, no. 11 (1984): 10-15.
"An Evangelical Perspective on Authority." *Prism* 1, no. 1 (1986): 4-22.
"All Israel Will Be Saved: Supersessionism and the Biblical Witness." *Interpretation* 43, no. 2
  (1989): 130-42.
"The Finality of Christ and Religious Pluralism." *Touchstone* 4, no. 3 (1991): 5-9.
"The Law and Gospel in Reformed Perspective." *Grace Theological Journal* 12, no. 2 (1991):
  181-87.
"Our Vocation to Holiness." *Faith and Renewal* 17, no. 2 (1992): 20-25.
"The Demise of Biblical Preaching." *Touchstone* 8, no. 4 (1995): 13-16.
"Evangelical Rationalism and Propositional Revelation." *Reformed Review* 51, no. 3 (1998): 169-81.

Selected Secondary Works

Callahan, James. "Bloesch, Donald G." *Evangelical Dictionary of Theology.* Edited by Walter
  Elwell. Grand Rapids: Baker, 1982.
Nash, Ronald H. *The Word of God and the Mind of Man.* Grand Rapids: Zondervan, 1982.
Noll, Mark. "The Surprising Optimism of Donald Bloesch." *Center Journal,* Summer 1984.
Van Essen, R. "A Theological Portrait: Dr. Donald G. Bloesch." Translated by Daniel W. Bloesch.
  Soteria: Evangelical Theological Reflection 3, no. 3 (1986).
Gier, Nicholas F. *God, Reason and the Evangelicals.* Lanham, Md.: University Press of America, 1987.
Keylock, Leslie R. "Meet Donald G. Bloesch." *Moody Monthly* 88, no. 7 (1988): 61-63.

McKim, Donald K. "Donald G. Bloesch." In *A Handbook of Evangelical Theologians*. Edited by Walter Elwell, pp. 388-400. Grand Rapids: Baker, 1993.

White, James Emery. *What Is Truth? A Comparative Study of the Positions of Cornelius Van Til, Francis Schaeffer, Carl F. H. Henry, Donald Bloesch and Millard Erickson*. Nashville: Broadman & Holman, 1994.

Deddo, Gary W. "Shapers of Modern Evangelical Thought: Donald Bloesch." *Religious and Theological Studies Fellowship Bulletin*, no. 6, January-February 1995, pp. 17-19.

Hasel, Frank M. *Scripture in the Theologies of W. Pannenberg and D. G. Bloesch: An Investigation and Assessment of Its Origin, Nature and Use*. New York: Peter Lang, 1995.

Colyer, Elmer M. "A Theology of Word and Spirit: Donald Bloesch's Theological Method." *Journal for Christian Theological Research* 1, no. 1 (1996). http://apu.edu/~CTRF/jctr.html

Murphy, Nancey. *Beyond Liberalism and Fundamentalism: How Modern and Postmodern Philosophy Set the Theological Agenda*. Valley Forge, Penn.: Trinity Press International, 1996.

Olson, Roger. "Donald G. Bloesch." In *A New Handbook of Christian Theologians*. Edited by Donald W. Musser and Joseph L. Price, pp. 67-73. Nashville: Abingdon, 1996.

Parker, David, "Donald G. Bloesch: Evangelical Theologian of Word and Spirit." In *From East to West: Essays in Honor of Donald G. Bloesch*. Edited by Daniel J. Adams, pp. 1-22. Lanham, Md.: University of America Press, 1997.

Rohrer, James R. "The Theologian as Prophet: Donald Bloesch and the Crisis of the Modern Church." In *From East to West: Essays in Honor of Donald G. Bloesch*. Edited by Daniel J. Adams, pp. 211-32. Lanham, Md.: University of America Press, 1997.

Dorrien, Gary. *The Remaking of Evangelical Theology*. Louisville, Ky.: Westminster John Knox, 1998.

Notes

Preface
[1]Daniel J. Adams, ed., *From East to West: Essays in Honor of Donald G. Bloesch* (Lanham, Md.: University of America Press, 1997).
[2]Donald G. Bloesch, *Essentials of Evangelical Theology*, 2 vols. (San Francisco: Harper & Row, 1978-1979), 1:ix-23 and 2:235-297.
[3]Thomas F. Torrance, *The Christian Doctrine of God, One Being Three Persons* (Edinburgh: T & T Clark, 1996).
[4]Donald G. Bloesch, *God the Almighty: Power, Wisdom, Holiness, Love* (Downers Grove, Ill.: InterVarsity Press, 1995).

Chapter 1: Donald G. Bloesch & His Career
[1]See the selected bibliography at the end of this book (p. 209) which also includes important secondary literature. For the most recent complete bibliographies of Bloesch's publications see Daniel J. Adams, ed., *From East to West: Essays in Honor of Donald G. Bloesch* (Lanham, Md.: University of America Press, 1997), pp. 233-49, and Donald G. Bloesch, *Theological Notebook,* 2 vols. (Colorado Springs: Helmers and Howard, 1989-1991), 2:181-97.
[2]Donald G. Bloesch, *Essentials of Evangelical Theology*, 2 vols. (San Francisco: Harper & Row, 1978-1979). *Essentials* has received extensive praise. See Frank Hasel, *Scripture in the Theologies of W. Pannenberg and D. G. Bloesch* (Frankfurt am Main: Peter Lang, 1996), pp. 162-63, for a sampling of commendation for from various reviewers of the book.
[3]In a poll of twenty evangelical theologians from around the country, Leslie Keylock found that Bloesch was at the top of the list of "most brilliant, creative evangelicals working in systematic theology." See Leslie R. Keylock, "Evangelical Leaders You Should Know: Meet Donald G. Bloesch," *Moody Monthly* 88, no. 7 (1988): 61. The publication of *Essentials of Evangelical Theology* appears to have precipitated a rather astonishing flood of systematic theologies from the broadly evangelical academic community. Hasel lists over a dozen examples, and there are others as well. See Hasel, *Pannenberg and Bloesch,* p. 170.
[4]I have experienced this firsthand when using *Essentials of Evangelical Theology* in the required theology courses at the University of Dubuque Theological Seminary (UDTS). *Essentials* has been used widely in seminaries and colleges. It has gone through a number of printings and has been translated into Korean, Russian, Serbo-Croatian and Polish. A number of Bloesch's books have been translated into other languages such as Korean, Japanese, Chinese, Turkish and Spanish. *Essentials* has been used as a text at a Presbyterian seminary in Seoul, Korea, and at the Baptist seminary at Odessa in the Ukraine.
[5]Bloesch has been repeatedly praised for the depth and breadth of his scholarship. See Hasel, *Pannenberg and Bloesch,* pp. 163-64, for examples in secondary literature. Bloesch's combination of scholarly erudition and deep piety has helped overcome North American evangelicalism's suspicion that one cannot have both. It is one of the reasons why a whole generation of students at the University of Dubuque Theological Seminary and abroad has found Bloesch and his writings so formative. He has brought to North American evangelicalism a vision of the urgent need for rigorous, uncompromising scholarship in service to the gospel.
[6]Bloesch has been quoted in *Newsweek* and *Time* and has been interviewed on radio.
[7]See Bloesch, *Essentials of Evangelical Theology,* vol. 1, *God, Authority and Salvation* (San Francisco: Harper & Row, 1978), 1:x-xi, 3-5, 13-17 and 20-21. Donald McKim characterizes Bloesch as seeking an alternative vision, a middle way, beyond liberalism and fundamentalism. See Donald McKim, "Donald G. Bloesch," in *Handbook of Evangelical Theologians,* ed. Walter A. Ewell (Grand Rapids, Mich.: Baker, 1993), pp. 391, 395.

[8]The biographical material contained in this article comes from archival material at UDTS, including an unpublished autobiography (Donald G. Bloesch, "An Incomplete Autobiography"), and also from personal interviews with Donald Bloesch and his mother, Adele Bloesch. Anyone doing serious research on Bloesch and his theology should examine the archival material in the Academic Resource Center at UDTS in Dubuque, Iowa.

Virtually all the information found in the several published biographical treatments of Bloesch are based primarily on Keylock's article "Evangelical Leaders," pp. 61-63. See McKim, "Donald G. Bloesch," pp. 388-400; and Roger E. Olson, "Donald G. Bloesch," in *A New Handbook of Christian Theologians*, ed. Donald Musser and Joseph L. Price (Nashville: Abingdon, 1996), pp. 67-73. Keylock's article, however, is based almost exclusively on Bloesch's unpublished autobiography. The exception is Hasel, *Pannenberg and Bloesch*, pp. 159-72. Hasel's treatment is the most careful and well-documented brief biographical summary, especially his copious references to secondary literature on Bloesch, including unpublished dissertations. McKim's article is the most insightful.

[9]In fact, Bloesch's father drove Niebuhr around in a horse and buggy when Niebuhr, as a young man, was raising money selling books. Bloesch, *Theological Notebook*, 1:xi.

[10]The Evangelical Synod of North America represents a blend of Lutheran and Reformed Pietism (the Lutheran element was dominant) and was composed primarily of immigrants from the Church of the Prussian Union. The confessional documents of the Evangelical Synod included Luther's *Small Catechism*, the *Augsburg Confession* and the *Heidelberg Catechism*. See Donald G. Bloesch, *Jesus Is Victor! Karl Barth's Doctrine of Salvation* (Nashville: Abingdon, 1976), p. 12, and Bloesch, "Incomplete Autobiography," pp. 4-5.

[11]Bloesch, *Theological Notebook*, 1:xi. Bloesch's maternal grandfather was a converted Jew. His paternal grandfather was converted at a Salvation Army meeting. Bloesch, "Incomplete Autobiography," p. 5.

[12]This family heritage in Pietism appears at various points in Bloesch's career and theology, including (1) his criticism of Karl Barth's soteriological objectivism, (2) his affinity for existentialism which stresses personal decision and human agency, (3) his uncompromising rejection of all forms of rationalism, (4) his continued interest in spirituality, (5) the overall soteriological focus of his theology, (6) his interest in religious communities, (7) his support of spiritual and theological renewal of the church.

[13]The influence of his maternal grandmother was important in his early years. She often gave him devotional literature that played a significant role in his spiritual maturation. Bloesch remembers reading the Bible and John Bunyan's *Pilgrim's Progress* at an early age. It was also in his childhood that Bloesch first encountered popular American evangelicalism through gospel songbooks that he found in his father's library: "I loved to go to the piano and play many of these hymns which were not included in the official Evangelical and Reformed hymnal." Confirmation was an important event for Bloesch, and he viewed it as a public profession of faith. Preparation for confirmation in the Evangelical and Reformed Church consisted of a year devoted to Bible study and a second year on the Evangelical Catechism, which represents a Reformed modification of Luther's Small Catechism.

The first year of Bloesch's high-school experience was in a one-room/one-teacher school in Monee. Bloesch had left-wing political inclinations in high school. He was an avid reader of *In Fact* magazine, which praised socialist countries. Bloesch, "Incomplete Autobiography," pp. 1-7.

[14]Ibid., p. 7.

[15]There were many evangelical students at Elmhurst College, though the professors in religion and philosophy were, according to Bloesch, "liberals." Bloesch started a discussion group called Christians in Action, which focused on theological and ethical issues. Another group of older students on the Elmhurst campus (mainly veterans of World War II), called the Gospel Team, influenced Bloesch. The Team was primarily a prayer and fellowship group that also sponsored trips to inner-city missions in Chicago; Bloesch always felt that it needed deeper theological foundations. Bloesch also participated in the Student Christian Movement and the

Pre-Theological Society. Ibid., pp. 8-9.

[16]Ibid., p. 10.

[17]Ibid., p. 11.

[18]Ibid. Few evangelical theologians are as well-read in process philosophy and theology as Bloesch. Bloesch also founded a student magazine at CTS called *Witness*. It was designed to counteract *Quest*, the official student magazine of the Federated Schools of Theology, though Bloesch actually wrote for both.

[19]Bloesch encountered neo-orthodoxy in the federated schools at Chicago, especially through visiting professors from Europe like the British Congregationalist Daniel Jenkins. For lists of Bloesch's theological mentors see Bloesch, *Essentials*, 1:xi, 4-5; Bloesch, *Theological Notebook*, 1:xi; and Hasel, *Pannenberg and Bloesch*, pp. 167-68.

[20]Bloesch wrote an insightful paper on Kant's philosophy at the University of Chicago that included an extensive theological evaluation of Kant. See Donald G. Bloesch, "A Theological Critique of Kant's Metaphysical Agnosticism" (December 23, 1953), in the archives at UDTS. Traces of Kant's critiques, especially his emphasis on the role of practical reason in the religious and ethical sphere, are evident in Bloesch's first volumes of Christian Foundations. See, for example, Donald G. Bloesch, *A Theology of Word and Spirit: Authority and Method in Theology*, Christian Foundations 1 (Downers Grove, Ill.: InterVarsity Press, 1992), pp. 21-22, 37, 39, 116, 282. Bloesch's doctrine of revelation and his theology of Word and Spirit are designed in part to overcome the Kantian problematic and its resulting skepticism regarding knowledge of the thing in itself *(Ding an sich)*.

[21]Hasel also correctly notes that Bloesch served several interim pastorates. Bloesch has had approximately five years of pastoral experience. See Hasel, *Pannenberg and Bloesch*, p. 161.

[22]Bloesch, *Theological Notebook*, 1:ix.

[23]Bloesch, "Incomplete Autobiography," p. 14.

[24]Bloesch had nearly completed a prior thesis, but his adviser, D. D. Williams, left for another school, and the graduate committee informed him that he would have to begin a new thesis under a new adviser (ibid., pp. 15-16).

[25]Ibid.

[26]Donald G. Bloesch, *Centers of Christian Renewal* (Philadelphia: United Church Press, 1964). Bloesch visited a variety of religious communities while in England, Scotland, Switzerland, France, Italy and Germany.

[27]Bloesch has also served as a visiting and/or adjunct professor at the University of Iowa School of Religion (1982), Ontario Theological Seminary, Toronto (summers of 1984 and 1992), Bethany Theological Seminary, Oakbrook, Illinois (January 1994) and Wheaton Graduate School of Theology, Wheaton, Illinois (August 1996 and May 1997). Bloesch has also been a resource scholar (1985-1993) and corresponding editor (1993-) for *Christianity Today*.

[28]See Bloesch, *Theological Notebook*, 1:xi. Roger Olson astutely observes that "more than anyone else, Bloesch brought the influence of the Swiss theologian, Karl Barth, to bear on North American evangelical theology." Olson, "Donald G. Bloesch," p. 67.

[29]In 1959 Alfred E. Ewald, president of Wartburg Seminary, invited the executive secretary of the World Council of Churches, Visser t'Hooft, to lecture in Dubuque. From that point onward ecumenical relations between the three theological faculties in Dubuque developed considerably. See Joseph L. Mihelic's unpublished "Survey of the History of the University of Dubuque 1846-1979" in the archives at UDTS.

[30]See Hasel, *Pannenberg and Bloesch*, p. 165, for Bloesch's reputation as a bridge builder. The pronounced ecumenical environment of the major part of Bloesch's career is a significant feature of Bloesch's personal and theological biography that Hasel has missed in his otherwise careful research on Bloesch. Bloesch has had longstanding personal contact with Roman Catholic, Lutheran, Presbyterian and United Methodist professors and students during his years at UDTS. This includes the classroom, committees, dialogues, joint worship, colloquies and informal conversation across these denominational lines. Bloesch's *The Battle for the Trinity:*

The Debate over Inclusive God-Language (1985) was published by a Roman Catholic press, Servant Publications, Ann Arbor, Michigan. Bloesch's contacts with Roman Catholics are far more substantive than Hasel realizes. All of this took place at the height of the ecumenical movement.

There are three key influences that Bloesch's interpreters often miss: (1) Bloesch's ecumenical involvements in Dubuque and beyond, (2) Art Cochrane's Barthian mentoring of Bloesch and (3) Bloesch's wife, Brenda, and her evangelical convictions and Wesleyan Methodist background.

[31]See McKim, "Donald G. Bloesch," p. 400.

[32]During a convocation the faculty wore white arm bands over the sleeves of their dark academic robes and distributed leaflets explaining their perspective. In January 1973 the faculty and staff of UDTS unionized and affiliated with the IHEA (Iowa Higher Education Association), the first seminary faculty in the country to do so. See Jim Miller, "Seminary Faculty, Students Protest," *Telegraph Herald* (Dubuque, Iowa), April 2, 1974. Also see Howard Wallace, "History of Faculty-Staff and Administration Bargaining," and Mihelic, "Survey of the History of the University of Dubuque," p. 62, both unpublished papers in the archives at UDTS.

[33]Bloesch is an accomplished musician who has played the piano, guitar and harmonica since he was a child. He has a fondness for gospel and country-western music.

[34]See the bibliographies in Adams, ed., *From East to West*, pp. 233-49 and Bloesch, *Theological Notebook*, 2:181-97.

[35]Richard Lovelace, "Renewal and the Future of Evangelicalism," *Renewal* 3, no. 3 (1983): 12. Quoted in Hasel, *Pannenberg and Bloesch*, p. 163.

[36]Bloesch indicated in an interview on January 14, 1997, that he considers his *Theological Notebook* to be possibly his most significant theological work. If all of his "notebooks" were published, there would be eight or nine volumes.

[37]See the bibliographies in Adams, ed., *From East to West*, pp. 233-49, and Bloesch, *Theological Notebook*, 2:181-97.

[38]Portions of this correspondence are now in the Donald G. Bloesch Collection in the archives at UDTS.

[39]Donald G. Bloesch, *The Future of Evangelical Christianity* (Garden City, N.Y.: Doubleday, 1983), p. 108. It is interesting to compare Bloesch with Clark Pinnock, who is also on the short list of premier evangelical theologians but whose theological trajectory has been in the other direction. Bloesch's confessional stance mirrors that of Barth in the Barmen days, in that Bloesch underscores the diastasis between the gospel and Western culture.

[40]Donald G. Bloesch, *Holy Scripture: Revelation, Inspiration & Interpretation*, Christian Foundations 2 (Downers Grove, Ill.: InterVarsity Press, 1994).

[41]Donald G. Bloesch, *God the Almighty: Power, Wisdom, Holiness, Love*, Christian Foundations 3 (Downers Grove, Ill.: InterVarsity Press, 1995).

[42]Donald G. Bloesch, *Jesus Christ: Savior & Lord*, Christian Foundations 4 (Downers Grove, Ill.: InterVarsity Press, 1997).

[43]Also see I. John Hesselink, "A Tribute to Donald Bloesch," on the occasion of Bloesch's retirement from teaching at UDTS on April 13, 1993, in the archives at UDTS.

Chapter 2: Locating Donald G. Bloesch in the Evangelical Landscape

[1]Donald G. Bloesch, *The Future of Evangelical Christianity* (Garden City, N.Y.: Doubleday, 1983), p. 15.

[2]Of course some nonfundamentalist evangelicals embraced the label "neo-evangelical," but by and large that label was rejected by the mainstream, conservative Protestants who led the evangelical Christian subculture that looked up to Billy Graham.

[3]Donald G. Bloesch, *Essentials of Evangelical Theology*, 2 vols. (San Francisco: Harper & Row, 1978-1979), 2:235.

[4]Personal correspondence from Donald G. Bloesch, February 21, 1997.

[5]Donald G. Bloesch, *The Evangelical Renaissance* (Grand Rapids, Mich.: Eerdmans, 1973), p. 8.

[6]Donald G. Bloesch, *A Theology of Word & Spirit: Authority & Method in Theology,* Christian Foundations 1 (Downers Grove, Ill.: InterVarsity Press, 1992), p. 31.

[7]Ibid.

[8]Bloesch, *Essentials,* 2:269.

[9]Ibid., 1:75.

[10]Bloesch, *Theology of Word & Spirit,* pp. 117-18.

[11]Ibid., p. 21.

[12]Ibid., p. 203.

[13]Ibid., p. 271.

[14]Bloesch, *Essentials,* 2:164.

[15]Donald G. Bloesch, *Holy Scripture: Revelation, Inspiration & Interpretation,* Christian Foundations 2 (Downers Grove, Ill.: InterVarsity Press, 1994), p. 27.

[16]Ibid., p. 127.

[17]Ibid., pp. 36-37.

[18]Ibid., p. 97.

[19]Randy Maddox, "The Necessity of Recognizing Distinctions: Lessons from the Evangelical Critique of Christian Feminist Theology," *Christian Scholar's Review* 17, no. 3 (1988): 307-23.

[20]See Bloesch, *Holy Scripture,* pp. 208-18. I am not aware of published criticisms of Bloesch's position against narrative theology, but many of narrative theology's evangelical proponents or sympathizers have privately commented negatively about Bloesch's treatment of it.

[21]Donald G. Bloesch, *God the Almighty: Power, Wisdom, Holiness, Love,* Christian Foundations 3 (Downers Grove, Ill.: InterVarsity Press, 1996), pp. 254-60. Again, Bloesch's critics have not published their expressions of dismay, but they do convey them verbally to those who ask. Their surprise and dismay at Bloesch's irenic but firm rejection of their proposal arises partially from the fact that in *The Evangelical Renaissance* Bloesch wrote: "Sovereignty in the biblical sense likewise entails omniscience. God knows the course of the future and the fulfillment of the future, but this must not be taken to mean that He literally knows every single event even before it happens. It means that He knows every alternative and the way in which His children may well respond to the decisions that confront them. The plan of God is predetermined, but the way in which He realizes it is dependent partly on the free cooperation of His subjects. This does not detract from His omnipotence, for it means that He is so powerful that He is willing to attain His objectives by allowing a certain room for freedom of action on the part of man" (p. 53).

[22]Donald G. Bloesch, *The Struggle of Prayer* (Colorado Springs: Helmers & Howard, 1988).

[23]Donald G. Bloesch, *The Battle for the Trinity: The Debate over Inclusive God-Language* (Ann Arbor, Mich.: Servant, 1985).

[24]See Bernard Ramm, *After Fundamentalism: The Future of Evangelical Theology* (San Francisco: Harper & Row, 1983).

[25]Leslie R. Keylock, "Evangelical Leaders You Should Know: Meet Donald G. Bloesch," *Moody Monthly* 88, no. 7 (1988).

[26]Cornelius Van Til, *The New Modernism: An Appraisal of the Theology of Barth and Brunner* (Philadelphia: Presbyterian & Reformed, 1947).

[27]Donald G. Bloesch, *Jesus Is Victor! Karl Barth's Doctrine of Salvation* (Nashville: Abingdon, 1976).

[28]Ibid., p. 133.

Chapter 3: "Fideistic Revelationalism"

[1]Donald G. Bloesch, *Holy Scripture: Revelation, Inspiration & Interpretation,* Christian Foundations 2 (Downers Grove, Ill.: InterVarsity Press, 1994), p. 13.

[2]Donald G. Bloesch, *Essentials of Evangelical Theology,* 2 vols. (San Francisco: Harper & Row, 1978-79), 1:4.

[3]Gordon R. Lewis and Bruce A. Demarest, *Integrative Theology,* 3 vols. (Grand Rapids, Mich.: Zondervan, 1987), 1:23.

[4]Richard A. Muller, "Scholasticism Protestant and Catholic: Francis Turretin on the Object and Principles of Theology," *Church History* 55, no. 2 (1986): 204.

[5]Franciscus Turrettinus, *Institutio theologiae elencticae* (Geneva, 1677-1685; reprint, Edinburgh, 1847), 1.5.4.

[6]Ibid., 1.2.6-7. See Muller, "Scholasticism," p. 205.

[7]Hence Charles Hodge's famous statement, "If natural science be concerned with the facts and laws of nature, theology is concerned with facts and principles of the Bible. If the object of the one be to arrange and systematize the facts of the external world, and to ascertain the laws by which they are determined; the object of the other is to systematize the facts of the Bible, and ascertain the principles or general truths which those facts provide." *Systematic Theology* (reprint, Grand Rapids, Mich.: Eerdmans, 1952), 1:18.

[8]Wayne Grudem, *Systematic Theology: An Introduction to Biblical Doctrine* (Grand Rapids, Mich.: Zondervan, 1994), p. 21.

[9]Lewis and Demarest, *Integrative Theology,* 1:23.

[10]Carl F. H. Henry, *God, Revelation and Authority,* 6 vols. (Waco, Tex.: Word, 1976-1983), 3:457.

[11]Ibid., 3:248.

[12]See the appendix of "Evangelical Rationalism and Propositional Revelation," in Donald G. Bloesch, *The Holy Spirit: His Works & Gifts,* Christian Foundations 5 (Downers Grove, Ill.: InterVarsity Press, forthcoming). Bloesch finds this approach exemplified in the work of Carl F. H. Henry.

[13]Lewis and Demarest, *Integrative Theology,* 1:27.

[14]Henry, *God, Revelation and Authority,* 1:244.

[15]Ibid., 1:199.

[16]Carl F. H. Henry, *Remaking the Modern Mind* (Grand Rapids, Mich.: Eerdmans, 1946), p. 247.

[17]Henry, *God, Revelation and Authority,* 1:394, 405; 2:136.

[18]Lewis and Demarest, *Integrative Theology,* 1:33.

[19]Donald G. Bloesch, *A Theology of Word & Spirit: Authority & Method in Theology,* Christian Foundations 1 (Downers Grove, Ill.: InterVarsity Press, 1992), p. 13.

[20]Bloesch, *Holy Scripture,* p. 48.

[21]Ibid., p. 50.

[22]Ibid., p. 48.

[23]Bloesch confesses that he sides with Barth against Brunner in their famous dispute over the "point of contact." (see *Theology of Word & Spirit,* pp. 153, 174).

[24]Ibid., p. 235.

[25]Bloesch, *Holy Scripture,* p. 12.

[26]Bloesch, *Essentials,* 1:75.

[27]Bloesch, *Theology of Word & Spirit,* p. 164.

[28]Ibid., p. 164.

[29]Ibid.

[30]Ibid., p. 176.

[31]Bloesch, *Essentials,* 1:75-76.

[32]Bloesch, *Holy Scripture,* p. 151.

[33]Ibid., p. 57.

[34]Ibid., p. 58.

[35]Ibid., p. 27.

[36]Bloesch, *Theology of Word & Spirit,* p. 38.

[37]Ibid., p. 115.

[38]Ibid., p. 59.

[39]Ibid., p. 39.

[40]Ibid., p. 19.

[41]Ibid.

[42]Ibid., p. 120.

[43]Ibid., p. 19.

[44]Bloesch, *Holy Scripture*, p. 54.

[45]Ibid., p. 15.

[46]Ibid., p. 301-2.

[47]Bloesch, *Theology of Word & Spirit*, p. 78.

[48]Ibid., p. 195.

[49]Ibid., p. 210.

[50]Ibid., p. 116.

[51]Bloesch, *Holy Scripture*, p. 40.

[52]Ibid., p. 41.

[53]Ibid., p. 44.

[54]Bloesch, *Essentials*, 1:62-63.

[55]Ibid., p. 63.

[56]Bloesch, *Holy Scripture*, p. 41.

[57]Bloesch, *Theology of Word & Spirit*, p. 203.

[58]Bloesch, *Essentials*, 1:58.

[59]Ibid., pp. 58-60.

[60]Bloesch, *Holy Scripture*, p. 160.

[61]Ibid.

[62]Ibid., p. 13.

[63]Ibid., p. 160.

[64]Ibid.

[65]Ibid.

[66]Bloesch, *Essentials*, 1:64.

[67]Bloesch, *Holy Scripture*, p. 159.

[68]Ibid., p. 178.

[69]Ibid., p. 190.

[70]Ibid., pp. 207-8.

[71]Ibid., p. 71.

[72]Bloesch, *Essentials*, 1:70.

[73]Bloesch, *Holy Scripture*, p. 202.

[74]Ibid., p. 190.

[75]Bloesch, *Essentials*, 1:71.

[76]Ibid., 1:71.

[77]Bloesch, "Evangelical Rationalism and Propositional Revelation."

[78]Bloesch, *Theology of Word & Spirit*, p. 257.

[79]Ibid., p. 260.

[80]Ibid., p. 262.

[81]Ibid., p. 229.

[82]Ibid., p. 267.

[83]Ibid., p. 253.

[84]Bloesch, "Evangelical Rationalism and Propositional Revelation."

[85]Bloesch, *Theology of Word & Spirit*, p. 268.

[86]Ibid., p. 114.

[87]Bloesch, *Holy Scripture*, p. 19.

[88]Bloesch, *Theology of Word & Spirit*, p. 21.

[89]This opinion was recently articulated by George A. Lindbeck, "Confession and Community: An Israel-like View of the Church," *Christian Century* 107, no. 16 (1990): 495.

[90]See, for example, George Herbert Mead, *Mind, Self and Society*, ed. Charles W. Morris (Chicago: University of Chicago Press, 1934, 1974), pp. 138-58.

[91]Robert N. Bellah et al., *Habits of the Heart: Individualism and Commitment in American Life* (Berkeley: University of California Press, 1985), p. 81.

[92]See, for example, Alisdair MacIntyre, *After Virtue*, 2nd ed. (Notre Dame, Ind.: University of Notre Dame Press, 1984), p. 221.

[93]Bloesch, *Essentials*, 1:ix.

[94]For a lengthier exposition of this criticism, see Elmer M. Colyer, "A Theology of Word and Spirit: Donald Bloesch's Theological Method," *Journal for Christian Theological Research* 1, no. 1 (1996). http://apu.edu/~CTRF/jctr.html

Chapter 4: Donald Bloesch on Revelation

[1]Avery Dulles, *Models of Revelation* (Garden City, N.Y.: Doubleday, 1983), especially at p. 115.

[2]Donald G. Bloesch, *Holy Scripture: Revelation, Inspiration & Interpretation*, Christian Foundations 2 (Downers Grove, Ill.: InterVarsity Press, 1994), p. 62. Cf. Donald G. Bloesch, *Essentials of Evangelical Theology*, 2 vols. (San Francisco: Harper & Row, 1978-1979), 2:3.

[3]Bloesch, *Holy Scripture*, p. 49.

[4]Donald G. Bloesch, *A Theology of Word & Spirit: Authority & Method in Theology*, Christian Foundations 1 (Downers Grove, Ill.: InterVarsity Press, 1992), p. 187.

[5]Bloesch, *Essentials*, 2:240-41.

[6]Bloesch, *Holy Scripture*, p. 50.

[7]Bloesch, *Essentials*, 1:62.

[8]Bloesch, *Holy Scripture*, p. 49; cf. p. 74.

[9]Ibid., p. 49.

[10]Ibid., p. 74, quoting Karl Barth, *Theology and Church* (New York: Harper & Row, 1962), p. 210.

[11]Bloesch, *Theology of Word & Spirit*, p. 190.

[12]Bloesch, *Holy Scripture*, pp. 51-52.

[13]Bloesch, *Essentials*, 2:270.

[14]Bloesch, *Theology of Word & Spirit*, p. 71.

[15]Bloesch, *Essentials*, 1:76.

[16]Bloesch, *Holy Scripture*, p. 57; cf. p. 18.

[17]Bloesch, *Essentials*, 1:70.

[18]Bloesch, *Holy Scripture*, p. 126.

[19]Bloesch, *Essentials*, 1:55.

[20]Ibid.

[21]Ibid., p. 78.

[22]Donald G. Bloesch, *God the Almighty: Power, Wisdom, Holiness, Love*, Christian Foundations 3 (Downers Grove, Ill.: InterVarsity Press, 1995), p. 77.

[23]Dulles, *Models of Revelation*, p. 210.

[24]Bloesch, *Holy Scripture*, p. 68.

[25]Bloesch, *Theology of Word & Spirit*, pp. 120-21, quoting Dulles, *Models of Revelation*, p. 223.

[26]Bloesch, *Theology of Word & Spirit*, pp. 120-21.

[27]Bloesch, *God the Almighty*, p. 66.

[28]Bloesch, *Essentials*, 2:242.

[29]Bloesch, *God the Almighty*, p. 60-61.

[30]Ibid., pp. 64-69.

[31]Bloesch, *Holy Scripture*, pp. 23-24, 41, 47.

[32]Bloesch, *Theology of Word & Spirit*, pp. 14-15.

[33]Bloesch, *Essentials* 1:61.

[34]Ibid., 2:238.

[35]Ibid., 2:240.

[36]Bloesch, *Theology of Word & Spirit*, p. 108.

[37]Ibid., pp. 108-9.

[38]Ibid., p. 109.

[39]Ibid., p. 27.

[40]Bloesch, *Essentials*, 1:139, quoting J. A. T. Robinson without specific reference. Bloesch is apparently relying on Robinson's *The Human Face of God* (Philadelphia: Westminster Press,

1973).
[41]Bloesch, *Theology of Word & Spirit*, p. 157.
[42]Ibid., pp. 29, 108.
[43]Ibid., p. 29.
[44]Ibid., p. 52.
[45]Vatican II, Pastoral Constitution on the Church in the Modern World, nos. 4, 11 and 44.
[46]Bloesch, *Essentials*, 1:46.
[47]Bloesch, *Theology of Word & Spirit*, p. 78.
[48]Bloesch, *Holy Scripture*, p. 52.
[49]Ibid., p. 63.
[50]Ibid., p. 78.
[51]Bloesch, *God the Almighty*, p. 78.
[52]Bloesch, *Holy Scripture*, p. 103.
[53]Ibid., p. 102.
[54]Ibid., p. 31.
[55]Bloesch, *Essentials*, 2:271.
[56]Bloesch, *Holy Scripture*, p. 115.
[57]Ibid.; cf. Bloesch, *Essentials*, 1:69.
[58]Bloesch, *Essentials*, 1:53.
[59]Bloesch, *Holy Scripture*, p. 48.
[60]Bloesch, *Theology of Word & Spirit*, p. 189.
[61]Ibid., p. 116.
[62]Bloesch, *Holy Scripture*, p. 160.
[63]Ibid., p. 13.
[64]Ibid., p. 193.
[65]Bloesch, *Essentials*, 1:57-58.
[66]Vatican II, Dogmatic Constitution on Divine Revelation, nos. 9 and 10.
[67]Ibid., no. 10.
[68]Bloesch, *Essentials*, 1:59.
[69]Vatican II, Decree on Ecumenism, no. 21.
[70]Bloesch, *Theology of Word & Spirit*, pp. 57-59.
[71]Ibid., p. 37.
[72]Bloesch, *Holy Scripture*, p. 75.
[73]Ibid., p. 76; cf. Bloesch, *Theology of Word & Spirit*, p. 241.
[74]Bloesch, *Essentials*, 2:285-86.
[75]Bloesch, *Theology of Word & Spirit*, p. 22.
[76]Bloesch, *Essentials*, 2:240.
[77]Bloesch, *Theology of Word & Spirit*, p. 272.
[78]Ibid., p. 59.
[79]Ibid.
[80]Bloesch, *Essentials*, 2:241; cf. 1:103.
[81]Ibid., 2:241.
[82]Bloesch, *God the Almighty*, p. 65-66.
[83]Bloesch, *Theology of Word & Spirit*, pp. 57, 219; cf. Bloesch, *Essentials*, 2:267. In an appendix
to the forthcoming fifth volume of his Christian Foundations series, Bloesch takes Carl Henry
and Wolfhart Pannenberg as exemplars of the "evangelical rationalism" he repudiates.
[84]Bloesch, *Theology of Word & Spirit*, p. 43.
[85]Bloesch, *Essentials*, 1:246.
[86]Ibid., p. 244.
[87]Ibid., p. 245.
[88]Bloesch, *Theology of Word & Spirit*, p. 52.
[89]Vatican II, Decree on the Church's Missionary Activity, nos. 11, 15; cf. Dogmatic Constitution
on the Church, no. 17.

[90]John Paul II, encyclical *Redemptor Hominis,* no. 11, with references to Justin and Clement of Alexandria; encyclical *Redemptoris Missio,* no. 28; encyclical *Veritatis Splendor,* no. 94; *Crossing the Threshold of Hope* (New York: Alfred A. Knopf, 1994), p. 81.

[91]Bloesch, *Essentials,* 1:246.

[92]Bloesch, *Theology of Word & Spirit,* p. 70.

[93]Ibid., p. 72, quoting Dulles, *Models of Revelation,* p. 143.

[94]Ibid., p. 96.

[95]Bloesch, *Theology of Word & Spirit,* pp. 112-13.

[96]Bloesch, *Holy Scripture,* p. 39.

[97]Ibid., pp. 40-45.

[98]Ibid., p. 45.

[99]Bloesch, *Theology of Word & Spirit,* p. 94.

[100]Ibid., p. 98.

[101]Ibid., p. 101, referring to the hymn "Lauda Sion" and especially the verse "Sed auditu solo tuto creditur."

Chapter 5: Donald Bloesch's Doctrine of Scripture

[1]Donald G. Bloesch, *Essentials of Evangelical Theology,* 2 vols. (San Francisco: Harper & Row, 1978-1979), 1:51-87.

[2]Elmer M. Colyer, "A Theology of Word and Spirit: Donald Bloesch's Theological Method," *Journal for Christian Theological Research* 1, no. 1 (1996); http://apu.edu/~CTRF/jctr.html

[3]Donald G. Bloesch, *Holy Scripture: Revelation, Inspiration & Interpretation,* Christian Foundations 2 (Downers Grove, Ill.: InterVarsity Press, 1994), p. 12. Elsewhere he speaks of Barth as "indubitably the most profound and creative theological mind since the Reformation" (*A Theology of Word & Spirit: Authority & Method in Theology,* Christian Foundations 1 [Downers Grove, Ill.: InterVarsity Press, 1992], p. 150).

[4]Bloesch, *Holy Scripture,* p. 13.

[5]Ibid., p. 14.

[6]Ibid., p. 15.

[7]Ibid., p. 14.

[8]Ibid., pp. 17-18.

[9]Ibid., p. 18.

[10]Ibid.

[11]Ibid., p. 19.

[12]Ibid.

[13]Ibid.

[14]Ibid., p. 26.

[15]Ibid.

[16]Ibid.

[17]Ibid., p. 26.

[18]Ibid., p. 27.

[19]Ibid.

[20]Ibid.

[21]Ibid., p. 31.

[22]Ibid.

[23]Ibid., p. 33.

[24]Ibid.

[25]Ibid., p. 40.

[26]Ibid., p. 42.

[27]Ibid., p. 40.

[28]Ibid., p. 42.

[29]Ibid., pp. 41-42.

[30]Ibid., pp. 42-43.

[31]Ibid., p. 43.
[32]Ibid.
[33]Ibid.
[34]Ibid., p. 44.
[35]Ibid.
[36]Ibid.
[37]Ibid., p. 47.
[38]Ibid., p. 67.
[39]Ibid., p. 49.
[40]Ibid., pp. 49-50.
[41]Ibid., p. 50.
[42]Ibid.
[43]Ibid.
[44]Ibid., p. 48.
[45]Ibid.
[46]Ibid., p. 51.
[47]Ibid.
[48]Ibid.
[49]Ibid.
[50]Ibid., p. 51-52.
[51]Ibid., p. 52.
[52]Ibid.
[53]Ibid.
[54]Ibid., p. 53.
[55]Ibid., p. 47.
[56]Ibid., p. 53.
[57]Ibid., p. 52.
[58]Bloesch, *Theology of Word & Spirit,* p 164.
[59]Ibid.
[60]Bloesch, *Holy Scripture,* pp. 119-20.
[61]Ibid., p. 120.
[62]Ibid.
[63]Ibid., p. 128.
[64]Ibid., p. 121.
[65]Ibid.
[66]Ibid., p. 95.
[67]Ibid., p. 105.
[68]Ibid., p. 107.
[69]Ibid.
[70]Ibid., pp. 108-9.
[71]Ibid., p. 111-12.
[72]Ibid., p. 114.
[73]Ibid.
[74]Ibid., pp. 115.
[75]Ibid., p. 116.
[76]Ibid.
[77]Ibid., p. 172.
[78]Ibid., p. 173.
[79]Ibid., p. 177.
[80]Ibid., p. 174.
[81]Ibid., p. 176.
[82]Ibid., p. 178.
[83]Ibid., pp. 178-79.

84Ibid., p. 190.

85Ibid.

86Ibid.

87Ibid., p. 20.

88Ibid., p. 33.

89Bloesch, *Theology of Word & Spirit*, p. 57.

90See the appendix "Evangelical Rationalism and Propositional Revelation" in Donald G. Bloesch, *The Holy Spirit: His Works & Gifts*, Christian Foundations 5 (Downers Grove, Ill.: InterVarsity Press, forthcoming).

91Ibid.

92Bloesch, *Holy Scripture*, p. 74.

93See Bloesch, "Evangelical Rationalism and Propositional Revelation."

94Bloesch, *Holy Scripture*, p. 80.

95Ibid., p. 103.

96Ibid., p. 216.

97See Bloesch, "Evangelical Rationalism and Propositional Revelation."

98Karl Barth, *Church Dogmatics* 1/1, *The Doctrine of the Word of God*, trans. Geoffrey W. Bromiley (Edinburgh: T & T Clark, 1975), p. xiii.

99Bloesch, *Holy Scripture*, p. 82.

100Søren Kierkegaard, *Concluding Unscientific Postscript*, trans. David F. Swenson and Walter Lowrie (Princeton, N.J.: Princeton University Press, 1941), pp. 97-113.

101Ibid., pp. 169-83.

102Søren Kierkegaard, *Philosophical Fragments, or A Fragment of Philosophy*, trans. David F. Swenson (Princeton, N.J.: Princeton University Press, 1936).

103Kierkegaard, *Concluding Unscientific Postscript*, pp. 190-92.

104While taking issue with Rogers and McKim at a number of points, Bloesch nonetheless agrees with their historical assessment. Even Clark Pinnock, however, who is in many ways in harmony with Bloesch's view of Scripture, acknowledges the effectiveness of John Woodbridge's pointed refutation of Rogers and McKim. See Clark Pinnock, *The Scripture Principle* (San Francisco: Harper & Row, 1984), p. xii.

105Daniel Fuller, "The Holy Spirit's Role in Biblical Interpretation," in *Scripture, Tradition and Interpretation*, ed. W. Ward Gasque and William Sanford LaSor (Grand Rapids, Mich.: Eerdmans, 1978), pp. 189-98.

106R. C. Sproul, John Gerstner and Arthur Lindsley, *Classical Apologetics: A Rational Defense of the Christian Faith and a Critique of Presuppositional Apologetics* (Grand Rapids, Mich.: Zondervan, 1984), pp. 21-22.

107Review of Stanley Grenz, *Theology for the People of God*, in *Christianity Today* 39, no. 2 (1995): 65-66.

108Karl Barth, "Evangelical Theology in the 19th Century," in *The Humanity of God*, trans. Thomas Wieser (Richmond, Va.: John Knox, 1960), p. 14.

109Ibid. p. 28.

110Kenneth Scott Latourette, *A History of the Expansion of Christianity* (New York: Harper & Brothers, 1945), 7:492.

111Bloesch, *Holy Scripture*, p. 215.

112Ibid., p. 68.

113Ibid.

114Ibid., p. 56.

115Emil Brunner, *The Divine-Human Encounter*, trans. Amandus W. Loos (Philadelphia: Westminster Press, 1943), pp. 112-13.

116John Newton Thomas commented that having destroyed the fundamentalist view of the Bible, Barth then proceeded to quote it as a fundamentalist would. See John Newton Thomas, "How Barth Has Influenced Me," *Theology Today* 13, no. 3 (1956): 368-69.

117Emil Brunner, *Our Faith*, trans. John W. Rilling (New York: Charles Scribner's Sons, 1954), p.

11.
[118]Bloesch, *Holy Scripture*, p. 68.
[119]Ibid., pp. 68-69.

Chapter 6: Jesus Christ in Bloesch's Theology

[1]We were both under care of the Northern Illinois Synod of the Evangelical and Reformed Church, seeing each other briefly at a Commission on Ministry meeting but going our separate ways.

[2]Bloesch drafted "The Dubuque Declaration" of the Biblical Witness Fellowship, and I wrote portions of the first Witness Statement of the Craigville Colloquies (1984) and the Statement of Purpose of the Confessing Christ movement (1993). Bloesch notes that "theologians of various persuasions are beginning to speak of a new confessional situation, a *status confessionis*, as the church finds itself engulfed in a crisis concerning the integrity of its message and the validity of its language. . . . People of faith may be called again . . . to engage in a new *Kirchenkampf* (church struggle)" (Donald G. Bloesch, *Jesus Christ: Lord & Savior*, Christian Foundations 4 [Downers Grove, Ill.: InterVarsity Press, 1997], pp. 243-44). I have made a similar case for the importance of centrist/confessing movements in "The Church of the Center," *Interpretation* 51, no. 2 (1997): 130-42. Currently both of us have written critiques of *The New Century Hymnal*, seeing it as a characteristic example of obeisance to ideologies of the day.

[3]Donald G. Bloesch, *Essentials of Evangelical Theology*, vol. 1, *God, Authority and Salvation* (New York: Harper & Row, 1978), and Gabriel Fackre, *The Christian Story: A Narrative Interpretation of Christian Doctrine* (Grand Rapids, Mich.: Eerdmans, 1978). Later came Bloesch, *Essentials of Evangelical Theology*, vol. 2 *Life, Ministry and Hope* (New York: Harper & Row, 1979), and Fackre, *The Christian Story*, rev. ed., 1984; 3rd ed., 1996; and *The Christian Story*, vol. 2, *Authority: Scripture in the Church for the World* (Grand Rapids, Mich.: Eerdmans, 1987).

[4]The ecumenical evangelical-evangelical ecumenical distinctions are made in Fackre, *Ecumenical Faith in Evangelical Perspective* (Grand Rapids, Mich.: Eerdmans, 1993), pp. vii-x. The conjunction "Savior, Redeemer and Lord" is from question 60 of the Evangelical Catechism, learned by Bloesch in his early years in the Evangelical Synod of North America.

[5]A usage Bloesch himself employs in his early work *The Christian Life and Salvation* (Grand Rapids, Mich.: Eerdmans, 1967), p. 53.

[6]See George S. Hendry, "Christology," in *A Dictionary of Christian Theology*, ed. Alan Richardson (Philadelphia: Westminster Press, 1969), pp. 51-64.

[7]As in John Murray, *Redemption Accomplished and Applied* (Grand Rapids, Mich.: Eerdmans, 1955, 1978).

[8]Charles Hodge, *Systematic Theology*, 3 vols. (New York: Charles Scribner's Sons, 1872), 1:313-732; 3:3-709. See also Augustus Strong, *Systematic Theology: A Compendium* (New York: Revell, 1907), pp. 665-888, with person, work and application, but only short discussions of election and law and "the ordinances of the Church" discussed under the separate rubric of "Ecclesiology."

[9]Representative systematics include the following:

Evangelical systematics: Millard Erickson, *Christian Theology* (Grand Rapids, Mich.: Baker, 1983-1985): pt. 7, "The Person of Christ"; pt. 8, "The Work of Christ"; pt. 10, "Salvation" (the *ordo*, including predestination); James Leo Garrett Jr., *Systematic Theology: Biblical Historical and Evangelical*, 2 vols. (Grand Rapids, Mich.: Eerdmans, 1990-1995): pt. 5, "The Person of Jesus Christ"; pt. 6, "The Work of Jesus Christ"; pt. 8, "Becoming a Christian and the Christian Life" (the *ordo*, including predestination); Gordon R. Lewis and Bruce A. Demarest, *Integrative Theology*, 3 vols. (Grand Rapids, Mich.: Zondervan, 1987-1994): vol. 2, pt. 2, "Christ's Atoning Provisions" (including person and work); vol. 3, pt. 1, "Personal Transformation."

Reformed systematics: Louis Berkhof, *Systematic Theology*, 4th rev. and enl. ed. (Grand Rapids, Mich.: Eerdmans, 1939, 1941): pt. 3, "The Doctrine of the Person and Work of Christ" (including natures, states and offices); pt. 4, "The Doctrine of the Application of the Work of Redemption" (the *ordo*, with predestination treated in pt. 1, "The Doctrine of God"); John H. Leith, *Basic Christian Doctrine* (Louisville, Ky.: Westminster John Knox, 1993): pt. 8, "Jesus Christ"; pt. 9, "The Work of Christ"; pts. 12-14, on faith, justification and sanctification; Daniel L. Migliore, *Faith Seeking Understanding: An Introduction to Christian Theology* (Louisville, Ky.: Westminster John Knox, 1991): pt. 8, "The Person and Work of Jesus Christ"; pt. 9, "The Holy Spirit and the Christian Life" (justification, sanctification, vocation).

Roman Catholic systematics: Francis Schüssler Fiorenza and John P. Galvin, *Systematic Theology*, 2 vols. (Minneapolis: Fortress, 1991): pt. 5, "Jesus Christ" (person and objective work); pt. 6, "Church"; pt. 7, "Sin and Grace"; Richard McBrien, *Catholicism* (Minneapolis: Winston, 1981): pt. 3, "Jesus Christ" (including person, work and sacramental presence); pt. 5, "Christian Existence—Ethical and Spiritual Dimensions" (including conversion, faith, discipleship).

[10]Assuming the definition of *evangelical* in the entry Gabriel Fackre, "Evangelical, Evangelicalism," in *The Westminster Dictionary of Christian Theology*, ed. Alan Richardson and John Bowden, rev. ed. (Philadelphia: Westminster Press, 1983), pp. 191-92.

[11]An evangelical "infallibilism" in the sense of unfailingly trustworthy in matters of faith and morals, rather than "inerrant" in science and history as well. See the writer's distinctions and discussion of Bloesch's hermeneutic in Fackre, *Authority: Scripture in the Church*, pp. 71-72.

[12]Bloesch is an "evangelical" also in its sixteenth-century Reformation meaning, as in his Evangelical Synod of North America origins and nurture in the Evangelical Catechism of that church.

[13]Distinctive aspects of Reformed theology discussed in Gabriel Fackre, "What the Lutherans and the Reformed Can Learn from One Another," *The Christian Century* 114, no. 18 (1997): 558-61, 563-65.

[14]Bloesch's father was a friend of Reinhold Niebuhr, and Bloesch wrote his doctoral dissertation at the University of Chicago Divinity School on Niebuhr.

While much influenced by the Reformed Barth, Bloesch's evangelical differences with him appear regularly. For example, in anthropology vis-à-vis Christology, Barth takes up "pride, sloth and falsehood" in turn *after* each christological theme (priest, king and prophet), whereas Bloesch deals with the Fall *before* the specifics of Christology. Here also is an example of Bloesch's appreciation for the Lutheran law-gospel distinction, albeit dealt with by Bloesch christologically.

[15]For example, Bloesch, *Christian Life and Salvation*, pp. 13-18.

[16]See "Reflections on the Theological Drift of the UCC: An Interview with Donald Bloesch," *The Witness*, Winter 1996, pp. 13, 16.

[17]See his review of the *New Century Hymnal* in *Christianity Today* 40, no. 8 (1996): 49-50 and comments on inclusive language in Bloesch, *Jesus Christ*, pp. 75-79.

[18]Bloesch, *Jesus Christ*, pp. 229-30.

[19]Ibid., p. 15.

[20]The title of the well-known book by Karl Menninger, *Whatever Became of Sin?* (New York: Hawthorne, 1973).

[21]A characterization that comes to mind as parallel to the title of a book by Bloesch: *The Battle for the Trinity: The Debate over Inclusive God-Language* (Ann Arbor, Mich.: Servant, 1985).

[22]Bloesch, *Jesus Christ*, p. 13.

[23]Ibid., pp. 69-70.

[24]Ibid., p. 56.

[25]Ibid., p. 55.

[26]Bloesch, *Essentials*, 1:129.

[27]Bloesch, *Jesus Christ*, p. 56.

[28]Ibid., pp. 57, 73.

[29]Ibid., p. 54.

[30]A theme anticipated in earlier works (Bloesch, *Essentials*, 1:130), but developed in detail in

conversation with Barth in Bloesch, *Jesus Christ,* chapter five.

[31]Bloesch, *Essentials,* 1:120-80, 2:174-210.

[32]Bloesch, *Jesus Christ,* pp. 83, 93, 104.

[33]Bloesch, *Essentials,* 1:122, 127; Bloesch, *Jesus Christ,* p. 57.

[34]A full chapter (ten) is devoted to this in Bloesch, *Jesus Christ.*

[35]Bloesch, *Jesus Christ,* p. 107.

[36]Ibid., pp. 118-19.

[37]For discussion of same see Bloesch, *Is the Bible Sexist?* (Westchester, Ill.: Crossway, 1982), 61-83; Donald G. Bloesch, *Battle,* pp. 1-67 and passim; Bloesch, *Jesus Christ,* pp. 75-79.

[38]Bloesch, *Jesus Christ,* pp. 144-58.

[39]Ibid., p. 158.

[40]Ibid., pp. 157, 162.

[41]Ibid., pp. 159-62.

[42]Ibid., p. 161.

[43]Ibid.

[44]Ibid., pp. 158, 160.

[45]Ibid., p. 226.

[46]Ibid., p. 170.

[47]Ibid., p. 169.

[48]Ibid., p. 162-63.

[49]Barth in *The Epistle to the Philippians,* cited in Bloesch, *Christian Life,* p. 63.

[50]Ibid., p. 64.

[51]Ibid., pp. 64-83. See also Bloesch, *Jesus Is Victor! Karl Barth's Doctrine of Salvation* (Nashville: Abingdon, 1976), pp. 118-22.

[52]See Waldron Scott in *Karl Barth's Theology of Mission* (Downers Grove, Ill.: InterVarsity Press, 1978), pp. 40-43.

[53]Bloesch, *Jesus Christ,* p. 179.

[54]For a collection of the same, as well as longer commentaries, see Bloesch, *Theological Notebook,* 2 vols. (Colorado Springs: Helmers & Howard, 1989-1991).

[55]Bloesch, *Jesus Christ,* p. 185.

[56]Bloesch, *Christian Life,* pp. 30-31.

[57]Bloesch, *Jesus Christ,* pp. 176-77.

[58]Bloesch, *Christian Life and Salvation;* Bloesch, *Jesus is Victor!;* Bloesch, *Essentials,* vols. 1 and 2; and Bloesch, *Jesus Christ.*

[59]Gabriel Fackre, "The Atonement," in *Encyclopedia of the Reformed Faith,* ed. Donald K. McKim (Louisville, Ky.: Westminster John Knox, 1992), pp. 13, 16.

[60]As documented by David F. Wells in *No Place for Truth: Or Whatever Happened to Evangelical Theology?* (Grand Rapids, Mich.: Eerdmans, 1993).

[61]See the paragraph reference in Bloesch, *Jesus Christ,* p. 158.

[62]As, for example, in the theologies of Hodge, L. Berkhof and Barth.

[63]An understanding of the atonement argued in Fackre, *Christian Story,* 3rd ed., pp. 134-51.

[64]So stated by Robert S. Franks in *The Work of Christ: A Historical Study of Christian Doctrine* (London: Thomas Nelson, 1962), p. 348.

While the Heidelberg Catechism, one of the three doctrinal symbols of Bloesch's Evangelical Synod and Evangelical and Reformed roots, features the threefold office in its christological section (question 31), the Evangelical Catechism of Bloesch's early training has no reference to it.

[65]See the "Decree on the Apostolate of the Laity," *Documents of Vatican II,* ed. Walter M. Abbott, S.J. (New York: Association Press, 1966), pp. 491-95. See also questions 31 and 32, *The Heidelberg Catechism* (Philadelphia: United Church Press, 1962), pp. 36-39.

[66]Nicholas Wolterstorff, *Until Justice and Peace Embrace* (Grand Rapids, Mich.: Eerdmans, 1983), pp. 2-22.

[67]Donald G. Bloesch, *Freedom for Obedience: Evangelical Ethics in Contemporary Times* (San

Francisco: Harper & Row, 1987), p. 234.

[68]Bloesch, *Jesus Christ*, pp. 242-43.

[69]While Bloesch associates Docetism today with views that reduce Jesus to a universal idea, this appears rather to be yet another version of Ebionism in which Jesus is an exemplar of a human value.

[70]Bloesch, *Jesus Christ*, p. 234.

[71]See *Interpretation*, April 1997, an issue devoted to the centrist phenomenon.

[72]Most recently, the Lutheran-Reformed Formula of Agreement and its antecedents, The Leuenburg Concord, the Lutheran-Episcopal Concordat, the Roman Catholic-Lutheran Agreement on Justification and the nine-denomination Consultation on Church Union with its doctrinal COCU Consensus. The World Council of Churches also has in its brief doctrinal statement the confession of Jesus Christ as "God and Savior," and its Faith and Order Commission's two recent documents *Baptism, Eucharist and Ministry* and *Confessing the Apostolic Faith* (based on the Nicene Creed) presuppose and/or articulate Chalcedonian orthodoxy.

[73]See Gabriel Fackre, "Reorientation and Retrieval in Seminary Theology," *Christian Century* 108, no. 20 (1991): 653-56.

[74]Bruce Marshall, "Aquinas as a Post-liberal Theologian," *The Thomist* 53, no. 3 (1989): 353-402, and its sequel, George Lindbeck, "Response to Bruce Marshall," pp. 403-6.

[75]See especially Wolfhart Pannenberg, *Systematic Theology*, trans. Geoffrey W. Bromiley (Grand Rapids, Mich.: Eerdmans, 1994), 2:386-96.

[76]Bloesch, *Jesus Christ*, p. 118.

[77]Ibid.

[78]Bloesch, *Is the Bible Sexist?* pp. 72, 73.

[79]Bloesch, *Battle for the Trinity*, p. 23 and passim.

[80]Bloesch, *Is the Bible Sexist?* p. 77.

[81]Ibid.

[82]Ibid., p. 72.

[83]Bloesch, *Jesus Christ*, pp. 188-89.

[84]Thus the difference in relations to the UCC between the two neoconfessional movements in the UCC, the Biblical Witness Fellowship and Confessing Christ.

[85]Bloesch, *Christian Life*, p. 30.

[86]Continuing to this day as in the North American Lutheran-Reformed dialogue and hopes for "full communion." See Keith F. Nickle and Timothy F. Lull, eds., *A Common Calling: The Witness of Our Reformation Churches in North America Today* (Minneapolis: Augsburg, 1993).

[87]A critique developed in Gabriel Fackre, *The Doctrine of Revelation: A Narrative Interpretation* (Edinburgh: Edinburgh University Press; Grand Rapids, Mich.: Eerdmans, 1997), pp. 137-48 and passim.

[88]Karl Barth, *Church Dogmatics* 4/3/1, trans. G. W. Bromiley and T. F. Torrance (Edinburgh: T & T Clark, 1961), pp. 477-78.

[89]At one point Bloesch seems to have the passage cited above in mind when he says he "does not share his [Barth's] expectation of a universal final salvation" (Bloesch, *Jesus Is Victor!* p. 118). However, there is an important distinction between "expectation" and "hope," the former an uncharacteristically Barthian assumption of our penetration of God's freedom, and the latter an acknowledgment of that freedom, but attention to evidences granted of what that might be in God's freedom for us in Jesus Christ.

Chapter 7: The Holy Spirit in the Theology of Donald G. Bloesch

[1]Donald G. Bloesch, *Essentials of Evangelical Theology*, 2 vols. (San Francisco: Harper & Row, 1978-1979).

[2]Donald G. Bloesch, *A Theology of Word & Spirit: Authority & Method in Theology*, Christian Foundations 1 (Downers Grove, Ill.: InterVarsity Press, 1992).

[3]Donald G. Bloesch, *The Evangelical Renaissance* (Grand Rapids, Mich.: Eerdmans, 1973), p.

21.

[4]Bloesch, *Theology of Word & Spirit*, p. 58.

[5]Ibid., p. 38.

[6]Ibid., p. 202.

[7]Ibid.

[8]Ibid., pp. 60-66.

[9]Ibid., pp. 234-41.

[10]Ibid., pp. 38, 58.

[11]Ibid., p. 60.

[12]For a full examination of Bloesch's view of the Bible, see Frank Hasel, *Scripture in the Theologies of W. Pannenberg and D. G. Bloesch* (Frankfurt am Main: Peter Lang, 1996).

[13]Donald G. Bloesch, *Holy Scripture: Revelation, Inspiration & Interpretation*, Christian Foundations 2 (Downers Grove, Ill.: InterVarsity Press, 1994), p. 87.

[14]Ibid., p. 38.

[15]Ibid., pp. 120, 125.

[16]Ibid., pp. 108-17.

[17]Ibid., p. 115.

[18]Ibid., pp. 181, 200, 206-8. See also Donald G. Bloesch, "A Christological Hermeneutic: Crisis and Conflict in Hermeneutics," in *The Use of the Bible in Theology: Evangelical Options*, ed. Robert K. Johnston (Atlanta: John Knox Press, 1985), pp. 78-102.

[19]Ibid., p. 126.

[20]Bloesch, "Christological Hermeneutic," pp. 98-102.

[21]Bloesch, *Theology of Word & Spirit*, p. 118.

[22]The phenomenon is similar to Barth's so-called actualism in biblical interpretation, in which the Bible is said ever-anew to become the Word of God. It sounds as if it could mean anything at all. But what evidence is there that Barth practices eisegesis or engages in fanciful interpretations? Both employ a christocentric focus which is thoroughly and classically Christian. The practice may be better than the theory. See Klaas Runia, *Karl Barth's Doctrine of Holy Scripture* (Grand Rapids, Mich.: Eerdmans, 1962), chap. 8.

[23]See the discussion in Gary D. Badcock, *Light of Truth and Fire of Love: A Theology of the Holy Spirit* (Grand Rapids, Mich.: Eerdmans, 1997), and John Thompson, *Modern Trinitarian Perspectives* (New York: Oxford University Press, 1994).

[24]Karl Barth, *Church Dogmatics* 1/1, *The Doctrine of the Word of God*, trans. Geoffrey W. Bromiley (Edinburgh: T & T Clark, 1975), p. 413.

[25]Donald G. Bloesch, *God the Almighty: Power, Wisdom, Holiness, Love*, Christian Foundations 3 (Downers Grove, Ill.: InterVarsity Press, 1995), pp. 185, 193, 197.

[26]Ibid., pp. 99-102.

[27]Ibid., pp. 99, 205.

[28]Ibid., pp. 254-61. His reference is to the open view of God found in Clark Pinnock et al., *The Openness of God: A Biblical Challenge to the Traditional Understanding of God* (Downers Grove, Ill.: InterVarsity Press, 1994).

[29]Bloesch, *God the Almighty*, p. 257.

[30]Donald G. Bloesch, *The Battle for the Trinity: The Debate over Inclusive God-Language* (Ann Arbor, Mich.: Servant, 1985), p. 53.

[31]Bloesch, *God the Almighty*, p. 190.

[32]Ibid., pp. 108-12.

[33]Bloesch, *Essentials*, 1:227, 246.

[34]By way of contrast, in my book *A Wideness in God's Mercy: The Finality of Jesus Christ in a World of Religions* (Grand Rapids, Mich.: Zondervan, 1992) there is an attempt to find a universal opportunity within history that retains better the importance of earthly decisions. Both positions are, however, wider hope standpoints.

[35]Bloesch, *Essentials*, 2:155-73; and Bloesch, *Evangelical Renaissance*, pp. 72 and 101-57.

[36]Bloesch, *Essentials*, 1:244.

[37]Ibid., 2:7.

[38]Ibid., 1:32.

[39]Bloesch, *Evangelical Renaissance*, p. 63; and Bloesch, *Essentials*, 1:202.

[40]Donald G. Bloesch, *Jesus Christ: Savior & Lord*, Christian Foundations 4 (Downers Grove, Ill.: InterVarsity Press, 1997), p. 178.

[41]Donald G. Bloesch, *Jesus Is Victor! Karl Barth's Doctrine of Salvation* (Nashville: Abingdon, 1976), pp. 111, 109.

[42]Bloesch, *Essentials*, 1:206-8.

[43]I appreciate what Bloesch says in *Essentials* (1:203-8, 220 n. 83), which reveals his struggle with the issue. However, I believe that a choice has to be made between monergism and synergism: there is no *tertium quid*.

[44]Ibid., 1:201.

[45]Not all Reformed theologians are monergists: for example, Harry Boer, *An Ember Still Glowing: Humankind in the Image of God* (Grand Rapids, Mich.: Eerdmans, 1990), and Vincent Brummer, "Can We Resist the Grace of God?" in *Speaking of a Personal God* (Cambridge: Cambridge University Press, 1992), chap. 3.

[46]For references, see note 4 on pages 268-69 of Clark Pinnock, *Flame of Love: A Theology of the Holy Spirit* (Downers Grove, Ill.: InterVarsity Press, 1996).

[47]Consider Robert V. Rakestraw, "Becoming Like God: An Evangelical Doctrine of Theosis," *Journal of the Evangelical Theological Society* 40 (1997): 257-69.

[48]Bloesch, *Essentials*, 2:11-15.

[49]Ibid., 2:107-9. I think he would agree with Jon Ruthven, *On the Cessation of the Charismata: The Protestant Polemic on Postbiblical Miracles* (Sheffield, U.K.: Sheffield Academic Press, 1993).

[50]Bloesch, *Essentials*, vol. 2, chap. 3.

[51]Bloesch, *Evangelical Renaissance*, p. 64. Also see Bloesch, *Essentials*, 1:206, 240.

Chapter 8: Bloesch's Doctrine of God

[1]Donald G. Bloesch, *God the Almighty: Power, Wisdom, Holiness, Love*, Christian Foundations 3 (Downers Grove, Ill.: InterVarsity Press, 1995).

[2]Ibid., p. 29.

[3]Ibid., p. 36.

[4]Ibid., p. 38.

[5]Ibid., p. 58.

[6]Donald G. Bloesch, "The Finality of Christ and Religious Pluralism," *Touchstone* 4, no. 3 (1991): 5-9.

[7]Bloesch, *God the Almighty*, p. 65.

[8]Ibid., p. 69. Bloesch is quoting Jürgen Moltmann, *God in Creation*, trans. Margaret Kohl (San Francisco: Harper & Row, 1985), p. 64.

[9]Ibid., p. 28.

[10]Ibid., p. 80.

[11]Ibid.

[12]Ibid., pp. 91-102.

[13]Ibid., p. 101.

[14]Ibid.

[15]Ibid., p. 102.

[16]Ibid., pp. 118-19.

[17]Ibid., p. 136.

[18]Ibid., p. 139.

[19]Ibid., p. 156-57.

[20]Ibid., p. 157.

[21]John Calvin, *Institutes of the Christian Religion*, ed. John T. McNeill, trans. Ford Lewis Battles, Library of Christian Classics 20-21 (Philadelphia: Westminster Press, 1960), 1.13.5, p. 128.

[22]Bloesch, *God the Almighty,* p. 166.

[23]Ibid., p. 167.

[24]Ibid., p. 199.

[25]James B. Torrance, *Worship, Community & the Triune God of Grace* (Downers Grove, Ill.: InterVarsity Press, 1996).

[26]Bloesch, *God the Almighty,* p. 261.

[27]Ibid.

[28]Ibid., pp. 262-63.

Chapter 9: Bloesch's Doctrine of the Christian Life

[1]The quotation from Kierkegaard appears as an epigraph in Bloesch's early book *The Christian Life and Salvation* (Grand Rapids, Mich.: Eerdmans, 1967), setting the tone for the vision Bloesch develops throughout the work.

[2]Donald G. Bloesch, *The Crisis of Piety: Essays Toward a Theology of the Christian Life* (Grand Rapids, Mich.: Eerdmans, 1968), p. 8.

[3]Donald G. Bloesch, *Centers of Christian Renewal* (Philadelphia: United Church Press, 1964).

[4]Donald G. Bloesch, *Essentials of Evangelical Theology,* 2 vols. (San Francisco: Harper & Row, 1978-1979).

[5]Bloesch, *Centers of Christian Renewal,* pp. 13-14.

[6]Ibid., p. 22.

[7]Bloesch, *Crisis of Piety,* p. 16.

[8]Donald G. Bloesch, *The Crisis of Piety,* 2nd ed. (Colorado Springs: Helmers & Howard, 1988), pp. ix-x. In the preface Bloesch indicates concern that while the church was not "silent in the face of social evils," its word seemed "to lack power and discriminating judgment" (p. xv).

[9]Donald G. Bloesch, *The Christian Witness in a Secular Age* (Minneapolis: Augsburg, 1968). Bloesch's unpublished dissertation on Reinhold Niebuhr's apologetics also deals with this.

[10]Ibid., pp. 9-11.

[11]Ibid., p. 11.

[12]Donald G. Bloesch, *The Reform of the Church* (Grand Rapids, Mich.: Eerdmans, 1970).

[13]Donald G. Bloesch, *The Ground of Certainty: Toward an Evangelical Theology of Revelation* (Grand Rapids, Mich.: Eerdmans, 1971).

[14]Throughout the period from the mid-sixties through the early seventies, Bloesch became more and more self-consciously "evangelical." It appears that the first time Bloesch refers to his position as "evangelical" and "catholic evangelical" is in *Crisis of Piety,* 1st ed., pp. 28, 33. However, Bloesch's acute theological mind could not but see problems within evangelicalism, and he has sought to correct and redefine it by bringing it more fully into dialogue with the Great Tradition of the church than any other North American evangelical theologian had previously done.

[15]This is evident even in the titles of other books Bloesch published during this period. See the selected bibliography in this book (p. 209).

[16]See chapter one of this book.

[17]See Donald G. Bloesch, *Jesus Is Victor! Karl Barth's Doctrine of Salvation* (Nashville: Abingdon, 1976), p. 10.

[18]Bloesch, *Christian Life,* p. 129.

[19]Ibid., pp. 25-29.

[20]Ibid., pp. 24-46, especially 25-26, 43.

[21]Ibid., pp. 42-46.

[22]Bloesch discusses the two poles or perspectives in significant detail in relation to the biblical witness and the history of Christian thought, and also in relation to the categories of mystery, paradox and dialectic, which are of strategic importance to his theological perspective. Ibid., pp. 13-18, 127-40, 141-42.

[23]Ibid., p. 23.

[24]Ibid., p. 141.

[25]Ibid., p. 18.

[26]Ibid., pp. 13-18, 127-40, 141-42.

[27]Ibid., pp. 128-29. Bloesch also calls this objectivism, emphasizing what God has done for us in Christ but neglecting the need for human participation or appropriation.

[28]Ibid. Bloesch also calls this subjectivism, emphasizing our apprehension of God or the gospel.

[29]Donald G. Bloesch, *A Theology of Word & Spirit: Authority & Method in Theology,* Christian Foundations 1 (Downers Grove, Ill.: InterVarsity Press, 1992).

[30]Ibid., p. 14.

[31]The Word and Spirit motif defines Bloesch's understanding of revelation, truth and authority. It also signifies his concern to affirm and unite the objective and subjective poles of revelation. In this way he hopes to overcome the incessant oscillation between the objective and subjective poles of the knowing relation that is characteristic of theological and philosophical conversation throughout the modern period. The rigorous application of this "Word and Spirit" theme throughout the first two volumes of Bloesch's systematic theology leads to some characteristic reformulations of the theological loci covered there.

[32]Bloesch, *Christian Life,* pp. 26-27.

[33]Ibid., pp. 29-30.

[34]Donald G. Bloesch, *Jesus Christ: Savior & Lord,* Christian Foundations 4 (Downers Grove, Ill.: InterVarsity Press, 1997), p. 11. Bloesch also says that "a holy life is not an appendage to our salvation, but the sign and evidence of the authenticity of our salvation," (p. 12).

[35]Donald G. Bloesch, *The Future of Evangelical Christianity: A Call for Unity amid Diversity* (Garden City, N.Y.: Doubleday, 1983), p. 133.

[36]Ibid.

[37]Bloesch, *Christian Life,* pp. 42-46.

[38]Ibid., p. 43.

[39]Ibid.

[40]Ibid.

[41]Ibid., pp. 43-44.

[42]Ibid., p. 44.

[43]Ibid.

[44]Indeed, Bloesch spends an entire chapter on each of the three tenses or dimensions of time in salvation and the Christian life. Chapter three, "The Divine Sacrifice," focuses on the objective basis and past dimension of salvation. Chapter four, "Bearing the Cross," deals with the present pole of salvation in the Christian life. Chapter five, "The Crown of Glory," treats the future dimension where soteriology is fulfilled in eschatology.

An additional chapter (chap. six, "The Christian Pilgrimage") outlines the interrelationship of the various dimensions of salvation and the Christian life. Here Bloesch discusses baptism (water and Spirit), the Lord's Supper and other means of grace; conversion as a break from the past but also a process that continues throughout life; a reconceived view of sainthood; the experiential element of faith; and also "a desert element"—all under the notion of Christian life and salvation as a pilgrimage.

A final chapter, "The Paradox of Salvation," returns to the central motif of his doctrine of the Christian life and salvation, the coincidence of divine agency and human agency.

[45]Ibid., p. 127.

[46]See Bonnie Miller-McLemore, *Also a Mother: Work and Family as Theological Dilemma* (Nashville: Abingdon, 1994), and Miroslav Volf's brilliant book *Work in the Spirit* (New York: Oxford University Press, 1991), which proposes a pneumatological alternative to a theology of work as vocation.

[47]Bloesch, *Christian Life,* p. 27.

[48]There is absolutely no question that Bloesch fully and unequivocally affirms the Trinity. The question I am raising is the place of the doctrine of the Trinity within the architectonics of Bloesch's theology. Both in *Essentials of Evangelical Theology* and in his seven-volume systematic theology, Christian Foundations, Bloesch thematizes his doctrine of God under the

rubric of God's sovereignty. The chapter in *Essentials* dealing with his doctrine of God is entitled "The Sovereignty of God," and the doctrine of the Trinity is covered in barely three pages (see Bloesch, *Essentials*, 1:35-37). Volume 3 in Christian Foundations, on Bloesch's doctrine of God, is entitled *God the Almighty: Power, Wisdom, Holiness, Love* (Downers Grove, Ill.: InterVarsity Press, 1995), and Bloesch devotes one chapter to "The Mystery of the Trinity."

[49]Eberhard Nestle, "Bengel als Gelehrter: Ein Bild für unsere Tage," in *Marginalien und Materialen* (Tübingen: J. J. Heckenhauer Buchhandlung), 1893, p. 8, but cf. pp. 29, 86 and 106, following Albrecht Ritschl, *Geschichte des Pietismus*, 3 vols. (Bonn: Adolph Marcus, 1880-1886), 3:64.

[50]Donald G. Bloesch, *The Struggle of Prayer* (Colorado Springs: Helmers & Howard, 1988); Bloesch, *Essentials*, 2:56-59. All of Bloesch's books dealing with the Christian life abound with references to prayer and its importance.

[51]Recent biblical scholarship has shown that there was undoubtedly a symbiotic relationship between spontaneous prayer and patterned prayer. Samuel Balentine, following M. Greenberg, surveys recent research and concludes, "The spontaneous and the prescribed in social behavior were always mixed. In interhuman as well as divine-human communication the patterned speech form, the conventional openings and closings, the traditional articulations in set situations, made spontaneity truly possible." See Samuel Balentine, *Prayer in the Hebrew Bible: The Drama of Divine-Human Dialogue* (Minneapolis: Fortress, 1993), p. 24, citing M. Greenberg, *Biblical Prose Prayer as a Window to the Popular Religion of Ancient Israel* (Berkeley: University of California Press, 1983), p. 44. My one criticism of Bloesch's work in this area is that this symbiosis between the spontaneous and patterned seems to be lacking. He appears to prefer spontaneous freedom in intercession, supplication and penitence over the patterned. See Bloesch, *Struggle of Prayer*, pp. 20 and 40-42.

[52]As Sebastian Moore said to Kathleen Norris, "God behaves in the Psalms in ways God is not allowed to behave in systematic theology." Norris, "The Paradox of the Psalms," in *Out of the Garden: Women Writers on the Bible*, ed. Christina Büchman and Celina Spiegel (New York: Fawcett Columbine, 1994), p. 222. The people who pray know that they can say more, maybe claim more, in prayer than in propositional formulas. Those who cannot find resolution in propositional argument might find a resolve through prayer sufficient to maintain fidelity to God, experience notwithstanding.

[53]Bloesch, *Crisis of Piety*, p. 16.

[54]Ibid. Bloesch draws a similar relationship between *theologia dogmatica* and *theologia practica* in Bloesch, *Christian Life*, p. 79.

[55]Bloesch, *Essentials*, 1:2.

[56]Donald Bloesch, "A Call to Spirituality," in *The Orthodox Evangelicals*, ed. Robert Webber and Donald Bloesch (Nashville: Thomas Nelson, 1978), p. 149.

[57]Bloesch, *Crisis of Piety*, p. 18.

[58]How this issue plays out for Bloesch is seen in his comparison between mysticism and evangelicalism. The problems in particular are in their differing conceptualities of the order of salvation. In sum, the mystical way develops in three stages: purgation, illumination and mystical union with God. The evangelical way can also be posited in three stages, variously described. In a reversal of the mystical way, evangelical soteriology posits this development: union with God in Christ, illumination and purgation. These correspond to the doctrinal loci of justification, sanctification and glorification. When lived as the shape of the Christian life, these doctrinal loci become awakening to faith, repentance and obedience.

Bloesch views the evangelical order of salvation as safeguarding both a radical theocentricity and a radical anthropocentricity. As for God, in the mystical way the boundary between God and humans is blurred, since the union achieved between the two comes close to a unity of being. When things get that metaphysical, the identities of both God and persons are not easily distinguished. If such distinctions are not maintained, then a genuine relationship between God and persons is largely precluded, and the relationship initially established between God and persons is only a stage on the way to unitive being.

The way in which these orders of salvation are set up is crucial to Bloesch's understanding of "radical" theocentricity and "radical" anthropocentricity. In the mystical way the process ends with God. In the evangelical way the process begins with God. In the mystical way, motivated by eros, one is elevated to share in union with God, whereas in the evangelical understanding God comes down, motivated by agapaic love, to establish a relation with those unlike him in character to the point of being his enemies.

The fruit of agape is more in the nature of communion than union. If the language of union is used, it will be to designate a moral union of wills, not a metaphysical union of being. If the mystical way succeeds, Bloesch's concern is that a theology of glory will replace a theology of the cross. In the union of human will with the will of God, the human will be plunged ever more into history with its contingencies and suffering. In part at least, God will be met in the world in the person who mediates God and God's will to us.

Put in this way, the evangelical mode of knowing God stresses a less direct, less immediate mode in that it relies on modes of revelation that sometimes hide God more than reveal him. For example, the way of Jesus Christ led more and more into ambiguity the nearer he came to his death. God seemed unavailable for rescue. How God fits into this story seemed at times no clearer to Jesus than to us, driving him to excruciating times of prayer.

In mysticism, on the other hand, by virtue of the union of the person with God, knowledge of God is far less mediated by history and mediated more by the direct and immediate presence of God. The closer one comes to union with God, the less God seems present *to* the person and the more the person is present in God. In evangelicalism God is always present *to* the person, never compromising the boundary between himself and the person. This brief discussion of evangelicalism and mysticism is a composite of the comparisons and contrasts Bloesch develops in several publications.

For the full treatment of this, see Jordan Aumann, O.P., Thomas Hopko and Donald G. Bloesch, *Christian Spirituality—East and West* (Chicago: Priory, 1968), pp. 165-78; Bloesch, *Crisis of Piety*, pp. 95-124; Bloesch, *Struggle of Prayer*, pp. 1-10, 97-130; and Bloesch, *Essentials*, 2:242-46.

Bloesch does devote a portion of his book *Struggle of Prayer* to some areas of convergence between mysticism and evangelical Christianity. For example, meditation does not lead to union with God but supplication (p. 120). Contemplation is "heartfelt attention to the things of God," but "neither meditation nor contemplation is to be regarded as true prayer" (p. 121). Since Bloesch regards true prayer as requiring the use of words, audible or inaudible (p. 50), I have wondered if the "rest" that belongs to the people of God in Hebrews is not also a form of prayer, even though perhaps wordless. Presence to and for each other does not require words, but communication and communion take place. If prayer is a constant struggle, it could become self-defeating. The invitation to rest is not necessarily an invitation to cease praying, but it is an invitation to enjoyment and rest.

[59]Bloesch, *Essentials*, 1:39.

[60]Ibid.

[61]Bloesch, *Jesus Christ*, p. 41.

[62]Ibid., p. 44.

[63]Bloesch, *Essentials*, 1:92-93.

[64]Ibid., 1:98-99.

[65]Bloesch, *Jesus Christ*, p. 145.

[66]Ibid., p. 161, and Bloesch, *Essentials*, 2:280-281.

[67]Bloesch, *Jesus Christ*, p. 161.

[68]Bloesch, *Future of Evangelical Christianity*, p. 133 and Bloesch, *Christian Spirituality*, p. 165.

[69]Bloesch, *Jesus Christ*, pp. 166-67.

[70]Ibid., p. 163.

[71]Ibid., p. 181; see also Bloesch, *Essentials*, 2:41-42, and Bloesch, *Christian Spirituality*, pp. 174-78.

[72]Bloesch, *Crisis of Piety*, pp. 84-85.

[73]This *(A Theology of Word & Spirit)* is the title of volume one of his systematic theology.

[74]Bloesch, *Jesus Christ*, p. 178, and Bloesch, *Christian Life*, pp. 25-28.

[75]Bloesch, *Crisis of Piety*, p. 69.

[76]Bloesch, *Jesus Christ*, p. 183.

[77]Donald Bloesch, *Theological Notebook*, 2 vols. (Colorado Springs: Helmers & Howard, 1989-1991), 2:66.

[78]Bloesch, *Jesus Christ*, p. 178.

[79]Bloesch, *Theological Notebook*, 2:145.

[80]Bloesch, *Crisis of Piety*, p. 46.

[81]Ibid., p. 90.

[82]Bloesch, *Christian Life*, p. 79.

[83]Bloesch, *Jesus Christ*, p. 11.

[84]Ibid.

[85]Bloesch, *Christian Spirituality*, p. 176.

[86]Bloesch, *Jesus Christ*, p. 181.

[87]Bloesch uses "evangelical devotionism" to describe his doctrine of the Christian life in his book *Crisis of Piety*, pp. 28-33.

[88]Bloesch, *Christian Spirituality*, pp. 180-81, and Bloesch, *Reform of the Church*, pp. 15-34.

[89]Bloesch, *Jesus Christ*, p. 184, and *Essentials*, 1:201-3.

[90]Bloesch, *Crisis of Piety*, p. 84.

[91]Ibid., pp. 28-29.

[92]Ibid., pp. 39-40.

[93]Ibid., pp. 66-69.

[94]Bloesch, *Theological Notebook*, 1:87. Also see 1:5.

[95]Donald G. Bloesch, *Freedom for Obedience: Evangelical Ethics in Contemporary Times* (San Francisco: Harper & Row, 1987), p. 81.

[96]Bloesch, *Struggle of Prayer*, p. 45.

[97]Bloesch, *Essentials*, 1:97.

[98]Ibid. Also see Bloesch, *Theological Notebook*, 2:61.

[99]Bloesch, *Theological Notebook*, 2:61.

[100]Ibid., 2:16.

[101]Paul Tillich, *The Protestant Era*, trans. James Luther Adams, abridg. ed. (Chicago: University of Chicago Press/Phoenix, 1957), p. x.

[102]Walter Brueggemann, *Praying the Psalms*, Pace Book (Winona, Minn.: St. Mary's, 1986), p. 79.

Chapter 10: Donald Bloesch as a Social Prophet

[1]Donald G. Bloesch, 1964, in *Theological Notebook*, 2 vols. (Colorado Springs: Helmers & Howard, 1989-1991), p. 186. The first two parts of this chapter summarize a much more extensive survey of Bloesch's career found in my essay "The Theologian as Prophet: Donald Bloesch and the Crisis of the Modern Church," in *From East to West: Essays in Honor of Donald G. Bloesch*, ed. Daniel J. Adams (Lanham, Md.: University of America Press, 1997), pp. 211-32.

[2]Donald G. Bloesch, *The Ground of Certainty: Toward an Evangelical Theology of Revelation* (Grand Rapids, Mich.: Eerdmans, 1971), p. 13.

[3]Donald G. Bloesch, "A Theology of Christian Commitment," *Theology and Life* 9, no. 4 (1966): 343.

[4]Ibid.

[5]This theme runs throughout his writings. See, for example, Donald G. Bloesch, "The Ideological Temptation," *Listening* 7, no. 1 (1972): 45-54.

[6]Donald G. Bloesch, *Freedom for Obedience: Evangelical Ethics in Contemporary Times* (San Francisco: Harper & Row, 1987), p. 265.

[7]On this theme see, for example, Donald G. Bloesch, "Burying the Gospel," pts. 1 and 2, *Christianity Today* 15, no. 25 (1971): 8-11; 16, no. 1 (1971): 12-14.

[8]Donald G. Bloesch, "The Challenge Facing the Churches," in *Christianity Confronts Modernity*, ed. Peter Williamson and Kevin Perrotta (Ann Arbor, Mich.: Servant, 1981), p. 215.

[9]Bloesch, *Ground of Certainty*, p. 174.

[10]Bloesch, "Ideological Temptation," pp. 51-52.

[11]Donald G. Bloesch, "The Christian and the Drift Towards War," *Theology and Life* 2, no. 4 (1959): 325. See also his essay "Vain Hope for Victory," *The Pulpit* 32, no. 1 (1961): 9-11. In January 1960, Bloesch signed a statement against weapons of mass destruction issued by the faculty of the University of Dubuque Theological Seminary (UDTS). This statement read in part: "There is . . . no conceivable end that justifies these means—neither the salvation of the West with what is here called Christian civilization, nor the salvation of the East with what is there called the achievements of the Socialist revolution. . . . All men and nations who follow the policy of war by mass extermination provoke the wrath of God and His just retribution." See Dubuque Theological Seminary Faculty, *Mass Extermination as a Means of Waging War* (Dubuque, 1960), in the archives at UDTS.

[12]Quotes are from a 1960 course syllabus, "Christianity and Secularism," pp. 20-21, in the archives at UDTS. See also Bloesch's essays "Biblical Religion vs. Culture Religion," *Theology and Life* 3, no. 3 (1960): 175-76; and "Syncretism: Its Cultural Forms and Its Influence," *Dubuque Christian American* 36, no. 2 (1961): 2.

[13]Donald G. Bloesch, "Billy Graham: A Theological Appraisal," *Theology and Life* 3, no. 2 (1960): 140-41.

[14]Bloesch, "Theology of Christian Commitment," pp. 335-36. See also Donald G. Bloesch, *The Reform of the Church* (Grand Rapids, Mich.: Eerdmans, 1970), pp. 145-55; and Donald G. Bloesch, "The Secular Theology of Harvey Cox," *The Dubuque Seminary Journal* 1, no. 2 (1966): 1-5.

[15]Donald G. Bloesch, "Prophetic Preaching and Civil Rights," *The Pulpit* 37, no. 2 (1966): 7-9. See also Bloesch, *Reform of the Church*, p. 170.

[16]Donald G. Bloesch, "This Immoral War: Why We Protest," archives at UDTS.

[17]See Bloesch, *Reform of the Church*, pp. 172-73.

[18]Ibid., p. 169. On the same theme also see Donald G. Bloesch, "Church Funds for Revolution?" *Christianity Today* 12, no. 15 (1968): 27-28; and Donald G. Bloesch, "The Meaning of Salvation," *Good News* 4, no. 4 (1971): 53-57.

[19]On this last issue see Donald G. Bloesch, "Intensive Farming," *Lutheran Forum* 2, no. 7 (1968): 4-6.

[20]Donald G. Bloesch, "Response to 'Theological Education and Liberation Theology' by Frederick Herzog et al.," *Theological Education* 16, no. 1 (1979): 16-18.

[21]Donald G. Bloesch, "Reply to Randy Maddox," *Christian Scholar's Review* 18, no. 3 (1989): 283.

[22]Donald G. Bloesch, "Liturgical Sexism: A New Dispute," *Eternity* 31, no. 6 (1980): 13. See also his review of Stephen Clark, *Man and Woman in Christ*, in *Christianity Today* 25, no. 8 (1981): 56.

[23]Donald G. Bloesch, *The Battle for the Trinity: The Debate over Inclusive God-Language* (Ann Arbor, Mich.: Servant, 1985). Quotes are from a University of Dubuque press release, October 30, 1985, in the archives at UDTS. See also Bloesch's essay "Living God or Ideological Construct?" *The Reformed Journal* 34, no. 6 (1984): 29-31.

[24]Donald G. Bloesch, *Is the Bible Sexist?* (Westchester, Ill.: Crossway, 1982); see also Catherine Gabe, "Dubuque Theologian Disputes Claims Bible Is Sexist," *Dubuque Telegraph Herald*, October 1, 1982.

[25]Donald G. Bloesch, "Beyond Patriarchalism and Feminism," *Touchstone* 4, no. 1 (1990): 10.

[26]Bloesch, "Theology of Christian Commitment," p. 327.

[27]Donald G. Bloesch, "God the Civilizer," in *Christian Faith and Practice in the Modern World*, ed. Mark A. Noll and David F. Wells (Grand Rapids, Mich.: Eerdmans, 1988), pp. 182-83.

[28]Donald A. McGavran, "Variations in Adjustments," in *Christopaganism or Indigenous Christianity?* ed. Tetsunao Yamamori and Charles R. Taber (South Pasadena, Calif.: William Carey

Library, 1975), pp. 167-68.

[29]Paul Hiebert, "Critical Contextualization," *International Bulletin of Missionary Research* 11, no. 3 (1987): 104-12.

Chapter 11: Donald Bloesch Responds

[1]Donald G. Bloesch, *Centers of Christian Renewal* (Philadelphia: United Church Press, 1964).

[2]Donald G. Bloesch, *Wellsprings of Renewal* (Grand Rapids, Mich.: Eerdmans, 1974).

[3]Donald G. Bloesch, *The Reform of the Church* (Grand Rapids, Mich.: Eerdmans, 1970).

[4]Donald G. Bloesch, *Freedom for Obedience: Evangelical Ethics for Contemporary Times* (San Francisco: Harper & Row, 1987).

[5]Donald G. Bloesch, *Jesus Christ: Savior & Lord*, Christian Foundations 4 (Downers Grove, Ill.: InterVarsity Press, 1997).

[6]Donald G. Bloesch, *The Future of Evangelical Christianity: A Call for Unity amid Diversity* (1983; 2nd ed., Colorado Springs: Helmers & Howard, 1988).

[7]Donald G. Bloesch, *A Theology of Word & Spirit: Authority & Method in Theology*, Christian Foundations 1 (Downers Grove, Ill.: InterVarsity Press, 1992), pp. 57-61.

[8]See ibid., pp. 61-66.

[9]Thomas F. Torrance, *The Doctrine of Grace in the Apostolic Fathers* (Edinburgh: Oliver and Boyd, 1948).

[10]Emil Brunner, *The Christian Doctrine of God*, trans. Olive Wyon (Philadelphia: Westminster Press, 1974), p. 74.

[11]Karl Barth, *Church Dogmatics* 4/3/1, ed. G. W. Bromiley and T. F. Torrance (Edinburgh: T & T Clark, 1961), pp. 292-96.

Contributors

Donald G. Bloesch, emeritus professor of theology, University of Dubuque Theological Seminary (United Church of Christ)*

Elmer M. Colyer, associate professor of historical theology, Stanley Professor of Wesley Studies, University of Dubuque Theological Seminary (United Methodist Church)

Avery Dulles, S.J., Laurence J. McGinley Professor, Fordham University (Roman Catholic)

Millard J. Erickson, Distinguished Professor of Theology, Truett Seminary, Baylor University (Baptist General Conference)

Gabriel Fackre, Abbot Professor of Christian Theology Emeritus, Andover Newton Theological School (United Church of Christ)

Stanley J. Grenz, Pioneer McDonald Professor of Theology and Ethics, Carey/Regent College; professor of theology and ethics, Northern Baptist Theological Seminary (Baptist Union of Western Canada)

Roger E. Olson, professor of theology, Bethel College and Seminary (American Baptist Churches, USA)

Clark H. Pinnock, professor of theology, McMaster Divinity College (Baptist Convention of Ontario and Quebec)

James R. Rohrer, formerly assistant professor of church history, Yushan Theological College and Seminary in Hualien, Taiwan; now assistant professor of religion, Northwestern College, Iowa (United Church of Christ)

Thomas F. Torrance, emeritus professor of Christian dogmatics, University of Edinburgh (Church of Scotland—Presbyterian)

John Weborg, professor of theology, coordinator of spiritual formation, North Park Theological Seminary (Evangelical Covenant Church)

*Indicates the church affiliation of the contributor.

Name Index

Subject Index